When Disasters Come Home

When Disasters Come Home

Making and Manipulating Emergencies in the West

David Keen

polity

Permission was granted by *Disasters* (Wiley) to re-use material previously published as David Keen, 'Does democracy protect? The United Kingdom, the United States, and Covid-19' (volume 45, issue S1, December 2021). This material appears in Chapter 6.

First published in 2023 by Polity Press

Polity Press
65 Bridge Street
Cambridge CB2 1UR, UK

Polity Press
111 River Street
Hoboken, NJ 07030, USA

ISBN-13: 978-1-5095-5062-3 (hardback)
ISBN-13: 978-1-5095-5063-0 (paperback)

A catalogue record for this book is available from the British Library.

Library of Congress Control Number: 2022945381

Typeset in 10.75 on 13 Adobe Janson
by Fakenham Prepress Solutions, Fakenham, Norfolk NR21 8NL
Printed and bound in Great Britain by TJ Books Ltd, Padstow, Cornwall

For further information on Polity, visit our website:
politybooks.com

Contents

Acknowledgements

Space is tight and I'll keep this short. But I am hugely grateful to friends, colleagues and family for innumerable suggestions and enormous patience. Special mention for my sister Helen for her kindness and encouragement. Aunty Ann has also been a great support – not least in chivvying me gently so that I (almost) met my deadlines. I'd also like to say a huge thank you to Louise Knight and Inès Boxman for their faith in this project and for their great patience and support through the writing process. Thanks to Steve Leard for a great cover design and to all at Polity for their editing and proofreading. Ruben Andersson has been a hugely important source of support, encouragement and intellectual input. Mark Duffield has been an inspiration here and at various points in my life. My students and colleagues at LSE have also engaged very interestingly with this topic. I'd also like to thank Maya, as well as Emma, Pascale and Heather in my writers' group. Among those who have been especially helpful with their feedback are Mats Berdal, Ali Ali, Thomas Brodie, David Dwan, Gopal Sreenivasan, Clare Fox-Ruhs and Martin Ruhs. Other supportive friends have been too numerous to mention individually but special thanks to Harti, Ade, Cindy, Cristina, Sam, Gunwoo, Chandima, Georgia, Nira, Thomas B., Jenny, Huw, David, Gordon, Jennifer, James, Angela, Freda, Haro, Eric, Rob, Patricia, Klaus, Martin C, Paul, Andreas and the St Antony's football community. A special thank you, too, to my daughter for her charm, humour and forbearance, making the writing process much happier. And most of all, I am hugely grateful to Vivian for her help with the manuscript, for putting up with all papers and the hours, and above all for keeping such a resolute faith in me. I dedicate this book to her: hers is the kind of kindness and sweetness of soul that might yet rescue us from all of this!

1

Disasters Coming Home

Just down the muddy road from a famine 'relief' centre with one of the highest death rates ever recorded anywhere in the world,[1] a northern Sudanese trader was hosting an elaborate feast. 'God sent me the famine', he told me before noting the large profits he'd made from transporting high-priced commercial grain to the Dinka people of southern Sudan, who were visibly emaciated, mostly unable to afford whatever grain had arrived in their vicinity, and subject to enslavement, hyper-exploitation and robbery on their northward journey. This was 1988 and northern Sudanese merchants were also involved in funding militias who were creating famine through mass theft of the Dinka's cattle.

Behind the scenes, the Sudanese government was desperate to access oil in the south by forcibly ejecting the Dinka from areas where rebels were opposing the extraction of oil. While encouraging the militia raiding through arms and impunity, the Khartoum government was also preventing the delivery of famine relief to the areas where it was most needed, instead forcing aid agencies to collude in forcible depopulation by focusing their aid only on the edge of the oil-zone. To be in an environment where famine was being *actively created* was deeply shocking.

It became increasingly clear that a range of important benefits were being anticipated and often actually extracted from disaster – and Sudan was hardly an isolated example of this. In the 1990s and 2000s, a growing body of research suggested that disasters in a great many poorer countries in Africa, Asia and Latin America were not simply a source of great suffering but also *an opportunity*. A dangerous and shifting mix of warlords, militias, traders, governments and rebels were routinely instrumental *in creating* disasters from which many key players were benefiting. That finding emerged strongly from my own investigations – in Sudan and also in Sierra Leone, Guatemala, former Yugoslavia, Sri Lanka, Iraq and on the Turkey–Syria border – as well as from a wide range of research by others.[2] Alongside the lesson that disasters have beneficiaries and functions, a related lesson was also becoming increasingly clear: that attempts to relieve these disasters were themselves being routinely undermined precisely by those who were benefiting or seeking to benefit.[3]

Of course, the 1980s was also the era of Bob Geldof and Live Aid, and this is what got me interested in famine in the first place. Critics of humanitarianism later came to speak of a 'white saviour complex', and there was a slightly unfortunate turn of phrase in the Live Aid anthem, 'Do they know it's Christmas?', which advised its listeners 'Tonight thank God it's them instead of you.' In the UK, the suffering certainly felt *a long way away*. Today, the world seems radically transformed in many respects, so that thanking God for this exemption seems increasingly ill-advised.

While Sudan and the breakaway state of South Sudan are still suffering from wars and famines, there has been substantial growth in many parts of Africa as well as some patchy progress towards democracy. Ethiopia made substantial progress in tackling famine (though the current war/famine in Tigray is a huge step backwards). In Asia, nations that were previously labelled as 'underdeveloped', most obviously India and China, have come surging through (despite major political and economic problems) to the status of major powers in the world economy.

Among Bob Geldof's 'saviours', meanwhile, the situation has deteriorated in significant respects. A wide range of situations suggest that disasters, and indeed the active manipulation of disasters, are actually 'coming home' to Western democracies. Before considering how and why this is playing out, I should clarify what I mean by 'disaster'.

The *Oxford Dictionary of English* defines a disaster as 'a sudden accident or natural catastrophe that causes great damage or loss of life'.[4] But while this may sound reasonable, it misses the possibility that a disaster may be very extended and it also tends to locate disasters within a framework of 'nature' that risks playing down human responsibility. The Merriam-Webster dictionary defines a disaster as 'a sudden calamitous event bringing great damage, loss, or destruction', but again we should note that not all disasters are 'sudden'. In the context of conflict-related disasters in particular, Mark Duffield has written insightfully about 'permanent emergencies' – a concept, as we shall see, that applies disturbingly well to the current situation in Western democracies as well as much of the rest of the world. Partly to avoid assuming that disasters are 'sudden' or 'natural', I use disaster in this book to mean 'a serious problem occurring over a short or long period of time that causes widespread human, material, economic or environmental loss'.[5]

Over the last two decades or so, nine high-profile disasters threatening Western democracies stand out (though there are certainly others). Six are relatively specific, involving high-profile events (many quite 'sudden'), and the other three are slow-burning disasters – the unfolding of deeper underlying processes.

First, then, there has been a significant problem of terrorism along with a complicated political backlash. The devastating attacks of 9/11 severely dented a sense of immunity to disaster that many people in America had previously enjoyed, with fear also reverberating in Europe and elsewhere. After this, there were other major terror attacks, including in Madrid in 2004, London in 2007 and Paris in 2015.[6] The threat of terrorism spurred and legitimized a resort to various kinds of emergency powers and increased domestic surveillance, both of which have now become relatively normal in Western democracies.

At the same time, there is convincing evidence that foreign policy in the Middle East, particularly the 'war on terror' from 2001, played a significant role in *generating* many of these terror attacks, so that violence backed by Western governments (and the US in particular) may in this sense be said to have 'come home' or even to have 'come home to roost'. Terrorism has been 'coming home' in at least two other senses. First, many jihadist attacks within Western democracies have had a significant *home-grown* element, with the perpetrators having lived in the West for a long time or even having grown up there (see e.g. Keen, 2006). Second, there has been a generally under-recognized but growing problem of *right-wing* terrorism perpetrated by white people. Between 2008 and 2017 far-right and white-supremacist movements were responsible for 71 per cent of extremist-related killings in the US (compared to 26 per cent for jihadist extremists).[7] The phenomenon need not have come as a revelation: after all, the second worst terror attack on American soil was carried out in Oklahoma City in 1995 by a white American Gulf War veteran, Timothy McVeigh and his associate Terry Nichols. One careful analysis noted that the 9/11 attacks were 'a gift' to peddlers of xenophobia and white supremacism, and that the 'war on terror' and increased domestic surveillance of Muslims also energized the far right.[8] Yet, in 2005 the US Department for Homeland Security had only one analyst working on non-Islamist terrorist threats.[9]

A second set of disasters increasingly affecting Western democracies has been weather-related. While such disasters have often been assumed to be a phenomenon primarily impacting Asia, Africa and Latin America, any 'immunity' among Western democracies is increasingly difficult to discern. We have seen hurricanes and floods wreaking destruction on New Orleans, New York and Puerto Rico, bushfires ripping through California, Australia, Turkey and Greece, and so on. In 2021, floods in Germany, Belgium and several other European countries shocked climate scientists when precipitation records were broken.[10] Meanwhile, extreme heatwaves were smashing records across the western United States and Canada. In Colorado in 2021 wildfires were raging *in December*. Matthew Jones at the University of East Anglia has reported an eightfold increase in forest wildfires in California over the past twenty years, with water scarcer and forests drying out.[11] In this rash of extreme weather events, climate change has been an important factor. We also need to look at policies that have helped to produce underlying *vulnerabilities* to existing weather events. A great deal of literature on disasters makes clear that hazards like extreme weather events or earthquakes translate into disasters via underlying vulnerabilities, so that a smaller earthquake in Haiti for example can cause more damage and more suffering than a bigger earthquake in Chile.[12]

A third disaster has been financial crisis, notably in 2007–8. The lasting impact of the 2007–8 crisis was exacerbated by policies of austerity. Programmes of 'structural adjustment' that had been associated with Africa and Asia and Latin America since the mid-1970s were now penetrating right into the heart of Europe, with Greece the worst affected and Italy, Spain, Portugal and Ireland and many others also suffering significantly. The erosion of sovereignty that many had bemoaned in the context of the Global South became rather clearly a feature of European politics,[13] playing a part in the rise of far-right parties like Golden Dawn in Greece.[14] The erosion of sovereignty also inserted itself into major American cities, as we shall see. It turned out that capitalism and its debt-collectors did not particularly discriminate between the Global North and the Global South, while debt, de-democratization and disaster proved to be close cousins within Europe and North America just as they had long been within other continents. Financial crisis recurred in the UK in 2022, to give one example, when the Truss government's planned tax cuts alongside heavy spending on energy subsidies sent financial markets into a tailspin.

A fourth set of disasters impacting Western democracies has been a complex array of humanitarian disasters around migration. These have included mass drowning in the Mediterranean, significant mortality in American deserts adjoining the border with Mexico, and inhuman conditions in camps for migrants in Europe as well as on the US–Mexico border and offshore from the Australian mainland. Then there has been the damage to political culture – hard to quantify but very significant nonetheless – that comes when fundamental human rights such as the right to asylum are not respected, when the ability of aid organizations to offer assistance or to speak about suffering is severely curtailed, and when 'hostile environments' are actively created both within Western democracies and on their geographical fringes.

A fifth disaster has been Covid-19. First detected in Wuhan, China, the coronavirus has been wreaking havoc in a number Western democracies as well as many other countries around the world. With Covid, we have seen the extra danger that arises precisely from the assumption that disasters are *somebody else's problem*.

A sixth disaster has been the war in Ukraine. (We might consider Ukraine a Western democracy since its government is elected and Ukraine is part of Europe.) The war in Ukraine, which has severely impacted on food supplies to many countries in Africa and the Middle East, is also impacting on democracies further west – for example through the movement of refugees, through rising energy prices, and even through the huge expenditure that some Western democracies (most of all the US) are making on weapons for Ukraine as well as on humanitarian assistance. Then there is the small matter of a possible nuclear war triggered by the tense confrontation between Russia and the NATO allies, at which point disaster would be seen, albeit briefly, to have come home with a vengeance.

Longer-Term Disasters

In addition to the six relatively 'sudden' and 'dramatic' disasters set out above, we need to consider three *underlying* disasters impacting strongly on Western democracies. As the book progresses, we will explore some of the ways in which longer-term underlying disasters are feeding shorter-term disasters, and vice versa. Disasters that appear to be sudden have often been the product of longer-term processes.

The first of the underlying disasters impacting on Western democracies (as well as the rest of the world) is an ongoing economic crisis linked to globalization, oligopolization, and automation. Particularly from the 1990s, capital became increasingly unregulated, hyper-mobile and able to search out relatively low-wage and low-regulation environments around the world, as well as boom-environments where pushing out large amounts of capital became (for a while) a kind of self-fulfilling prophesy of quick profits.[15] Robert Wade, Professor of Political Economy and Development at the London School of Economics, has noted 'After the collapse of the Soviet Union around 1990 and the opening to trade of China, India and other large developing countries at around the same time, the global labour force roughly doubled', thereby greatly weakening the bargaining power of labour and raising the share of profits in world gross domestic product (GDP).[16] A set of complex processes, acting together, have tended to marginalize or simply render redundant the labour of millions of workers within Western democracies, though manufacturing output itself has held up much better than most of the traditional industries.[17] As some countries have rapidly industrialized, others have suffered partial de-industrialization.[18] In the industrial Midwest of the US, scrap metal from devastated industries was literally shipped to China, thanks largely to the migration of jobs (and, incidentally, the cheap rates for ships that were emptied of Chinese products when they *arrived* in the US).[19] Globalization, often envisaged as a kind of 'export' of democracy and free markets to the entire world, has had the effect of 'importing' into the West some of the *chronic precarity and superfluity* that has long been fostered in the Global South.

Linked to globalization, and fuelled also by a range of government policies, has been an escalation of inequality (for example in the UK and the US). Between 1978 and 2012, the share of wealth enjoyed by the richest 0.1 per cent of the population in the United States rose from seven per cent to fully 22 per cent, a reversion to the level of inequality that had prevailed before Roosevelt's New Deal politics emerged in the wake of the 1929 financial crash. The share of wealth enjoyed by the top one per cent of the US population had reached 42% by 2012.[20] That inequality has contributed to a vulnerability to disasters – both personal disaster and wider societal disasters – among a vast swathe of the population. Financial crisis in turn fed into underlying structural problems (including through a boost to automation that was reflected, for example, in production recovering more quickly than employment after the 2007–8 crash).

A second underlying crisis is climatological. So called 'natural disasters' have never been less natural, and no part of the world is exempt from this existential problem. The number, severity and impact of our current weather-related disasters is increasing significantly in comparison to even the late twentieth century.[21] Severe weather-related disasters have increasingly been occurring within temperate as well as tropical zones.[22] And future escalations seem certain in the context of global warming and a widely predicted rise in conflict and migration (or at least *attempts* to migrate). Of course, weather-related disasters are hardly novel and the saying goes that there is nothing new under the sun. But even this phrase takes on new meaning when a drastically thinning ozone layer escalates the impact of the sun itself. At the same time, protection policies make a difference, and the voluntary or enforced neglect of domestic infrastructure has increased vulnerabilities to weather-related (and indeed geological) disasters. We will see this vulnerability in the case of New Orleans. The terrible Greek wildfires of 2021 were made worse by cuts in the firefighters' budget that had been forced through by EU, European Central Bank and IMF officials in the context of the country's debt crisis.[23]

A third underlying disaster has been a political crisis. The precise *nature* of this crisis depends on who you ask: in fact, one person's 'disaster' is likely to be another person's 'solution'. This disparity itself betrays a wider political problem, which is arguably itself a disaster: there has been a shrinking of shared truths and shared political spaces. In this connection, Pankaj Mishra has pointed to 'a severely diminished respect for the political process itself'.[24] Retreating into 'alternative realities' has become commonplace, with right-wing populists often leading the way. As this book develops, we will get a better idea of some of the problems growing up around the 'alternative realities' that our current political moment has thrown into prominence. In particular, we will see that once a proper analysis of causes and effects has been set aside, relevant belief systems have often been defended through intimidation and even violence.

The rise of right-wing populism has seen a growing intolerance, an increasing resort to emergency powers, and a significant erosion of democratic norms. Major crises in Western democracies have included not only Brexit in the UK and Trump in the US but also the ascendance of openly racist and homophobic political parties in many countries. Again, many of the things that Western publics have tended to associate with 'faraway' conflict-affected countries are today increasingly evident within Western democracies that had seemed, at least in the late twentieth century, largely immune. These include the progressive surrender of authority to the executive, assaults on press freedom, denunciations of minorities, constitutional 'coups', threats against parliamentarians and judges, the politics of the 'strongman', and even the possibility of secession and all the conflict that this tends to bring with it.[25] In the US, a country where political crisis has been especially intense, 2020 saw escalating protests against police violence, with the President actively inflaming the underlying rage and racial tensions before going on to incite an attempt to overturn the November presidential elections – an extraordinary blow to democratic norms.

A System of Disasters

A kind of 'emergency politics' is significantly shaping many political systems across the world, and Western democracies are far from immune. It may be that globalization is now helping to 'import' into Western democracies not only the large-scale superfluousness and precarity afflicting the rest of the world but also some of the *emergency politics* that many influential actors in the Global South have for some time been fostering and using to distract, absorb and suppress the energies of discontented populations.[26]

In several countries where I have myself investigated disasters (including Sudan, Sierra Leone and Sri Lanka), a key part of politics has come to be the instrumentalization of disaster and emergency, while a second important part has been the attempt to limit the political fall-out from disaster. This second aim points towards an agenda of *legitimizing* disaster. This project seems to be becoming more central in many Western democracies, too. Indeed, making, manipulating and legitimizing disasters and 'emergency' are habits that appear to be embedding themselves within Western politics.

It would of course be incorrect to suggest that disasters impacting Western democracies are *something new*. Such a view would require a remarkably short-term memory that took no account of two world wars, of all manner of weather-related disasters and economic catastrophes in the twentieth century and earlier and, indeed, of the way democracy in Germany's Weimar Republic succumbed to the rise of Nazism and its accompanying horrors. Even in the last decades of the twentieth century, we should not forget the devastation wrought by AIDS, the destruction effected by wars in the former Yugoslavia, the terrorism in Oklahoma, Ireland, Britain and Spain, and so on. I personally remember the feeling in the 1980s that nuclear war was possible and even imminent, so current anxieties on that score are also hardly new.

As a further proviso, we should note that what felt like safety for many people in Western democracies in the later decades of the twentieth century clearly did not feel like safety for many others. Much of the difference depended on race or ethnic identity. In the US from the 1970s millions of people suffered the evolving disaster of mass incarceration, with Black and Hispanic populations disproportionately affected.[27]

What *would* perhaps be fair to say, though, is that a period of *relative* calm and safety for most people in Western democracies since the end of the Second World War has been giving way, in the twenty-first century, to a politics in which making and manipulating disasters has become increasingly common. A proliferating array of disasters are today feeding into each other in ways that are profoundly disturbing and ways that we need to understand much better.

Terrorism, weather-related disasters, financial crisis, humanitarian crises among migrants, Covid, Ukraine, structural economic crisis, climate crisis and political crisis: while the list of crises or disasters now impacting on Western democracies is certainly a long one, we should also notice that these various disasters tend to be treated *separately*. Quite rightly, there are specialists in each of these topics, specialist journals and specialists specializing in special aspects of each specialism. There are, of course, significant advantages in taking complex problems one at a time. But again, we also need a much better awareness of the ways in which these crises *relate to one another*. We need to acknowledge the diversity of disasters that are impacting Western democracies as well as the rest of the world. We need to be clear-sighted on which are being hyped and which are being underplayed. And we need to recognize that these crises are strongly feeding into each other in what amounts to a mutually reinforcing system of emergency-and-response, a politics of emergency that tends to feed voraciously off itself.

Bread and Circuses

In this book, I emphasize the salience of a 'politics of distraction'. Our three underlying disasters are major drivers of many more immediate and apparently sudden disasters but are typically not addressed effectively amid a succession of high-profile responses to the more visible and sudden disasters. Worse, when Western governments respond with a drive for increased 'security' – allocating additional resources for the military, building walls, and bolstering abusive governments that offer to cooperate in a 'war on terror' or in 'migration control' – these responses tend not only to bypass the underlying problems but to *exacerbate* them.[28]

One key mechanism here is this shoring up of repressive governments that say they are going to tackle terrorism or migration. A second mechanism is that underlying problems fester and proliferate when high-profile security measures absorb huge amounts of tax revenue. The cost of these various 'security systems' is sucking the lifeblood from systems of public health and social security, which in turn feeds back into vulnerability to disaster.

Today's overlapping disasters offer important opportunities for political manipulation as well as important economic opportunities for the expensive apparatus of deterrence that has been constructed around a variety of much-trumpeted 'threats', whether 'terror', 'drugs' or 'mass migration'. In effect, a sense of threat is being hitched to policies that generate more suffering – and more 'threats'. Meanwhile, an emphasis on 'building walls' tends dangerously to reinforce a pre-existing sense of 'immunity' to collective problems.

Today, we may say that a range of relatively spectacular emergencies like migration crises and terrorism have acquired an important 'function' in distracting Western populations from deeper-lying crises that major vested interests would prefer to leave unaddressed or even actively to worsen. As part of this, Western electorates have been invited to 'buy into' magical solutions for a range of high-profile crises.

Even the peculiar 'political emergency' that was Trump-as-President seems to have served as something of a distraction from the economic and political processes that put him in power in the first place. Today's proliferating disasters suggest a disturbing relevance for the old saying that grievances can be contained within a policy of 'bread and circuses'. For disasters themselves – and the trumpeted responses to proclaimed disasters – have become a kind of continuous political 'theatre'. Like plays, disasters hold the potential to awaken us to important underlying problems but all too often serve to keep us in a state of distraction and morbid entertainment.[29]

Magical Thinking and Self-Reinforcing Systems

Influenced by colonialism (and in turn helping to shape it), a common way of thinking and writing has been to construct societies outside

Europe, Australasia and North America as driven by emotions, passions, irrationality and magical thinking, while Western societies are seen to have embraced science and efficient bureaucratic modes of governance.[30] In my own work on disasters in the Global South, I have tried to bring out the very considerable extent to which these 'far away' disasters were *all too rational*, with a range of vested interests helping to drive destructive processes (both from within and outside the disaster-affected countries). Of course, such interests interacted with emotions in complex ways, and I also became interested in, for example, the complex interaction of economic accumulation and shame (or more broadly the interaction of greed and grievance) during the civil war in Sierra Leone.[31]

A related project, and part of the intention in this book, is to highlight the complex interactions of interests and emotions in relation to disasters unfolding in the Global North. This project invites not only an exploration of the various mundane functions that these disasters may be serving, but also of the extent to which they are being driven by *magical thinking*, a phenomenon that seems increasingly to be embedding itself in the politics of Western democracies as an integral part of our disaster-producing system. Understanding this is all the more urgent since the fragile protection afforded by democracy would seem to be significantly eroded when popular sentiment is stirred up in ways that *promote* or even *welcome* disaster – often through the promotion of beliefs that lack scientific backing.

By 'magical thinking', incidentally, I mean the belief that particular events are causally connected, despite the absence of any plausible link between them. The term has been used in different ways by various thinkers, and has been commonly invoked in anthropology.[32] Psychoanalytic thinking also rests heavily on a variety of conceptions of the magical, and Freud showed that in mental illness the magical side of human thinking often takes precedence. In *The Unconscious*, Freud observed that 'The neurotic turns away from reality because he finds either the whole or parts of it unbearable.'[33] In *Totem and Taboo*, Freud suggested that people with neurosis 'are only affected by what is thought with intensity and pictured with emotion whereas agreement with external reality is of no importance'.[34] The obsessions of neurotics 'are of an entirely magical character. If they are not charms, they are at all events counter-charms, designed to ward off the expectations of disaster with which the neurosis usually starts.'[35] Freud saw a connection between the belief systems of neurotics and those he called 'primitive' people 'who believe they can alter the external world by mere thinking'.[36] Yet he also wanted to stress that such a flight from reality among those with neurosis comes at a huge cost in terms of both human suffering and the difficulty of recovering. As psychoanalyst Thomas Ogden explained, 'magical thinking subverts the opportunity to learn from one's lived experience with real external objects'.[37]

In *Totem and Taboo*, Freud linked 'magical thought' with the 'omnipotence of thought'.[38] He saw 'primitive' magical belief systems as mirroring the baby's reaction to its earliest experiences. He noted that a baby may wish for the breast and, if the breast appears, the baby may attribute this to the power of its own thoughts (hence the 'omnipotence of thought'). But a baby who remains purely in the realm of thought (and forgets, for example, to kick and scream when hungry) might not even survive.[39] Freud argued that the temptation to wish away an unpleasant reality and even to construct a new one with our own thoughts is not left behind at this moment when the baby 'gets real', but rather is put into a place where a lifelong competition with reality-based thinking can begin.

While we often think of the process of development and modernization as bringing progress and empowerment, Freud portrays this modernization as a kind of *disempowerment*, at least in terms of how humans experience their own power. Thus, he notes in *Totem and Taboo*, 'At the animistic stage men ascribe omnipotence to themselves.'[40] This is because, while spirits proliferate, humans think they can influence them. Somewhat similarly, in 'the religious stage' humans transfer the sense of omnipotence to the gods 'but do not seriously abandon it themselves, for they reserve the power of influencing the gods in a variety of ways according to their wishes'.[41] In the scientific stage, Freud wrote, omnipotence has been abandoned, and 'men have acknowledged their smallness and submitted resignedly to death and to the other necessities of nature'.[42] Yet that degree of humility and powerlessness is a tough thing to embrace, as Freud well understood. While Freud often tended to push the concept of magical thinking *onto others* ('neurotics', 'primitives'), it would be more realistic to suggest, particularly in light of Freud's own account of an increasing sense of impotence as human history unfolded, that magical thinking retains very considerable appeal around the world.

It will be important to keep in mind both the appeal and the drawbacks of magical thinking when we come to consider the role of political delusions in relation to today's overlapping disasters. At the same time, we should also keep in mind the dangers inherent in pointing the finger at particular beliefs and *labelling* them as magical thinking or as irrational. How can we know what is delusional and what isn't? And in pointing the finger at the delusions of others, are we drawing a veil over our own?

As the discussion in the book unfolds, I also draw significantly on the fascinating insights of Hannah Arendt, who serves as an important guide throughout. Indeed, the book is intended – in part – as an exploration of the continuing relevance of Arendt's work. A German-born Jewish political philosopher who fled from Nazi-occupied France to the United States, Arendt contributed hugely to our understanding of violent propaganda and totalitarian reflexes. She showed how and why a fictional and highly destructive view of the world could become plausible. In so doing, she illuminated the magical thinking that lay close to the malignant heart of fascism.

Of course, there are dangers in importing insights on totalitarianism into non-totalitarian contexts, and nothing in this book is intended in any way to minimize the horrors of the either the Holocaust or the Soviet totalitarianism that Arendt also analysed. But we should remember that Arendt herself was profoundly concerned to understand how a democracy (like the Weimar Republic) could transition to something far more authoritarian and abusive, and some of her later work (for example on the Vietnam War) attempted to understand how democratic governments could embrace mass killing *abroad*, with damaging consequences also for domestic politics. In a contemporary context where threats to democracy have become significantly more prominent, it is surely no accident that there has been a surge of interest in Arendt's work. To the extent that contemporary Western democracies are today exhibiting elements of the dangerous, deluded and anti-democratic tendencies that Arendt analysed in *The Origins of Totalitarianism*, we should not conclude either that a move further in this direction is inevitable or that there is some kind of 'equivalence' or even near-equivalence between twentieth-century totalitarianism and what is happening now. But the current moment does feels like a very dangerous one, and one in which we are actually *obligated* to look at history (including some of its most horrific episodes) in search of lessons and pointers. It also feels like a propitious moment to tap into Arendt's remarkable wisdom.

We should note, incidentally, that in *The Origins of Totalitarianism* Arendt did not actually employ the term 'magical thinking'. Nevertheless, her entire book was a notable exploration of the collective capacity to travel into a world of dangerous delusions. At times, Arendt did use the term 'wishful thinking'. She noted for example that the 'non-totalitarian world' indulges in 'wishful thinking' and 'shirks reality in the face of real insanity',[43] adding that there is a 'common-sense disinclination to believe the monstrous'.[44]

As the current book proceeds, we will begin to see how magical (or wishful) thinking and self-interest have proven to be 'blood brothers' in fuelling a range of disasters, whether in democratic or undemocratic contexts. Very frequently, politicians have seen some kind of domestic political advantages in stirring up a sense of crisis (a financial crisis, a migration crisis, a political crisis etc.). Some of these crises have been real, some have been underplayed (like climate change), and some have been greatly exaggerated (like the 'migration crisis').

Part of magical thinking may be the belief that the preferred way of handling these various emergencies is the *only way* they can reasonably be handled. This closes down debate and protects unrealistic solutions. Today in Western democracies – as has so often been the case around the world – critics of how these crises are currently being defined and manipulated risk being incorporated into a conveniently expandable category of 'the enemy'. This process tends to feed the underlying political emergency, which centres to a significant extent on the *delegitimizing of dissent* and the *inability to learn*.

As part of our investigation of today's overlapping disasters, we urgently need to look at the degree to which they – like so many that have unfolded further afield – are being actively manipulated and even, in some cases, manufactured. We need to understand the various political, economic and psychological functions that are being served by this dysfunctional system of emergency-and-response. No doubt the functionality of contemporary disasters in Western democracies is rarely as obvious as it was in the Sudanese famine with which we began our discussion. But the emerging functions of today's overlapping disasters do need to be examined if we are to provide a proper explanation of why these disasters have taken the form they have, why they have been so severe, and why they have proliferated and persisted. A key part of the problem in Western democracies today, as so often in Sudan and many parts of the Global South, has been that the underlying functions of overlapping disasters have helped to undermine attempts to relieve them, contributing greatly to the ineffective or actively counterproductive nature of responses.

Much of classical thinking about politics and economics suggests *self-correcting* systems that benefit from in-built 'checks and balances': thus a price rise will lead to increased production and hence a fall in prices; a rise in executive power will be reined in by the legislature and the judiciary; an incompetent government will be voted out of power. Of course, such checks and balances have by no means disappeared, and we might take the election of Joe Biden following Trump's failures with the coronavirus as a reminder that democracy remains a vital defence against disaster. But many of our present-day political dysfunctions do nevertheless have the quality of being *self-reinforcing*. Indeed, we are confronted with a politics that in many ways is thriving on the very crises it is helping to produce. It's quite common to hear talk of the 'slippery slope' towards totalitarianism, and this expression should itself remind us that some routes to catastrophe have a kind of self-reinforcing quality. Certainly, this 'slippery' quality is something that Arendt can help us to understand.

We need to look more closely at blowback, which the *Oxford Dictionary of English* defines as the 'unintended and adverse effects of a political action or situation'.[45] Unfortunately, rather than changing fundamental policies in response to manifestations of blowback, many politicians in contemporary Western democracies are busy *taking advantage of crisis* and *incorporating blowback into their political strategies*. Yet this process – in many ways familiar from the Global South, as we shall see in Chapter 2 – tends only to deepen the underlying political crisis, a vicious circle that we need to find a way to fix.

North, South, East, West

From a Western or Northern perspective, disasters have been rather conveniently and complacently assumed to be far away from Western democracies, and this tendency seems to have been encouraged by assumptions around the *otherness* of 'the South' and 'the East'. Very often, the prevailing assumption has been that bad things happen only to '*them*', while Western democracies are involved only in the sense of being *potential saviours*.

Yet disasters are today 'coming home' in at least three senses. First, having for a long time been seen as confined to the Global South (and to some extent the East), disasters, including political disasters, have become an increasingly obvious feature of Western democracies. Second, the nature of Western politics is shifting so that the *manipulation* of disasters, whether domestic, global or some combination of the two, is becoming (or we might say becoming *once again*) a key feature. Third, violence perpetrated in 'far away' countries (whether in the contemporary era or as part of historical colonialism) is now coming home, or 'coming home to roost', as various kinds of blowback or 'boomerang effects' take a heavy toll on Western politics and society. Today's overlapping disasters, not least those impacting the West itself, should be opening our eyes to the major role that Western democracies are playing (and have played in the past) in generating them. The export of disasters in the form of colonialism and modern-day imperialism has found a potent counterpoint not only in blowback but in the instrumentalization of blowback.

In the past, others have remarked on such 'boomerang' effects, and it will be helpful to keep their views in mind. The Martinican author and politician Aimé Césaire argued that colonization decivilized and brutalized the colonizer, stirring race hatred at home and propelling the continent of Europe towards 'savagery' before eventually, in the ultimate 'boomerang effect', finding expression in the racialized violence of Nazism.[46] The French philosopher Michel Foucault also referred to colonial models being brought home in a 'boomerang effect' or 'internal colonialism'.[47]

Arendt also noted 'the boomerang effect of imperialism upon the homeland'. In the wake of the First World War and a Versailles Treaty that took away Germany's colonies, Arendt noted, 'The Central and Eastern European nations, which had no colonial possessions and little hope for overseas expansion, now decided that they "had the same right to expand as other great peoples and that if they were not granted this possibility overseas, [they would] be forced to do it in Europe"'.[48] In other words, the persistent allure of empire and expansion found an outlet in the pursuit of *Lebensraum* in the east. Of course, the primary actor here was Germany.

Today, we must try to understand the *contemporary* manifestations of such rebound effects, not least when it comes to the lasting effects of colonialism and the more immediate effects of the 'war on terror'. Both sets of effects have been incorporated into a renewed politics of intolerance within the West.

While it has been common to use European history to interpret and chastise, say, Africa (with its 'lack of a Weberian state', its 'painfully slow progress towards modernization', and so on), the possibility of learning lessons 'the other way around' has been relatively little explored. But this represents a major missed opportunity. 'What if we posit', as anthropologists Jean and John Comaroff suggest, 'that, in the present moment, it is the so-called "Global South" that affords privileged insight into the workings of the world at large?'[49] And what if political trends in the old Cold War 'East', for example in Poland and Hungary, are also harbingers of a political world to come?

We should note here that terms like 'North', 'South', 'East' and 'West' are extremely problematic. There's a danger that the North/

South and East/West binaries will reify and solidify the relevant distinctions, making the categories seem somehow permanently different and irreconcilable as well as homogenous.[50] The Comaroffs themselves suggested that there were enclaves of 'the South' in 'the North' and vice versa,[51] and we know that countries like China, Paraguay and Botswana have broken through to a 'middle-income' category, sometimes with spectacular success,[52] while southern capital now props up or owns signature businesses in Europe and North America.[53] Michelle Lazar notes that it's 'important to see the "North" and "South" as relational categories, mutually constitutive, and entangled'[54] and, of course, a key part of this relationship has been colonialism. Rather than being hamstrung by the limitations of the North/South distinction, a key aim in this book is to move beyond this distinction and to explore some dynamics and dangers that are operating *globally*.

When it comes to the distinction between 'East' and 'West', this is hardly definitive either. For one thing, we may observe that countries can move between these categories: it seems to 'help' if they embrace the right blend of markets, democracy and pro-US allegiance (as we have seen with Japan and South Korea). In its violent transition from Communism, Yugoslavia's ambiguous status also blurred the lines. When it collapsed into war in the 1990s, some politicians and commentators concluded that nothing could be done about these 'ancient ethnic hatreds', while Balkans expert Susan Woodward suggested that the region was effectively being redefined (with the help of such language) as 'not Europe'.[55] This 'othering' manoeuvre may have helped to preserve a sense of immunity in Europe further west, while also discouraging intervention. More generally, Maria Todorova argues that the Balkans has an uneasy status as *semi-oriental*, a region that is always trying to shed 'the last residue of an imperial [i.e. Ottoman] legacy'.[56] It would seem, too, that old stereotypes about the inherent 'brutality' or 'otherness' of 'the East' are easily revived – and Russia's vicious war in the Ukraine has given ample encouragement to this reflex.

As the Cold War wound down, references to 'the East' became less common. The term was an uncomfortable one in any case, not least in the light of Edward Said's influential 1978 book *Orientalism*.[57] Yet it is notable that references to 'the West' have continued to be absolutely normal[58] (and of course 'the West' is in the subtitle of the current book).

Again, my intention is not to reify a binary distinction but rather to consider important things that many countries may have in common, across whichever binary divide. One danger in drawing any sharp line between 'East' and 'West' is that disturbing developments in countries of the old 'eastern bloc' (such as Hungary and Poland) will be taken as somehow separate from – and irrelevant to – political trends in democracies in Western Europe and North America.[59] Yet, as Anne Applebaum reminds us in her perceptive book *Twilight of Democracy*, there is nothing particularly 'Eastern' or 'Western' about the process by which economic crisis, resentment and frustrated ambition has fuelled the rise of right-wing populism.[60]

More hopefully, a growing number of people are resisting our disaster-producing politics in diverse and creative ways, and again this process has important precedents and parallels in the Global South. As Western populations' sense of 'immunity' diminishes in the context of global heating and Covid-19 in particular, a sense of vulnerability is making many people more open to radical solutions that challenge our disaster-producing politics. But there is also a political backlash against the protesters, a process of delegitimizing protest and painting dissent as extremism. A key risk is that this backlash serves to consolidate our current disaster-producing system.

In Chapter 2 (Lessons from 'Far Away'), I set out a number of conclusions arising principally from my investigations of disasters around the word, emphasizing the functions of these disasters as well as the degree to which politics has turned on limiting political fall-out from these disasters. The chapter looks at disasters in the Global South as a threat to government legitimacy and it examines the way poor responses to these disasters have been legitimized. It also looks at how disasters have been explained and who bears the costs – and how these considerations shape the future trajectory of disasters.

Chapter 3 (A Self-Reinforcing System?) explores the extent to which emergencies have become a staple of Western politics, justifying a growing resort to various kinds of emergency measures. I argue that today various disasters are tending to reinforce the policies that generated them, so that we risk being caught in a self-reinforcing system rather than a self-correcting one. A key pitfall has been a collective focus on consequences rather than causes.

Chapter 4 (Emergency Politics) looks at how Trump instrumentalized a sense of insecurity and existential threat, and it positions Trump's politics within Arendt's wider analysis of the allure of norm-breaking and even cruelty. The chapter goes on to consider the 'politics of distraction' within both the US (where Democrats have played their part as well as Republicans) and the UK. It also examines the contribution to emergency politics that has been made by escalating debt, including in municipal governance within the US.

Chapter 5 (Hostile Environments) looks at some of the functions of the human suffering that has accompanied the tightening of migration controls. The chapter shows how European and US 'outsourcing' of migration-control has yielded a number of political as well as economic payoffs, even as it has fed into humanitarian disasters and undermined the right to asylum. Meanwhile, the causes of outmigration have been powerfully stoked, not least when deals have been struck with authoritarian regimes and abusive militias from Turkey to Libya and Sudan. Deterring migration – when taken to its logical conclusion – has involved fostering human rights violations both in 'transit' countries and in 'recipient' countries (as with the so-called 'hostile environment' in the UK). The chapter draws on fieldwork in the migrants' camp in Calais, France, as well as research by many others, to show how suffering among migrants has been artificially created and has served identifiable functions. The chapter also looks at how hostility to migrants/refugees has been extended to those who are trying to help them as well as to others who may be associated with the migrants/refugees in some way; this is another sense in which disaster may plausibly be said to be 'coming home'.

Chapter 6 (Welcoming Infection) looks at responses to Covid, another disaster 'coming home'. Focusing particularly on the US and the UK, the chapter asks what has made these countries so vulnerable and why democracy has not offered greater protection. It also asks about the impact of Covid-19 on democracy itself. One major source of vulnerability, it is suggested, is that at key points in the crisis infection itself was reconceptualized as *a good thing*.

Chapter 7 (Magical Thinking) looks at how our disaster-producing system is being legitimized through the resort to various kinds of magical thinking. The magical thinking that infuses, shapes and legitimizes the current disaster-producing system has important psychological functions even as it also helps to solidify the more prosaic political and economic interests that are bolstering this disaster system. In this chapter, I draw again on Arendt's work, not least in analysing how patently ludicrous and destructive ideas can acquire considerable appeal and plausibility under particular conditions.

Chapter 8 (Policing Delusions) looks at the defence of magical thinking – often a *violent* defence – and at how this is feeding our overlapping disasters. The chapter examines this process particularly in relation to the 'war on terror'.

In Chapter 9 (Action as Propaganda), I argue that what Arendt calls 'action as propaganda' – broadly, the use of violent action to make false claims appear more and more true as time goes by – has been an important technique through which our disaster-producing politics has been sustained and legitimized. While not all the elements of 'action as propaganda' have been intended or planned from the outset, there are many kinds of violence that have conveniently created legitimacy for themselves, giving little reason to change course.

Chapter 10 (Choosing Disaster) looks at the way disaster-producing policies have been encouraged by particular framings and especially by framing politics as a choice between a 'lesser evil' and some allegedly more disastrous alternative. This manoeuvre rests on a number of dubious assumptions. It depends on successfully evoking a sense of (impending) disaster while playing down the abuse of human rights that is involved in 'averting' it. It also depends on an underlying 'science' or theory that is rarely spelled out with sufficient clarity or scepticism. This takes us back to some of the key points in Chapter 7 as we explore the strange 'alliance' that has today been formed by 'science', magical thinking and self-interest.

Chapter 11 (Home to Roost) returns to the idea that disasters are 'coming home'. Within an emerging *system of suffering*, we may say that disasters are not just coming home but also *coming home to roost*. 'Home to Roost' was the title of an article by Arendt that discussed the domestic impact within the US of the Vietnam War, and some of the dynamics she highlighted remain extremely relevant today. In the context of various kinds of 'blowback' from policies that have long contributed to 'far away' disasters, a number of democratic leaders, mostly but not exclusively right-wing populists of one kind or another, have been peddling what we might call *the wrong solution for the wrong emergency*. This reflex has unfolded in the context of underlying economic disasters (and a broader political crisis) that preceded the most prominent right-wing populists and *made them possible*. To ignore these conditions is again to focus on symptoms rather than underlying problems.

2

Lessons from 'Far Away'

With crisis of one kind or another becoming increasingly normal in Western democracies, it seems like a good time to look to some of the countries around the world where crisis has for some time been an integral part of 'normal'. Such a focus, clearly important in its own right, will also give us some significant questions to ask in relation to Western democracies. My own investigations have included research in wartime and post-war environments, research on organized crime, research in famine zones, research in countries affected by genocide, and research on various kinds of humanitarian intervention.

Summing up any 'lessons' from such a wide-ranging set of events in many different places will always be a complex task with many pitfalls. It would also, of course, be unwise to try to apply lessons mechanically from 'the Global South' to 'the Global North'. The problematic nature of these categories has been mentioned, including the blurred lines between them. I should note, too, that my own focus on 'complex emergencies' illuminates only one aspect of countries in the 'Global South' that in many cases have experienced an enormous rush of creativity, energy and growth.[1] In any case, the crises that I have been able to investigate at first hand in the Global South are not in any sense 'representative'; some investigations, moreover, went much deeper than others.

Having said all that, I do think the study of an emerging 'emergency politics' in Western democracies can be enriched by experiences with emergencies elsewhere. The point, ultimately, is not to reify the 'North'/'South' distinction but to move beyond it towards a better understanding of some dangerous political dynamics that are currently operating – albeit with very considerable variation – *around the world*.

In the discussion that follows, I elaborate on five main 'lessons' in five subsections. First, disasters have *beneficiaries*, and understanding this helps us to explain why disasters happen. Second, *democracy* may not protect against disaster. Third, disasters can acquire a certain *legitimacy* (or at least the perception thereof), and we need to understand how this works. Fourth, the way disasters are *explained* affects not only the disaster but also future disasters. Fifth, the distribution of *costs* within a disaster plays a big part in determining the response and how the disaster evolves over time. The aim is not to 'apply' these lessons to the various disasters affecting Western democracies but to keep them in mind as a tool for understanding.

Beneficiaries

Disasters have typically, and for understandable reasons, been presented as relatively sudden shocks that bring overwhelmingly adverse effects. But a closer look at a number of disasters that have unfolded in Africa, Asia and Latin America suggests that they may be better regarded as *complex systems* and *extended episodes* from which *benefits* have been extracted by certain groups. These benefits, moreover, have tended to go a long way towards explaining why the disasters have occurred in the first place, why they have often persisted for long periods, and why they have frequently mutated from one form to another.

What *use* is the phenomenon that everyone seems to be denouncing? Foucault applied this question to the institution of imprisonment[2] and even to the *gulag* under Soviet Communism.[3] The question can also be instructively applied to famines, wars and other disasters.[4]

Certainly, a complex and shifting system of benefits can help to explain the 1988 Sudanese famine with which this book began. Significantly, many of the powerful actors who were benefiting (or who stood to benefit) were also able to *stoke* the famine – whether through militia raiding, through controlling population movements, or simply through blocking famine relief. In terms of economic processes (and in line with economist/philosopher Amartya Sen's famous analysis of market mechanisms in *Poverty and Famines*),[5] the famine was fuelled by rising grain prices and by falling livestock and labour prices. But these price changes were not only calamitous for the famine victims; they were also *advantageous* for those who were able to sell grain and buy livestock or labour. And some of these beneficiaries were also able to *deepen* the famine from which they were benefiting or hoped to benefit – for example by funding militias or bribing railway workers not to deliver relief. All this suggests that we need to understand the *functions* of famine as well as its immediate causes. Here Sen's theoretical perspective needs to be supplemented by the less well-known work of Indian sociologist Amrita Rangasami, who documented the economic instrumentalization of famine in colonial and post-independence India and portrayed famine as a process of *asset transfer* in which interventions typically occurred once the main benefits had been extracted.[6]

On top of the exploitative market mechanisms operating during the 1988 Sudan famine, there was a great deal of looting by militias that were supported by the Sudanese government. Militiamen stole cattle on a massive scale, so that assets were transferred from victim to beneficiary groups via simple theft as well as via market mechanisms. When people fled the area of most intense famine and violence, moreover, they were vacating land that was coveted for its oil and grazing land. At the time, the Sudanese government was under strong pressure to pay back escalating international debt, and Khartoum was ready forcibly to depopulate oil-rich areas (notably via the militia raids) in order to do so.

In terms of *political* and *military* benefits from famine, there was also the prospect of weakening rebels by starving or driving northwards members of the Dinka ethnic group, a group that was seen as lending key support to the rebel Sudan People's Liberation Army (SPLA). At the same time, there was also an attempt by the Sudanese government to turn discontented groups against each other – notably by turning the grievances of disgruntled Arab groups in the north of Sudan against the even more marginalized southerners (via arming the Arab militias and granting them impunity). Many of these Arab groups had themselves been victims of a 'development' process that was said to be turning Sudan into a regional 'breadbasket'.[7] Having stirred the conflict in this way, the Sudanese government then presented it as an inevitable manifestation of long-standing 'ethnic tensions' – a convenient abnegation of responsibility and one that helped to insulate it against the charge of genocide.

Significantly, Khartoum's 'divide and rule' strategy extended both backwards and forwards in time, and this tells us that the tactic was not simply an improvised abuse but an habitual mode of governance. 'Divide and rule' had certainly been an integral part of British colonial domination in Sudan, and toleration of Arab pastoralists' slave raiding was part of this system. Going *forwards* from the 1988 famine, Omar al-Bashir, who became Sudanese head of state in a 1989 military coup, managed to stay in power *for three decades* via policies that violently divided civil society in a succession of civil wars and related famines. Bashir was the epitome of the 'successful' leader in a chronically 'failed' state, a gifted and cynical practitioner not only of 'divide and rule' but of what we can reasonably call 'emergency politics'. His regime exemplified what Chabal and Daloz, in their influential book *Africa Works*, called the 'instrumentalization of disorder'.[8] We will have plenty of reasons to return to this idea of instrumentalizing disorder when we come to discuss the overlapping emergencies in contemporary Western democracies.

Adding to the complexity of motives contributing to the 1988 famine was the blocking of relief by local government officials in northern Sudan, officials who (for diverse political, security, economic and health reasons) often wished to deter famine migrants from staying in areas to which they had been forcibly displaced. This further underlines the complexity of motivation in the unfolding catastrophe, and it shows how genocide may in practice be a *project of expulsion* supplemented by a *project of exclusion*. (This way of looking at genocide is relevant, too, when it comes to the Nazi Holocaust itself, as Christopher Browning and David Wyman have shown in different ways.)[9] More recently, we have seen the expulsion of civilians from war zones in the Global South alongside a project of *refusing to receive them* in the Global North.[10] Again, we need to keep in mind that disaster is not simply a case of chaos or (at the other extreme) a well-coordinated conspiracy; it routinely arises from *the interaction of complex, diverse and often self-interested agendas*.

The Sudan case also shows the importance of *blowback*, another recurring theme in this book. In practice, in the context of many disasters around the world, blowback – the adverse consequences that bounce back on the perpetrator of earlier destructive policies – has often been incorporated into an intensification of abuse. Before Sudan's second civil war began in 1983, a process of geographically uneven development had fostered widespread grievances in both northern and southern Sudan, and grievances in southern Sudan escalated when it seemed that the benefits of newly discovered oil would head straight to Khartoum. When a variety of discontents erupted into the 1983 rebellion, insurrection was itself used to justify an *intensification* of political repression and economic exploitation. In the process, those ethnic groups who had fallen partially below the protection of the law in peacetime (including the Dinka) fell further below the protection of the law in wartime, while others (like the Arab militias) were in effect raised above the law. The escalating exploitation that resulted came to include a revival of human slavery. In his 2005 book *State of Exception*, Italian political philosopher Giorgio Agamben examined the concentration camp as a kind of model or paradigm for a wider societal process in which certain groups could be killed and *it would not count as a crime*. Sudan in 1988, whether at the Meiram famine camp or more broadly, exemplified this terrifying possibility, and it showed how a pushback against exploitative policies was in effect instrumentalized to deepen exploitation.

The tragedy also illustrates a more general point that is of relevance far beyond Sudan, whether in the Global South or Global North: a crisis cannot be neatly separated from more 'normal' times but rather will tend to have its *origins* in these earlier times. The structures of inequality, vulnerability and exploitation that become extremely obvious during war or other disasters are usually already in existence in the pre-disaster period.[11] Crisis may also, as noted, be a chance to *deepen* underlying inequities and exploitation.

Sudan's 1988 famine demonstrated that while poverty can create a significant vulnerability to famine even when overall food supplies are adequate (as Sen famously showed), at the same time certain types of *wealth* can also create vulnerability – not least among those who live in resource-rich areas but lack the political muscle to protect their assets or natural resources from those who are ready to resort to violence. The famine also showed that those lacking political muscle may also find it hard to stake a claim to disaster relief within the institutions of their own society.

The functions of this humanitarian disaster, meanwhile, were revealed most clearly by official Sudanese government hostility towards relief operations and in particular towards any aid agencies or individual aid workers who tried to highlight or challenge the government's destructive priorities. If a disaster is in some sense *useful* (whether economically, politically, militarily or because of some combination of these factors), then those who try to *relieve* the disaster are likely to be obstructed, criticized, and even targeted with violence. We have seen this phenomenon in Ethiopia, Syria, Yemen and many other disaster-affected countries. Again, this dynamic will prove extremely important when we come to examine the manipulation of disasters and the suppression of dissent within contemporary Western democracies.

In her well-known 2007 book *The Shock Doctrine*, Naomi Klein argued that corporate interests had seized on disasters in the US,

Iraq, Russia, Chile and many other parts of the world – generally as a way of rolling back the state and enhancing their own profits.[12] Klein highlighted destructive processes of privatization and she stressed the global influence of Milton Friedman and colleagues at the University of Chicago in pushing this neoliberal agenda from the 1970s onwards. *The Shock Doctrine* was an important and extraordinarily gripping contribution to our understanding of disasters – not least in the analysis of the brazen profiteering that surrounded the so-called 'reconstruction' of Iraq after the 2003 US-led invasion and of the damaging effects of neoliberal ideology during the response to Hurricane Katrina which hit the southern United States in 2005.

Klein's earlier research – notably her exposé of capitalist greed and exploitation in *No Logo* – provided a perfect springboard for her dive into corporate greed in the context of disasters, and she brought out big money's links to political power in the US in particular. At the same time, Klein was not herself coming from a background in humanitarian emergencies or drawing extensively on the literature on the use and abuse of disaster in the Global South that had been gaining prominence since the late 1980s. My own research – and the work of other academics in a similar vein – showed that the instrumentalization of disaster extended much more widely than international corporations and their political allies. It also suggested that local agency was a key driver. Very often, it is international actors who have been 'played' by local actors who understand the stakes and the context much better.[13] Many national governments around the world have *appeared* to sign up to a global war (the 'war on Communism', the 'war on terror', the 'war on drugs', the 'fight against illegal migration'), while actually seeking to make money, to stay in office, or to expand the power of the state. We need to investigate not only the agendas set in Washington (or Chicago) but also the complex agendas of many *local* actors and the diversity of agendas that has driven many disasters.[14]

A second point to stress is that we need to understand the political as well as the economic instrumentalization of disasters.[15] *Pace* Klein, many of those manipulating disasters may be more interested in *increasing and abusing* the power of government than in 'rolling back' the state. The extension of state power – for good or ill – is observable not just in many disasters in the Global South but also in the aftermath of the First World War in Europe and North America as well as in reactions to the Great Depression.[16]

When we look closely at disasters in the Global South, we find complex and evolving systems that have flourished amid widespread violence, systems where power has not simply been imposed by international superpowers but rather has been exercised *at a great variety of levels*.[17]

An important and related conclusion from mutating disasters in the Global South is that we need to keep an open mind about ends and means in emergencies. In counterinsurgency operations and counterterrorism operations the aim is not necessarily to defeat an insurgency or to defeat terrorism. Other important aims have included political repression and economic exploitation. Sometimes these relatively hidden agendas have been enthusiastically pursued *under the cover* of counterinsurgency or a counterterrorism operation, with ends and means becoming to some extent inverted. At the extreme, it may be more advantageous to keep a war going than to win it, while ending a 'state of emergency' may be seen by important vested interests as self-defeating. In wartime or peacetime, a common way for governments and warlords to extract benefits (whether nationally or internationally) is to promise to rein in violence that they themselves are stirring up.[18] On the whole, violence is not something that resides *outside of* politics but rather it is something *integral* to politics (as again in Chabal and Daloz's 'instrumentalization of disorder'.)[19] These dynamics can help us to think about the ways in which violence and the idea of 'chaos' are currently being instrumentalized within Western democracies – not least by those who are stirring up violence and 'chaos' behind the scenes. Very often these people are not trying to destroy the system but to manipulate it to their own advantage – perhaps by putting themselves forward as the solution to problems that they are hyping and even stoking.

Democracy's Fragile Protection

In *Hunger and Public Action* (1989), Sen and Drèze famously argued that democracy and a free press prevent famines.[20] The authors pointed to the very severe famines under colonial rule and Communist totalitarian regimes and they suggested that democracy and a free press actively protect against famines since any failing politicians can be voted out of power, while a free press will *show* that they are failing. In effect, Sen and Drèze were suggesting the existence of a self-correcting system. That message was clearly a reassuring one for those countries that have democratic systems and a relatively free press, particularly since the idea that democracies prevent famines would seem to extend – on the same logic – to other disasters. But, while democracies do provide some protection (particularly when they are functioning in genuinely democratic ways), we need to be careful here.

Strikingly, the 1988 Sudan famine unfolded under a government that was democratically elected, albeit within a very flawed political system. Equally strikingly, the humanitarian disaster in Sri Lanka in 2008–9 unfolded under the watch of an elected government. Indeed, Sri Lanka was a well-established democracy. There are several other examples of humanitarian disasters, including famines, that took place under the watch of elected governments.[21] Within a democracy, six main sources of vulnerability to disaster stand out.

First, some types of disaster may be considered *acceptable*. Sen and Drèze themselves point to the compatibility of Indian democracy and endemic malnutrition even as they suggest that democracy eliminates outright famine. Sen and Drèze's discussion of famine and democracy was helpfully supplemented by Alex de Waal. In his book *Famine Crimes* and related articles, de Waal noted that while India's history of severe colonial famines tended to make any declaration of famine a political liability for post-independence politicians, nevertheless this taboo around famine had arisen within a *very particular* historical and political context. More specifically, the collective memory of colonial famines meant (in theory at least)[22] that famine after independence was politically unacceptable. De Waal stressed that preventing famines demands that famine be made into a 'salient political issue',[23] adding that it was important to mobilize shame strategically with this in mind. In particular, it was important to nurture some kind of 'anti-famine contract' and to challenge discourses around the inevitability of so-called 'natural disasters'.[24] While de Waal concurred with Sen and Drèze that democracies are much better than autocracies when it comes to preventing famine, de Waal's analysis also highlighted that disasters may or may not be *seen* as disasters; this can create vulnerabilities within democracies as well as autocracies.

A second source of vulnerability for democracies is that some groups, as noted, may lack the political muscle that would allow them to protect themselves from disasters. The 1988 Sudan famine illustrated that even under an elected government some groups could neither protect themselves from violence nor make an effective claim to relief. In this case, the Dinka had a subordinate status within Sudan and representation for southern groups like the Dinka had been further eroded by disruptions during the civil war, which saw southern representation being cut almost in half in 1986.[25]

A third reason why democracy may not protect against disaster is that there may be some perceived or actual advantage in promoting suffering among particular groups. We have noted some of the relevant political and economic agendas in Sudan. In Sri Lanka, the electoral benefits of stirring up hostility towards the Tamil minority were often considerable and, well before the 2008–9 disaster, this kind of ethnic politics had played a part in deflecting frustrations arising within the poorer parts of the majority Sinhalese population.[26] Alongside the physical assault on the Tigers and on Tamil civilians in 2008–9, there was a parallel project of economic accumulation that saw many of President Rajapaksa's family members benefiting from forcible corporate takeovers. Former UN spokesperson on Sri Lanka Gordon Weiss was prompted to comment in his insightful book *The Cage* that 'the war and its aftermath provided an ideal opportunity to loot the country's coffers'.[27] While it is easy to imagine that democracies protect against disasters, a rather general source of scepticism here centres on the possibility that a majority will vote (at the extreme) to eliminate a minority. Although the media and the judiciary may protect against such an eventuality, we should not assume that they will. Less starkly, politicians may simply exploit an aggressive brand of ethnic politics to get elected (with consequences that may also turn out to be severe).

That brings us to a fourth source of vulnerability to disaster within democracies: while elected politicians may indeed feel threatened by disasters on their watch (as Sen and Drèze correctly emphasize), this threat may serve as an incentive to *distort the information environment* and to *cover up* a disaster rather than preventing or relieving it. When Sen and Drèze emphasized the protection against famine that democracy provides, they tended to bracket *democracy and a free press* as if these went naturally together. Yet the case of Sri Lanka exemplifies the possibility that democracy and a widespread bullying of journalists may exist alongside one another, and it shows how the intimidation of journalists can greatly erode the protection against disaster that a democracy provides.

A fifth problem is that the mere existence of a democracy may give *false reassurance* in terms of the apparent immunity to disaster, perhaps for citizens and perhaps for international actors who deduce the absence of catastrophe from the presence of democracy. International diplomats were conscious that the government during that 1988 Sudan famine was an elected government (with an Oxford-educated prime minister to boot) – and a potential buffer between authoritarian governments in Libya and Ethiopia. In 2008–9, an abusive Sri

Lankan government was given international credit for the country's long-standing democracy as well as for its relatively strong record on economic development.

A sixth problem is that democracies may themselves be eroded, so that the existence of a democracy at one point in time does not necessarily protect from disaster a little later, or indeed from the disaster that is the collapse of democracy. Notoriously, Hitler rose to the position of Chancellor through democratic mechanisms (albeit with a large dose of intimidation), and then used Article 48 of the Weimar Republic constitution to suspend key legal protections and freedoms in the context of the 'emergency' of the Reichstag fire and the alleged Communist plot that this fire was said to reveal.

In their general study of *How Democracies Die* (2019), Steven Levitsky and Daniel Ziblatt noted:

> Since the end of the Cold War, most democratic breakdowns have been caused not by generals and soldiers but by elected governments themselves ... elected leaders have subverted democratic institutions in Georgia, Hungary, Nicaragua, Peru, the Philippines, Poland, Russia, Sri Lanka, Turkey, and Ukraine ... Elected autocrats maintain a veneer of democracy while eviscerating its substance.[28]

Underlining the need to be alert to such stealthy de-democratization, the authors note that such processes have often been portrayed as a *defence* of democracy – for example an attempt to revive democracy through cleaning up corruption or through challenging some kind of 'deep state' or hidden conspiracy. Bringing the analysis 'home' to the US, Levitsky and Ziblatt warned: 'American democracy is not as exceptional as we sometimes believe. There's nothing in our constitution or our culture to immunize us against democratic breakdown.'[29]

Legitimizing Disaster

A third key 'lesson' from many disasters around the world is that such catastrophes have often been given a damaging aura or veneer of legitimacy through the way they have been framed and presented. In any disaster, we need to take heed of some general advice given by Michel Foucault. Foucault emphasized that it's important to ask which ways of speaking are being ignored or forgotten and which are taken up and made use of, by whom, and for what kinds of reasons. Who gets to define the crisis? Who gets to define the greatest threats and the best ways of meeting these threats? What is considered inevitable and what is seen as changeable? What is the relevant 'science' that is brought to bear, by whom, and for which kinds of purposes? And how do such things *change*?

While the functions of disasters have often helped to make these calamities acceptable to powerful actors, governments may still *fear* disasters as a possible threat to political legitimacy. While this may apply even to autocratic governments, it is likely to be a particular concern for a democratic government. Part of covering up a disaster may be to present an unhelpful response as a helpful one. To the extent that democracies are *especially* worried about their legitimacy, they might even be especially tempted to misrepresent both the original disaster and the response.

Experience in the Global South suggests that when there have been attempts to cover up disasters or to present unhelpful responses as helpful, these damaging exercises have generally involved *framing* disasters in particular and contentious ways. We need to understand how this has been done. Long before Trump and his aides made the concept of 'alternative facts' notorious, a wide range of national and international officials had shown a remarkable ability to build 'alternative realities' around a variety of humanitarian disasters.

Very often, elements of cover-up have been promoted not just by governments in disaster-affected countries (be they autocratic or democratic) but also by diplomats and aid workers with strong links to Western democratic countries. Even as human suffering has escalated in a war or a famine, powerful players (including many within the international community) have very often 'agreed to agree' that responses have been appropriate and effective. Such damaging fictions have routinely been cemented by host government intimidation of aid workers and by flows of money within the aid system, with resources often accruing to those who *claim* to have addressed humanitarian problems rather than those who have *actually* addressed them.[30] Aid agencies may be reluctant to embarrass the donor governments that fund them or that help to create and implement the legal frameworks in which they operate. Crucially, there have also been strong incentives for aid workers to refrain from analysis that embarrasses or provokes the national governments that preside over, and frequently fuel, disasters.

In Sudan in 1988, violence and exploitation flourished amid international discussions that projected 'success'. For example, aid organizations were able to present a late response as a prompt one by defining famine as mass mortality (rather than Rangasami's long and violent process of asset-depletion).[31] Meanwhile, aid organizations' emphasis on counting 'numbers of displaced' and on measuring their thin-ness tended to sideline social and political processes and, more specifically, to crowd out any helpful analysis of *why* these people were displaced and *why* they were malnourished.[32] In general, a depoliticized way of speaking helped create space for a highly politicized – and human-made – famine.

A key strategy for governments has been bullying aid workers and using the prospect of humanitarian access as a means of keeping aid workers silent. This has happened repeatedly in Sudan (including in 1988). It also happened in spades in 2008–9 in Sri Lanka, where aid agencies were subject to a variety of threats and attacks[33] and also forced to sign a 'memorandum of understanding' with the government that effectively prevented them from speaking about human rights abuses or even about the inadequacy of humanitarian assistance.[34] Somewhat similarly, as the Myanmar government forces attacked the Rohingya (escalating from 2016), the government pushed strongly for the Myanmar Red Cross to take the lead with humanitarian assistance, apparently attracted by the organization's disinclination to speak publicly.[35] This is an 'advantage' that the Red Cross and Red Crescent movement retains even in contemporary 'migration emergencies', as seen for instance along Europe's southern borders.

Tragedies like those in Sudan, Sri Lanka and Myanmar illustrate an important general point – namely that when a disaster is serving political or economic or military functions, attempts to relieve the disaster may only be allowed on a piecemeal basis and on condition that aid organizations participate in certain kinds of silence and distortion. Stepping outside that depoliticized mode is likely to bring accusations that you are part of the problem – or, at the extreme, part of the enemy. Veteran MSF aid worker Fabrice Weissman has suggested that the political manipulation of relief is not simply an obstacle to the delivery of relief; it is a *condition for its existence*. In other words, it is because you are *useful* that you are allowed to work. Part of the political manipulation of relief is precisely the project of engineering certain kinds of silence. Again, when we turn to look at 'migration emergencies' in contemporary Western democracies, we will see that aid agencies are facing some similar dilemmas in terms of access versus advocacy – and we will see that they risk contributing to an 'alternative reality' that props up abuses.

Major aid donors have also sometimes justified miserable levels of relief with the claim that they have succeeded in 'not creating dependency'. This highlights the possibility that, even in the midst of the worst disaster, there may be some greater disaster, even if it's just a *moral* disaster, that has allegedly been averted through weak or non-existent assistance. Again, we will have reason to revisit the idea that minimal assistance is somehow a 'lesser evil' when we look at disasters in the Global North.

In 2008–9, the Sri Lankan government was able to present its vicious policies towards the Tamils as part of the global 'war on terror'. The government also drew heavily on the totalitarian playbook when it came to implementing abuse and projecting power. Significant here was telling 'big lies' and being willing to back them up with violence and intimidation. This pushed official discourse, even aid agency discourse to a large extent, in the direction of an 'alternative reality'. A chilling example of a 'big lie' came when Sri Lankan President Mahinda Rajapaksa declared that not a single person had been killed in what the government chose to call a 'humanitarian operation' to rescue Tamils from Tamil Tiger rebels in 2009 – a military operation that in reality involved the mass shelling of Tamil civilians within a government-declared 'safe zone', killing perhaps 40,000 men, women and children.[36] This lie was matched by the claim that Tamil civilians were being rescued and benevolently housed in 'welfare centres', though many were bussed there without choice and kept in detention behind barbed wire. The government's working definition of the enemy was strategically expanded in ways that policed the relevant lies and delusions. A particularly effective technique here was accusing critics, including those within the humanitarian aid community, of being sympathizers or supporters of the rebel Tamil Tigers.

Part of legitimizing a disaster is seizing on the fashionable language of the day, and perhaps even using it to present the disaster as *a good thing*. In relation to Darfur, Susanne Jaspars has shown that Sudanese government officials have often been skilled at talking international 'aid-speak' even while ruthlessly pursuing their own political objectives. For example, when the Sudanese government came to see Darfur's camps for displaced people as centres for rebel organization and subversive politics, the government enthusiastically took up the international mantra that one should shift quickly from 'relief to development', moving towards 'self-sufficiency' and 'sustainable livelihoods'. Displaced people were also forcibly ejected from camps on the grounds that these camps were promoting 'dependency'. In addition, the camps were said to be promoting 'the political economy of war', demonstrating once more Khartoum's ability to pick up on and instrumentalize the terminology and debates in the aid world.[37] Somewhat similarly, in the DRC and Somalia, for example, a push for 'resilience' and for a shift from 'relief to development' was used to cut emergency aid.[38] The experienced and astute aid worker Nicholas Stockton suggested in 1998 that an excessive concern with 'fuelling the political economy of war' was helping to *undermine* humanitarian aid to the DRC.[39]

In the 1980s and 1990s, criticism of aid (either as fuelling conflict or simply ignoring an underlying human rights disaster) fed into a growing concern that humanitarian aid should *Do No Harm*, the title of an influential 1999 book by Mary Anderson. This 'Do No Harm' framework emerged primarily because of manipulation of aid by abusive governments like those in Sudan and Ethiopia as well as by the Hutu militias in the Democratic Republic of the Congo – and there was much to recommend the framework. But, in the context of a global 'war on terror', the need to 'Do No Harm' and be 'conflict sensitive' was taken up in perverse ways and became part of the ideological justification for withholding aid from rebel-held areas that were said to be incubating terrorism.[40] In effect, the old habit of depriving rebel areas of aid was reinvented, this time with the help of the anti-terrorism agenda and the 'Do No Harm' framework.[41] When we come to look at the suffering of migrants/refugees in contemporary Western democracies (and on the geographical fringes of these countries), we will see how a set of damaging and often violent policies has also been justified in terms of 'doing no harm' (as in the often-relentless official focus on not helping 'the smugglers' and not encouraging 'dangerous journeys').

Violence often generates an aura of legitimacy for itself. For example, in the 1988 famine in Sudan, when civilians unconnected to rebel groups were attacked, this indiscriminate violence tended to push these groups *towards* the rebels.[42] The expanding rebellion in turn created legitimacy for intensified violence against (expanding) 'rebel areas', with economic goals to the fore. Such cases can be seen as illustrating Arendt's concept of 'action as propaganda', a concept that again will prove extremely helpful when we come to examine disasters in Western democracies. As noted, 'action as propaganda' essentially refers to actions that make false propaganda appear more true over time. In *The Origins of Totalitarianism*, Arendt referred to 'the advantages of a propaganda that constantly "adds the power of organization" to the feeble and unreliable voice of argument, and thereby realizes, so to speak, on the spur of the moment, whatever it says'.[43]

The conflict in Syria also showed how Arendt's 'action as propaganda' could operate in wartime. In the context of the Arab Spring, peaceful political protests in Syria were a huge threat to the authoritarian Assad regime. But the government's vicious crackdown prompted an armed rebellion that proved much easier for Damascus to delegitimize, both domestically and internationally. Moreover, by releasing *jihadi* extremists from prison, by partially exempting ISIS areas from attacks, and by promoting criminality and terrorism via covert cooperation and the imposition of scarcity, the Assad regime actively fostered some of the most criminal and extremist elements *within* the rebellion. This created a situation in which influential officials and journalists (including Boris Johnson shortly before he became UK Foreign Secretary) could paint Assad as a 'lesser evil' in comparison to ISIS.[44]

In Chapter 10 we will explore the damage that *the 'lesser evil' argument* has done in relation to disasters unfolding in the Global North. Here, I mean essentially the argument that one should do harm in the present if it will prevent a greater harm in the future. In this context (as we saw with the example of ISIS in Syria but the phenomenon extends much more widely), extremists may become *oddly useful*, not least in legitimizing the extreme measures of those who say they are pre-empting extremism.[45] We have seen that, in the context of many humanitarian interventions in the Global South, depriving people of aid has itself been presented as a 'lesser evil' in comparison to the 'greater evils' that allegedly arise from providing *substantial* aid – 'greater' evils like 'fuelling war', stoking 'the political economy of war', supporting terrorism, undermining resilience, and so on.[46] As part of this discourse, the potential embarrassment of failing to prevent or relieve a disaster has routinely been 'explained away' with reference to some kind of 'science' or theory: the theory that withholding aid will undermine terrorism, for example, or the argument that offering only minimal food relief will cleverly support local markets. In practice, various critiques of humanitarian aid (including, incidentally, those to which I contributed) have been manipulated, hijacked, distorted and selectively appropriated in ways that have often reinforced violent and exploitative processes, not least by reinforcing the anti-aid lobby.

Dangerous Explanations

A fourth 'lesson' from disasters in the Global South is that explanations for disasters routinely *feed into* disasters. Again, this will be important when we come to consider disasters in Western democracies. The contributing role of explanations is especially clear when those explanations involve scapegoating – and the best-known example is the scapegoating of the Jews by the Nazis in the aftermath of the First World War, with the Jews being blamed both for starting and losing this war.[47] Another example of turning on an 'internal enemy' was the mass internment of Japanese Americans during the Second World War. If we go back much further in history, we find many other instances where explanations for disaster have fed strongly into violence (as for example when the Black Death plague was blamed on Jews who were alleged to be poisoning the wells).[48]

When it came to Rwanda's 1994 genocide, one important contributing factor was blaming Tutsi civilians for the Rwandan army's military setbacks. Abetted by Hutu extremist propaganda, the army made a call to arms against an internal Tutsi 'enemy' that was said to have betrayed their country by helping the Rwandan Patriotic Front rebels to advance from Uganda. In Mahmood Mamdani's words, the army and associated Hutu militias 'turned around to face the enemy within', presenting themselves as trying to 'purify the nation and rid it of all impurities that detracted from its strength'.[49]

In Sierra Leone's civil war in the 1990s, various fighting groups feared 'betrayal' by civilians; this fed into an escalating cycle of anti-civilian violence and increased civilian hostility towards these fighting groups. Women were sometimes blamed as a particular source of 'betrayal'. In my own research in Sierra Leone, one man held hostage in 2000 by a rogue army faction called the West Side Boys told me that six women attached to the group were accused of witchcraft in response to the thwarting of that faction's military progress. In effect, overconfidence was feeding into the search for internal enemies (a tendency, as we shall see, that extends much more widely). In the case of the soldiers who killed those six women, they had been told that if they just fired two shots, UN peacekeepers would run away. 'But these boys were getting blocked', the former hostage recalled. 'They were not making progress. They have an exaggerated idea of their own power, maybe a kind of indoctrination.'

Magical thinking was an important part of the war in Sierra Leone, and it was often harnessed to very practical agendas like inspiring the courage necessary to stand up to opponents or to secure access to valuable resources such as diamonds. As Patrick Muana has pointed out, 'For a counter-insurgency to succeed, [the] myth of RUF [Revolutionary United Front rebels'] invincibility had to be challenged by an even greater myth with the requisite psychological force to restore confidence in the displaced population.'[50] The civil defence forces (who stood up to the twin threat of government and rebel soldiers) were routinely attributed with supernatural powers, and carried a range of magic charms such as fly whisks, mirrors and shells to boost these powers. They were said to be immune to bullets provided that sacred taboos were kept.[51] Importantly, where magic charms did not succeed in protecting fighters, the conclusion was sometimes drawn that protective taboos (like sexual abstinence) had been insufficiently adhered to; stricter observance, conversely, would bring back the desired protection. Again, we will have occasion to revisit this reflex in a very different political context. Whether in the Global South or the Global North, we need to understand how disasters are explained and how *this* may feed into the production and legitimization of *future* disaster.

Quite often this has a *moral* dimension. Drawing particularly on his experience in Uganda, Tim Allen has stressed that a peace process is often accompanied by some kind of project of 'moral reform' in which key actors attempt to assert or reassert their dominance within the purported reinvention of a moral order.[52] We can also see a revealing example of a concern with 'moral reform' in Jason Hickel's anthropological work, published in 2015, among the Zulu ethnic group in South Africa.[53]

Hickel found that suffering around poverty, crop failures, deaths and miscarriages was commonly attributed to breaches in the moral order. These breaches were seen as displeasing the ancestors, who had withdrawn their protection as a result. While one might expect such traditional belief systems to be eroded by modernity, Hickel showed how modernization often *reinforced* traditional beliefs. He described the idealized homestead as a material embodiment of the moral order that many rural Zulu have seen as embattled. On a practical level, what disrupted the traditional homestead most substantially was apartheid and the mass exploitation of Black labour in urban areas. But many Zulu migrants were blaming poverty and other economic and social problems on the progressive gender and sexual politics of the ruling African National Congress party. More specifically, blame was directed at official policies permitting abortion, endorsing homosexuality, supporting single mothers and more generally granting equal rights to women and children. These initiatives were presented as upsetting the moral order, distressing the ancestors, disrupting the idealized homestead, and thereby jeopardizing prosperity and fertility. In this way, the disappearance of a golden age was linked to the non-observance of certain taboos. Of course, it is difficult to be sure how universal such reflexes are, and Western anthropology has sometimes emphasized the strangeness and exoticism of 'far-away' rituals and beliefs. But the inclination to magical thinking and the inclination to respond to setbacks with calls for moral reform can plausibly be seen as fundamentally *human*. Certainly, when we come to discuss responses to disasters and suffering within contemporary Western democracies, these reflexes seem to be rather strongly in evidence.

A different set of dangers arises when explanations for disasters are generated within the humanitarian system, though these too can point towards victim-blaming and scapegoating. Susanne Jaspars' long-term work in Darfur, Sudan, shows that international assistance has generally been limited by a very narrow view of humanitarianism that emphasizes the actions and responsibilities of individual aid recipients, while typically not addressing or even discussing the underlying conflict or the destructive role of the Sudanese government. The type of humanitarianism that has been practised has also tended to sideline the need to put proper health systems in place.[54] Amid continuing high levels of violence, donors' food security assessments have focused on consumption, on dietary diversity, on hygiene habits, and on income and expenditure. In this mode, responsibility for any suffering implicitly lies with target populations who adopt 'the wrong behaviours' while conflict itself is largely wished away.

More generally, Mark Duffield has pointed to a growing 'bunkerization' of aid workers hemmed in by security protocols. Many have relied increasingly on 'remote management' and on the quantitative data generated by technology rather than in-person conversations. As humanitarian crisis deepened in Darfur in the early 2000s, Duffield discovered that the UN was using algorithms to estimate the changing size of the camps there. Such estimates could be made, in Duffield's words, 'without the need to go there'.[55] Assistance was increasingly being delegated to machines; so too was *thinking itself*.[56] Yet Darfur has basically been stuck in a what Duffield has called a 'permanent emergency' with continuing high levels of violence and displacement that firmly stand in the way of 'development'. Such a situation cannot be fixed by apps.

Duffield and Jaspars' work speaks to a far-reaching depoliticization of a highly politicized space. The bland language (and figures) in which aid agencies conduct much of their discussion – at least their *public* discussion – is also closely related to intimidation, most often intimidation by the government in the country where they are operating. In understanding disasters anywhere in the world, it's important to understand how abusive governments have tried to maintain legitimacy by restricting flows of information.

A final area where explanations have been deficient is explaining peace. Why does peace happen, and what kinds of peace are possible? Wars have often been attributed to 'mindless violence', with peace seen as arriving when people 'come to their senses'. But this way of thinking and speaking is not very helpful for understanding why peace turns into war, why war turns into peace, or what kind of peace (often a violent and exploitative one) is actually emerging from a war. In Guatemala in 2002, I looked at how security structures adapted to a 'peace' that threatened their prestige and material interests; these structures were finding a renewed role in the 'war on crime' and the 'war on drugs'. Meanwhile, the extreme inequalities that had fuelled the war were generally not being tackled.[57] In a shift to peace, many of the underlying functions of war – social control, distraction from class grievances, legitimacy for security forces – are likely to *remain in place*. Peace is a modification, albeit often a substantial one, of a war system.

Naturally, the aim of 'getting back to normal' is often expressed in the wake of wars and other disasters – reconstructing the economy, rebuilding the institutions, resettling the refugees, and so on. But, even if one could reconstruct the precise political and economic conditions prevailing at the outset of a war (and assuming external factors are constant and discounting any war-weariness), then wouldn't the war just break out all over again – for the same reasons as before? This raises a question that might be asked in relation to *any* disaster: isn't the process of reconstruction and the process of 'getting back to normal' actually a rather direct route back to the vulnerabilities and grievances that created the disaster in the first place? Again, this consideration will be highly relevant when we look at Covid, for example – or even at the 'disaster' of Trump.

Uneven Costs

In many disasters in the Global South, the shifting distribution of suffering has strongly affected the *trajectory* of the disaster. In the Global North, too, we need to ask what effect the distribution of risks is having on the willingness of those in power to tackle key underlying problems.

Whether it's a war or a famine or some other disaster, the magnitude and timing of interventions seems to be dictated less by the intensity of the suffering than by the changing distribution of costs and risks that the disaster involves for powerful players. Insofar as people feel insulated from the costs of a disaster, they may have little interest in relieving or preventing it. And these things can change. For example, a famine relief operation may be promoted when rural famine victims *bring their problems to the towns*. The *trajectory* of the disaster will be strongly influenced by the shifting distribution of costs arising from these disasters, as well as the shifting distribution of benefits.[58]

When considering the uneven costs arising from disaster, we should also note that the suffering of disaster victims may or may not translate into costs for national or international officials or aid workers, all of whom may have some responsibility for relieving or preventing disaster but also important political or security reasons for *not* getting involved. Large-scale publicity may bring about a major (and often belated) response as the *costs of inaction* suddenly exceed the (economic and political) costs of action, something that Peter Cutler noticed in relation to the belated international response to the Ethiopian famine in the mid-1980s.[59] Part of insulating aid workers against costs has been the system of fortified aid compounds and related 'remote management' highlighted by Duffield, so that even as the humanitarian system adapts to insecurity, it risks understanding it less and less.[60]

When it comes to the costs of disasters, a key problem is that different groups tend to have different views on what *constitutes* a disaster and which kinds of costs should be prioritized. Underpinning vulnerability to disasters is the fact that relatively powerless groups generally do not get to *define* the crisis. They do not get to determine when an intervention is necessary, what kind of intervention it should be, or even to declare in retrospect whether the intervention has been helpful. In their research on responses to Covid in South Sudan, Alice Robinson, Peter Justin, Naomi Pendle and colleagues found that these problematic responses were strongly constrained by local perceptions that *other crises* (including conflict, nutrition, and a range of health threats) were more pressing, along with the common belief that a drastic response to Covid would *exacerbate* these other crises.[61] When government officials or aid workers advised people to prioritize Covid, moreover, the willingness to accept this advice was found to depend on the degree of trust that had been built up historically (often quite low). In the case in South Sudan, the perception that Covid was a 'white disease' – and also that foreign countries were interested in protecting *themselves* – has been part of the mistrust. In these rather unpromising circumstances, telling people that they are misguided or irrational is less helpful than taking their priorities seriously, trying to understand how and why their priorities and perceptions arise, and attempting to figure out how welfare can be maximized when people face multiple problems. This speaks to what is a much wider difficulty when it comes to the overlapping disasters affecting Western democracies as well as the rest of the world: for those who are prioritizing a strong response to Covid or global warming or some other disaster, what account are they taking of those who face multiple short-term crises (many of them economic) and who may take a radically different line on which 'disaster' should be prioritized?

Conclusion

We have seen that disasters are actively produced by a range of actors who frequently benefit from disaster in some way. Many of the benefits are opportunistic and local agency tends to be very considerable. At the same time, the disaster system as a whole tends to acquire a kind of functionality, or a diverse set of functions, that helps to sustain it. Democracies do not necessarily protect against disaster – particularly against suffering among those with relatively little political influence in their own societies. The vulnerability of such groups is compounded when disasters and relief failures are painted as legitimate. At the same time, explanations for disasters – especially when they involve scapegoats and when they let abusive governments off the hook – can easily feed into current and future disasters. Meanwhile, an understanding of who is bearing the main costs (and how this shifts over time) can help us to understand how a disaster evolves.

Again, our analysis of the functions, legitimizations, explanations and costs of disasters within the Global South raises a number of important questions that will be pertinent when we look at the overlapping disasters within Western democracies. Who benefits from disasters? In what ways do they benefit? What are the political benefits? What are the economic benefits? And what role do the beneficiaries play in shaping the disaster (including through blocking attempts to relieve it)? Who bears the main costs and how does this shape the evolving disaster? To what extent is disaster and relief failure presented as legitimate, and how is this done? Who gets to define which disasters are prioritized? How do explanations for disasters feed into future disasters? Who hypes which definition of the enemy? What do they gain from this process? How does the definition of the enemy mutate over time, and with what consequences?

When it comes to disasters affecting Western democracies, it will again be important to look at who has political muscle and who doesn't. Rather than assuming that democracy and a free press prevent disasters, it will be important to ask how much protection democracy and a 'free press' actually provide, and to whom. What are the safeguards against picking on minorities, and are they being eroded? With any government, whether authoritarian or democratic, whether in the Global North or the Global South, whether in the 'East' or the 'West', a key question is *which parts of the population* a government is interested in defending, and which (at the extreme) are seen as *worth sacrificing*.[62]

In many parts of the world, disaster-creating policies have been generated and defended through magical thinking as well as through the use of 'action as propaganda' and through a politics of the 'lesser evil'. All of these phenomena were highlighted by Arendt in relation to totalitarianism. All have been important in disasters in the Global South. And all will be important when we come to look at how crises within Western democracies are being generated and legitimized.

When 'alternative realities' are created and sustained, there is usually an element of lying as well as an element of magical thinking. Either way, alternative realities may be defended and deepened through a process of violence. Whether in relation to disasters in the Global South or the Global North, we need to ask not just how magical thinking has arisen (and with what consequences) but how magical thinking has been *defended* (and with what consequences). Under Communist regimes in China, Cambodia and the Soviet Union, fantastical and destructive visions of development were ruthlessly defended through an ever-widening circle of mass persecution and even human-made famine.[63] The system could not admit it was on the wrong path and this obstinacy constantly widened the circle of enemies.

3

A Self-Reinforcing System?

Today, several overlapping disasters, both within and beyond the Global North, are reinforcing each other through a variety of mechanisms that we need to understand much better. A key element in this emerging system is that a number of disasters, whether slow-burning or more sudden and dramatic, are being used to bolster the policies and the toxic politics that helped to generate them. High-profile and shorter-term disasters are tending to feed underlying economic, ecological and (longer-term) political disasters while these underlying disasters are also fuelling the more high-profile and shorter-term emergencies.

Part of the problem is that politics is centring increasingly on the manipulation of 'blowback' from earlier disasters. Again, this suggests that we may be moving towards a system that is actually *self-reinforcing* rather than self-correcting, a system that in effect feeds on its own failures. In other words, we face the frightening spectre of a 'positive feedback loop'[1] as opposed to a 'negative feedback loop' that brings systems back closer to a previous state. This echoes many contexts in the Global South, where disasters like war and famine have routinely fed into each other and where anti-democratic and other abusive elements have frequently thrived on the very disorder that they have helped to create.

One influential way of analysing the politics of emergency in the last two decades has been securitization theory, which emerged from Copenhagen in the 1990s. Securitization theory centres on the observation that important issues are sometimes taken outside the sphere of normal politics via 'speech acts' that present the relevant issue as a matter of life-and-death, thereby legitimizing extraordinary measures. There are different variations of the theory, some more sophisticated than others.[2] But, particularly in its purest and original form, the approach posits a relatively sudden and speech-driven shift to emergency politics. Today, however, we have something more like a *permanent emergency*, a paradoxical term that Mark Duffield coined primarily in relation to long-running conflicts in the Global South and which he subsequently employed in analyses of global systems.[3] Rather than a sudden shift or a *moment of transition* into a politics that has been radically securitized, the politics of emergency in Western democracies is today a notably extended one, with individual emergencies ebbing and flowing and emergency powers rising and (sometimes) falling. Emergency politics is better seen as a fluctuating system than a single event, and the general direction of travel within this complex system seems clear enough; some kind of emergency politics is becoming more and more 'normal'.

A Focus on Consequences

We have pointed to the role of magical thinking within the current disaster-producing system but, of course, a magician is not a practitioner of magical thinking; rather, the magician exploits the fact that *we want to believe*, while simultaneously mastering the art of distraction. The magician's trick depends on directing and redirecting our attention. A key part of the current politics, similarly, is distracting attention. More often than not, this means getting the audience to focus on *consequences rather than causes*.

That dangerous focus was insightfully explored by Nafeez Ahmed in an important and relatively little-known 2011 article in *Global Change, Peace and Security*. Ahmed pointed to the intersection of global ecological, economic and energy crises, noting for example that rising energy prices (reflecting 'post-peak' global production) had helped to drive the rapidly rising food prices that in turn helped to fuel famine (for example in Somalia in 2011) and political unrest (notably in the Middle East).[4] Characterizing current policy responses as influenced by (and in turn shaping) the discipline of international relations (IR) in particular, Ahmed observed:

> … orthodox IR has no means of responding to global systemic crises other than to reduce them to their symptoms. Indeed orthodox IR theory has largely responded to global systemic crises not with

> new theory, but with the expanded application of existing theory to 'new security challenges' such as 'low-intensity' intra-state conflicts; inequality and poverty; environmental degradation; international criminal activities including drugs and arms trafficking; proliferation of weapons of mass destruction; and international terrorism.[5]

Ahmed argued that this emphasis on 'new security challenges' 'actually *guarantees greater insecurity* by promoting policies which frame the "non-traditional" issues purely as amplifiers of quite traditional threats'.[6] In this way, '... a preoccupation with "security" ends up becoming an unwitting accomplice in the intensification of insecurity'.[7] In these circumstances, escalating crises have not been eliciting transformation but instead are held to require relatively powerful states 'to *radicalize* the exertion of their military-political capacities to maintain existing power structures, *to keep the lid on*' (my emphasis).[8] In another telling passage, Ahmed referred to the origins of global environmental, energy and economic crises in social, political, economic and ideological structures, noting:

> it is often assumed that these contemporary structures are largely what need to be 'secured' and protected from the dangerous impacts of global crises, rather than transformed precisely to ameliorate these crises in the first place.[9]

That need for transformation has also been emphasized by many others: for example by Naomi Klein, in her well-known books *This Changes Everything* and *No Is Not Enough*. Klein has rightly stressed that dealing with climate change means huge investment in the public sphere (renewable energy, public transport, energy efficiency), which in turn means taxing the wealthy.[10] Yet it's already clear that weather-related disasters are being used to shore up systems of security and political reflexes, which are themselves disaster-producing, so that the danger of a self-reinforcing system once again looms into view.[11]

Commenting on reconstruction efforts after Hurricane Katrina broke the levee system in New Orleans and caused widespread flooding and displacement of people there and more widely in Louisiana, Klein observed, 'What stands out is the commitment to wage all-out war on labour standards and the public sphere – which is bitterly ironic, because the failure of public infrastructure is what turned Katrina into a human catastrophe in the first place.'[12] Even *after* Katrina, critical infrastructure was neglected – rebuilding levees, for example, and modernizing pumps. The destruction of much of the public housing in the wake of Katrina (despite often minor damage) left poorer residents – disproportionately people of colour – vulnerable to rising rents, while also impeding the return of displaced residents.[13] Tax credits and subsidies in New Orleans were largely focused on enterprise zones and failed to incentivize adequate supplies of affordable housing, with the benefits going disproportionately to large firms and high-income residents.[14] Meanwhile, poor neighbourhoods were forced to compete with each other for public resources.[15] Gotham notes that the prevailing mode of 'recovery' in New Orleans had the effect of undermining the meaning and working definition of citizenship, particularly since assistance came to depend largely on the ability to pay.[16] One civil-rights organizer said the poor official response to Katrina 'convinced us that we had no caretakers'.[17] Such perceptions tend to jeopardize political cohesion and stability in *any* society, and we know that failure to respond properly to weather-related and geological disasters has been an important source of political instability in many parts of the world.[18]

Particularly after 9/11, the US emergency response machinery was focused to a large extent on the possibility of terror attacks.[19] The budget of the Federal Emergency Management Agency (FEMA) had been cut, along with federal funds to boost New Orleans' poorly constructed levee system,[20] which had been badly maintained by the US Army Corps of Engineers.[21] Notwithstanding these failings, President George W. Bush concluded from the catastrophe that the military should have a *greater* role in reacting to future disasters.[22] Of course, it's true that the military can often react quickly to disasters. But, apart from the failings of the army's engineers' corps, there was the wider problem of the country's emergency management having evolved conjointly with preparations for nuclear and terrorist attacks. This was part of what took attention away from infrastructural vulnerability to disasters like Katrina. More broadly, so much money and attention had been lavished on the US military and on foreign wars that there seemed to be precious little left for protecting the domestic population.

A related and again potentially self-reinforcing aspect of disasters is that underlying problems like climate change get securitized while threatened populations are turned into *threatening* populations.[23] Again, this process could be seen in responses to Hurricane Katrina in New Orleans. As Klein recalls in a typically vivid passage, 'Checkpoints were set up to trap people in the flooded parts of town. On Danziger Bridge, police officers shot Black residents on sight (five of the officers ultimately pled guilty, and the city came to a 13.3-million settlement with the families in that case and two other similar post-Katrina cases).'[24] Vigilantes combed the streets looking for looters. Private security guards were showing up fresh from Iraq.[25]

More broadly, the US military has been positioning climate change as a huge threat to which it has many of the answers. Yet, again, this amounts to 'keeping the lid on': it legitimizes massive spending on a huge military machine; it keeps funds away from necessary infrastructure; it reinforces the militarism of others; and it helps to sustain the massive contribution that the US military (along with other militaries around the world) is making to greenhouse gas emissions.[26]

From Washington or London or Paris, government officials may look out at the world and see a growing list of security threats that demand an ever-greater emphasis on security and the use of force. But this fearful perspective is strongly influenced by the self-interest and blinkers of the security structures themselves and, crucially, it tends to miss the extent to which these various threats are being actively stoked precisely through various kinds of securitization.[27]

A parallel problem exists at the domestic level, where the many effects of neoliberal policies are often seen as some kind of 'threat' that an even more right-wing politics will somehow be able to address. The far right has often promoted and benefited from this reflex. As Neil Davidson and Richard Saull put it:

> The far right has been able to claim that a series of outcomes – including the marginalization and non-assimilation of ethnic minorities, dependence on the welfare state and the disproportionate numbers of non-whites in prison – are because of inherent cultural identities and practices within such groups ... Culture is left as the only explanatory residue for apparent behavioural traits that do not conform to a 'meritocratic' neoliberal subjectivity.[28]

In terms of systems that feed off their own shortcomings, we should note too that in the financial world there has been a proliferation of financial instruments designed to price and manage the risks that are associated with extreme weather events, so that uncertainty around the climate itself becomes an opportunity for profit.[29] Meanwhile, some companies have been buying up large amounts of land (for example, in China, South Korea and South Sudan) on the basis of climate change projections, of anticipated rainfall in different regions, and of expected rises in food prices.[30] Such adaptations can be expected in any disaster and not all of them are bad. But, whenever there are benefits from crisis, the information environment can quickly become polluted.

A disaster-producing system will always produce a desire to seal oneself off or to insulate oneself from the costs. This has been explored by Klein in *No Is Not Enough*, for example, and by Ruben Andersson in *No Go World*, which explores (among other things) an aid system increasingly obsessed by its own security. In terms of Mark Duffield's work, a key contribution came in his 2001 book *Global Governance and the New Wars* which foreshadowed Ahmed's argument in many respects.[31] Duffield argued that managing 'emergency' has increasingly meant sealing oneself off from disasters, notably by trying to 'contain' refugee flows, while the underlying causes of precarity and insecurity have been dangerously and systematically set aside.

It was in his 2019 book *Post-Humanitarianism* that Duffield gave the most systematic analysis of 'permanent emergency', including the links with the extreme mobility of capital and with technological innovation and automation. Building on his 2007 book *Development, Security and Unending War* and on the distinction he drew there between 'insured' and 'uninsured' populations, Duffield used *Post-Humanitarianism* to highlight how a growing hegemony of market-based approaches had effectively rendered huge populations around the world 'surplus to requirements' – either unemployed or living a very precarious life, with minimal social security being provided by the state or the international community.[32] Emphasizing that precarity is something increasingly afflicting the Global North as well as the Global South, Duffield drew attention to an increasingly important fault-line between those lucky enough to be mobile and those stuck in their locality (with all the lack of bargaining power that this implies). The costs of shocks such as the 2007–8 financial crisis have been loaded disproportionately onto the immobile, while anger among these groups has fuelled variations of populist nationalism. For Duffield, governing precarity has involved increasingly sophisticated systems that rely on new technology. To a significant degree, this removes human decision-making from the equation, often generating a misleading aura of objectivity around ostensibly depoliticized responses. In terms of humanitarian and welfare interventions, there has been a rhetorical focus on building 'resilience' and 'self-reliance' and on improving the decision-making of the poor. But this, as we saw with Jaspars' work on Darfur in Sudan, can easily shade into victim-blaming while narrowing the scope for addressing the delusions, violence and exploitation that underpin disasters.

While not focusing explicitly on global systems, the Italian political philosopher Giorgio Agamben has explored the links between the obsession with 'security' and the kinds of underlying inequality and superfluity that Duffield has been highlighting. In fact, if we consider the work of Ahmed, Duffield, Jaspars, Klein and Andersson alongside the work of Agamben, then we can begin to see rather clearly how the international system for responding to disasters and human suffering more generally has embraced a dangerous focus on *consequences rather than causes*. That kind of focus is also a pretty good summary of international failings in relation to the 1988 famine in Sudan. Agamben makes the habitual focus on consequences explicit when he suggests that while once the aim of policy-makers was 'to rule the causes', by contrast 'modernity pretends to control the effects'.

Importantly, Agamben refers to 'the paradoxical convergence today of an absolutely liberal paradigm in economy with an unprecedented and equally absolute paradigm of state and police control'.[33] On similar lines, Cunningham and Warwick note that capitalism pushes for deregulation and is ostensibly opposed to any state influence in the economy but that this habit 'coexists with, and in fact relies upon, a massive expansion of authoritarian state power and complex regulatory regimes (often now enforced at a transnational level)'.[34] In this way, an ongoing violence (and indeed a major role for the state) appears to be necessary for the reproduction of capitalism – at least in its more unregulated forms. In the US, there has been a spectacular and extraordinarily cruel rise in mass incarceration,[35] a massive human disaster with about two million people currently in prisons and jails. While the causes are complicated, it is no coincidence that this extraordinary expansion has taken place alongside an equally extraordinary escalation in inequality. Meanwhile, adherence to 'free market' ideology has proceeded quite happily alongside huge state spending not just on prisons but on defence, border security, policing, and so on.

Debt and De-Democratization

Coping with the effects of an increasingly unregulated capitalism also encouraged processes of de-democratization that have in effect 'come home' to Europe and the US from countries where taking away sovereignty is part of a long and inglorious colonial and postcolonial 'tradition'. In the 1980s people in Africa, Asia and Latin America commonly found that high levels of debt were greatly undermining the autonomy of national governments (whether elected or not), while vesting power in a group of distant officials (notably inside the International Monetary Fund and World Bank) who imposed spending cuts, privatization and other 'free market' measures designed to improve the ratio of exports to imports and promote debt repayment. Pressure to democratize the Global South sat oddly with this taking away of decision-making power.[36] Such 'structural adjustment' was an important cause of Sierra Leone's terrible civil war in the 1990s, and wreaked considerable havoc elsewhere.

One of the shocks of 'disasters coming home' was when that loss of sovereignty after the 2007–8 financial crash was extended to Greece and, to a lesser extent, other European countries like Spain, Portugal, Italy and Ireland. It's hard to imagine the US being dictated to in such a way and, indeed, the US has been able to use the attractions of the dollar and its control over financial markets to maintain huge balance of payments deficits and in this sense to live persistently beyond its means.[37] However, if we shift our attention to *cities within the US*, we can see how debt *has* actually brought a substantial loss of sovereignty.

Consider Detroit. Having suffered a devastating loss of jobs in car manufacturing in particular as well as widespread lay-offs in the public sector, the city reeled from the financial crisis in 2007–8. There were 100,000 home foreclosures in the four years from 2011. Many of those affected had taken out subprime mortgages whose 'teaser' rates (sometimes starting at one per cent and then jumping quickly to 10 or even 17.5 per cent) disguised how unaffordable they would become.[38]

By 2011, Detroit was one of the cities across the state of Michigan that were deep in debt. The Michigan state legislature passed a law radically increasing the power of emergency managers so as to deal with the fiscal crisis. In his detailed study of overlapping crises in Detroit, Josiah Rector notes that financial crisis led not only to debt and austerity but to the 'suspension of democracy in Michigan's Black-majority cities'. By 2014, half of Michigan's Black residents (and only two per cent of the state's white residents) lived in cities that were governed by unelected emergency managers. Under the rule of emergency managers, repayments to banks were prioritized, budgets were cut, pensions were reduced, and the price of utilities rose sharply.[39] Michigan's 'Public Act 4', hastily approved in March 2011, authorized emergency managers to override the authority of the city mayor, the city council and the school board; it even allowed for locking local officials out of their email accounts.[40] Bankruptcy itself cost Detroit 164 million dollars (payable to Jones Day, from which firm the emergency manager had been hired, and other legal firms).[41] More generally, the highly technical nature of many municipal debt products allowed financial service firms to encourage local officials to 'leave the driving to us', further weakening democratic accountability.[42]

Carl Schmitt famously said that 'Sovereign is he who decides on the exception',[43] noting also that 'the legal system itself can anticipate the exception and can "suspend itself"'.[44] We've noted, too, that the Weimar Republic made provision for such an eventuality in its Article 48, which provided for the President to suspend important freedoms in the event of a major threat to public order, thereby opening the door to the suspension of freedoms within (rather than the abrogation of) the Weimar constitution as the Nazis rose to power. In Detroit, it turned out that sovereignty did not actually reside in the Detroit city council or in the people of Detroit but could quickly be taken away in the context of an emergency.

Rector's careful study describes the city's contracts for privatizing water as 'notoriously corrupt'.[45] And the human consequences came quickly. In the five years from 2014 at least 300,000 people had their water supply cut off, a bitter irony in a city adjoining America's fourth biggest lake. This was a human disaster that led to protests from the United Nations. With real incomes falling, the price of water had been rising rapidly due to partial privatization along with startling levels of corruption in the contracts for service providers. These rising water prices were part of the city's response to financial crisis, reflecting not just the crash of 2007–8 but some bizarre borrowing practices, notably interest 'swap' deals in which city officials bet on rising interest rates.[46]

The outsourcing and budget cuts that were pushed through under emergency management also led to increased copper and lead toxicity in Detroit's water supply. Meanwhile, the nearby city of Flint was under emergency management to pay its debts when water supplies were switched from lake water to the Flint river, where high concentrations of corrosive matter meant that toxic lead and copper leaked from pipes into the water supply, finding its way into people's bloodstreams.[47] In the longer term, drastic cuts under emergency management did nothing to make places like Flint more attractive to live, something that was essential if their revenue-base was to be revived.[48]

We may say, in fact, that cities like Detroit and Flint have experienced a variation of the loss of sovereignty documented by Klein in relation to Puerto Rico, which lacks representation in Congress but is subject to US law and which found in 2016 that its economy was placed into the hands of an unelected Financial Oversight and Management Board.[49]

Of course, the effects of debt play out differently in different societies. But the consequences for democracy are rarely good. In Hungary, a socialist government lost credibility from austerity policies forced upon the country by the EU and IMF, and this paved the way for Viktor Orbán's electoral success in 2010. This success, along with a reliance on bond markets rather than the IMF for financing, helped Orbán to implement his own brand of 'financial nationalism', maintaining the sovereignty of his government in the face of pressures from the EU and the IMF and implementing a range of repressive political measures (measures, incidentally, that did not deter support from the bond markets).[50] Despite some nationalizations, Orbán has mostly pursued neoliberal policies, including tax concessions to large companies, removing labour protections, and implementing sharp cuts to social services and welfare benefits.[51] As part of this emerging system, 'special supertaxes have been used to pillage whole sectors, including banking, telecommunications, insurance, and household energy'.[52] Income tax has been reduced for the rich while higher value-added tax has hit poorer people disproportionately. Punitive public works schemes have been established, for which pay has been very low.[53] With poverty rising, Kornai observes, 'the poorest are stigmatized and the homeless are chased out of cities by mayoral decree'.[54] Alongside all this, and in line with Agamben's analysis, spending on policing has been rising. Indeed, Stubbs and Lendvai-Bainton comment that Hungary is well on the path to a 'carceral state'.[55] We can see from this case that maintaining 'sovereignty' in the face of debt can come at a huge price (both socially and politically), just as losing sovereignty also tends to be extremely damaging.

We know that anger against elites in Western democracies was dampened by growth and credit in the 1990s and early 2000s. But the 2007–8 financial crisis and the national debt that governments took on was a chance to re-think the drastically deregulated system that produced this crisis. Yet in the US much of the anger surrounding this crisis was deflected – notably by the 'Tea Party' movement – from the financial elites to 'big government', which was painted as unfairly and unnecessarily bailing out the banks.[56] Again, we see evidence of a self-reinforcing system that turns the blowback from disasters into an advantage and into a kind of *doubling down* on disaster-creating habits. In the UK, the financial crisis also reinforced disaster-creating policies. The Conservative Party won the 2010 election on a platform of austerity, while the Labour Party took much of the blame for 'running up the national debt', a debt stemming in large part from its role in bailing out the banks under Prime Minister Gordon Brown. That austerity, in turn, was part of the context for the self-harming politics of Brexit. In directing their fire at Trump and Johnson and so on, even the would-be critics of the establishment were in danger of distracting from the underlying processes that *produced* these leaders. Again, we may detect a dangerous focus on consequences rather than causes.

Where the root causes of major social and economic problems are neglected, suffering will escalate and the need to tackle, or at least to be *seen* to tackle, consequences will correspondingly increase. Agamben notes that the neglect of causes and the focus on effects means that governments 'will be obliged to extend and multiply controls', not least through biometrical security measures. In these circumstances, 'While the state of exception was originally conceived as a provisional measure, which was meant to cope with an immediate danger in order to restore the normal situation ..., security reasons constitute today a permanent technology of government.' Again, we are not talking about the 'one-off' shift to emergency politics that the early securitization theory posited. In typically provocative mode, Agamben notes that modern-day high-tech surveillance would have made the extermination of the Jews 'total and incredibly swift', adding that '... according to a sort of fatality or unwritten law of modernity, the technologies which have been invented for animals, for criminals, strangers or Jews, will finally be extended to all human beings'.[57] He gives the example of video surveillance, originally conceived for the prisons and now tracking the public movements of everyone,[58] and he suggests that the unspoken governing principle is now that 'every citizen is a potential terrorist'. Such a state cannot be properly regarded as democratic or even *political*, Agamben argues. Indeed, he refers to 'a process of increasing depolitization', and suggests (with characteristic optimism!) that terrorism and the State are bound together 'in an endless vicious spiral'.

Three Dreams

Clearly, today's proliferating disasters are a major wake-up call. Yet rather than waking, we seem to be remarkably gifted at incorporating these escalating alarm calls into a riveting and ultimately debilitating dream. For Freud, a key function of dreams was that they helped us to stay asleep.[59]

Perhaps what we are dealing with is not one dream but three. For a long time (and often spanning the major political parties in Western democracies), the dominant dream centred on endless growth and the expansion of global trade and on living standards that were expected to rise with each generation. Internationally (and particularly as seen from Washington), there was a dream of liberating the world and spreading democracy and markets. In the 1980s, when I was living in Houston, Texas as a student, I remember an extraordinary and energizing sense that everything was possible as well as a strange (and probably irrational) sense that America was simply so big and so removed that global problems could not really make an impact.

Even when pursued by 'moderates' like Bill Clinton and Tony Blair, the dream of endless progress had a shadow side in its determination to resist the 'backward forces' who stood in the way of progress. Lurking in the shadows of the idea that 'history is on our side' (which Bush as well as Blair proclaimed so loudly) were the diverse resentments (from Detroit to Baghdad) of those who had been made to feel that history was actually passing them by. For many, even the vestiges of optimism had turned into what Lauren Berlant called a 'cruel optimism', where something that is desired (like the American Dream) becomes an obstacle to flourishing, while 'people are worn out by the promises they have attached to'.[60]

Concealed in shadows of the claim that 'all decent and reasonable people' agree on the path to progress, was the message, not always unspoken and certainly written in logic, that dissenters were indecent or unreasonable.[61] Behind the claim of 'consensus' was a rather adversarial stance towards those who did not subscribe.[62]

If self-conscious moderation was in this sense more dangerous than it appeared, several events and processes helped to puncture the shared dream of progress, among them: 9/11, the debacles in Iraq and Afghanistan, the 2007–8 financial crisis and (in the background) the creeping superfluity of millions in 'developed' countries as globalization and automation literally did their work.

But when the dream of progress acquired an increasingly nightmarish quality, the sleeper did not awake but simply found a new dream, or at least many millions did. According to the promises of contemporary right-wing populism, underlying problems would magically recede when a series of identifiable 'enemies' (from migrants, to criminals, to gays, to bureaucrats in Brussels) were denounced, neutralized, eliminated or rejected. Broadly, this has been a politics of scapegoating. This new dream offered to push aside, however fleetingly, the shame and free-floating anxiety of thwarted hopes and official disparagement. Particularly for older voters, there was also a dream of returning to a 'golden age' when things were better (and when they, not quite incidentally, were young).

From Trump to Johnson, from Salvini to Orbán, we have seen a growing tendency to elect self-proclaimed 'strong leaders' who promise some kind of national revival. But these promises – like those of advertising that were analysed by Raymond Williams in the *New Left Review* in 1960 – are essentially *magic systems* that fetishize particular solutions ('build a wall') while being chronically unable to fix the major underlying problems and emotional discontents on which they continually feed. As with a consumer purchase, the immediate 'feel good' effect is generally more notable than any substantive or longer-term benefit.

Today, there is sometimes an implication that if you do not subscribe to the officially endorsed definition of the priority emergency, then you have again stepped back into the ranks of the unreasonable and indecent, such as the 'anti-vaxxers' who were labelled as non-citizens by French President Macron. In Canada, truckers' protests at vaccination regulations saw Prime Minister Justin Trudeau invoking the country's Emergencies Act and condemning what he called a 'small fringe minority' who were 'holding unacceptable views'.[63] At the same time, right-wing populist politicians have fed on reservoirs of mistrust and habits of condescension among privileged actors: one key message is that 'liberal intellectuals' want you to be worried about global warming or Covid when you are naturally more worried about your job and the food on your table; another is that they will look down on you for your priorities.

Of course, the perils of labelling people as 'stupid' or 'irrational' might also extend to my own label of 'magical thinking'. But it's important to underscore the point that scapegoating is not going to solve real-world problems. It's a massive cause of confusion and false hope as well as being cruel in itself. A second 'defence' here is that I am trying to get beyond a *condemnation* of magical thinking and to move closer to an understanding of what makes magical thinking attractive and plausible. Finally, I am trying to move beyond some influential stereotypes about *who it is* that engages in magical thinking.

That brings us to a third dream, a dream that may bring some respite from the alarming spectacle of the second, but also brings a new set of problems that has been insufficiently recognized. According to this third dream – understandably beloved of many liberals and left-leaning individuals – it was right-wing populists like Trump and Johnson who became the overriding problem or enemy, the latest demon-figures whose elimination would magically heal both politics and the economy.

But a key danger here is that this new fantasy of elimination removes or greatly reduces the felt need to consider deeper underlying political and economic processes that created these populist purveyors of magic in the first place. Indeed, part of the appeal of this third dream has resided precisely in *removing* the need to look deeper. The danger here is that Trump, Johnson and company become themselves a kind of 'useful enemy', while the passion for denouncing helps to forestall a fundamental re-think about why so many citizens lost faith in politics and the state in the first place. Here, as so often, we are in danger of laying magic upon magic. We are entering the world of delusions through another door. Part of how a disaster-producing system renews itself is precisely through such delusions and the current definitions of 'the enemy' that these delusions involve. Returning for a moment to our discussion of disasters in the Global South in Chapter 2, we are in danger of letting a desire to 'get back to normal' feed into the reconstruction of the system and the grievances that created the disaster in the first place.

Conclusion

Some systems are self-regulating, and in the opening chapter we noted the example of rising prices leading (in theory) to increased production and then to falling prices. A disaster may delegitimize a government that presides over it – and corrective action may be designed to ward off this threat to legitimacy. Attempts to infringe democratic norms might be expected to lead to increased opposition (from the public, from the press, from the judiciary etc.), creating additional pressure to rein in executive power. Again, such 'self-correcting' mechanisms have certainly not disappeared in today's world. Some were notably invigorated under Trump.

But today we are witnessing the emergence of a functional-but-dysfunctional system that continuously feeds on its own failures. The system is functional, in large part, because it facilitates a spectacular accumulation and concentration of wealth, not least through the electoral success of parties that support this concentration of wealth. It is *dysfunctional* because it fuels suffering, poverty, inequality, conflict, environmental destruction and a heating planet. In other words, it fuels disaster.

Within the current disaster-producing system, high-profile responses to trumpeted disasters (like sending in the navy or building walls to stop migrants/refugees) represent magical (but politically and economically profitable) solutions to a range of underlying economic, ecological and political disasters that powerful interests would rather not address.

It's important to look not just at the disasters that threaten us but at the instrumentalization of these disasters – whether these are real, hyped up or simply imagined – within systems of control that themselves can plausibly be depicted as disasters in many crucial respects. A key part of this emerging system is a *politics of distraction*. This mode of governance – whether in relation to climate change, crime, drugs, terror, the so-called 'migrant crisis', Brexit, or the coronavirus – is primarily concerned with the world of appearances and the world of consequences and is intrinsically ineffective in addressing underlying socio-economic problems.

Within a highly charged and polarized atmosphere, right-wing populist leaders have been focusing on very particular emergencies, and selling very particular solutions. In many ways, we are getting *the wrong solution for the wrong disaster*. It points to the functions of emergency – and a permanent state of emergency – in shoring up inequitable systems in a manner long familiar from the Global South. At the same time, we need to recognize that people define disaster differently. Again, if they are looking economic disaster in the eye and have not encountered a state that helps them, they are not likely to prioritize the disaster that more privileged groups are foregrounding. And they may be easily swayed by a politics of distraction, perhaps one that involves imposing a greater pain on someone else.[64]

We need to notice that magical thinking has a range of *functions*, whether economic, political, psychological, or all three at once. In this, it resembles the disasters that it feeds. Although magical solutions are very unlikely to 'work' in any very constructive sense, the pursuit of magical solutions often yields substantial payoffs – and this is pivotal in explaining why such 'solutions' retain their allure. Whether in the Global South or the Global North, the magical and the mundane are combining in complex ways. Very often, they are being *purposefully and cleverly* combined. Here, it's important to note that as reality gets worse (as Arendt observed in 1951), a *flight* from reality is likely to become more tempting.[65] So, in an escalating series of crises, many strands of magical thinking may be expected to become more rather than less pronounced. In turn, this will create increased opportunities for those (of whatever political persuasion) who are selling delusions or perhaps embracing elements of magical thinking themselves. So the politics of distraction may be expected to intensify. And the political instrumentalization of disaster may be expected to worsen. *Pace* Sen and Drèze, democracy and the desire to be re-elected may not protect against disaster because re-election is often being sought precisely through the manipulation of disaster.

When we are scared, moreover, we cannot see things very clearly. 'Crisis blocks thought', as Joseph Masco puts it;[66] in particular, it blocks thought about what created the crisis.[67] A constant sense of crisis, paradoxically, keeps the recognition of crisis at bay. That is a key reason why fear is so useful politically. Given the situation we are in, we need, in some sense, *to panic*. But clearly an actual panic will prevent clear thinking about how to get out of the crisis, as well as playing into the hands of those for whom thoughtlessness is at once a boon and a habit. How we can panic and 'not panic' is a conundrum that requires a guru much wiser than myself. But it may be helpful, at least, to try to think more clearly about the system we are in and the many uses to which disasters are being put.

4

Emergency Politics

Accepting his party's nomination at the 2016 Republican National Convention, Trump declared: 'Our convention occurs at a moment of crisis for our nation. The attacks on our police, and terrorism in our cities, threaten our very way of life. Beginning on 20 January 2017, safety will be restored.'[1] That claim to be making people safe again was central to Trump's campaign, and Trump showed no lack of confidence in his ability to put things right, whether domestically or internationally. In March 2016, for example, he had tweeted: 'Another radical Islamic attack, this time in Pakistan, targeting Christian women and children. At least 67 dead, 400 injured', adding with his trademark modesty 'I alone can solve.'[2] Trump saw his 'tough' stance on security issues as pushing up his ratings, and there is evidence that he was right.[3]

Having won the 2016 presidential elections, Trump and his team continued milking the 'security' cow, highlighting crises both real and imagined. In February 2017, for example, Trump said the murder rate in the US was the highest for 47 years, and he would fix it. (In reality the murder rate was about half its 1991 level.)[4] Quickly ordering a travel ban on seven Muslim-majority countries, Trump pointed to the terror attacks in Brussels, Nice and Paris and then added, 'Look at what's happening last night in Sweden. Sweden!'[5] There had actually been no terror attack in Sweden (though Trump had apparently just watched a TV documentary about the country).[6] One of Trump's top aides Kellyanne Conway was meanwhile referring to the 'Bowling Green massacre', a terrorist outrage in Kentucky whose one redeeming feature was that it did not actually take place. Defending Trump's travel ban, Conway said:

> I bet it's brand-new information to people that President Obama had a six-month ban on the Iraqi refugee program[7] after two Iraqis came here to this country, were radicalized and were the masterminds behind the Bowling Green massacre.[8]

Commenting further on this phantom massacre (and feeding the Trump narrative about 'fake media'), Conway also complained, 'Most people don't know that because it didn't get covered.' In a way this was brilliant: you invent something and then castigate the media for ignoring it. What *had* happened in Bowling Green, Kentucky – for those who still like a spoonful of reality with their morning news – was that two Iraqi men living there were arrested in 2011 over a failed attempt to send money and weapons to Al Qaeda in Iraq.[9] With White House press secretary Sean Spicer having referred three times in the previous month to a non-existent terrorist attack in Atlanta,[10] the invention of disaster had become a habit.

It was back in 1918 when American journalist and essayist H. L. Mencken remarked that 'The whole aim of practical politics is to keep the populace alarmed (and hence clamorous to be led to safety) by an endless series of hobgoblins, all of them imaginary.'[11] Today, while crisis is certainly not always imaginary, the manipulation of crisis is again a recurring theme. In 2020, with protests against police violence breaking out in American cities, President Trump tried to boost his bid for re-election by describing an America under attack – this time from 'anarchists, agitators, rioters, looters and flag burners'.[12] Trump was again positioning himself as the solution. While not actually confessing to provocation, Kellyanne Conway noted with alarming frankness on *Fox and Friends*, 'The more chaos and anarchy and vandalism and violence reigns, the better it is for the very clear choice on who's best on public safety and law and order.'[13]

Trump's serial manipulations of crisis, and Conway's admission that chaos actually *helps*, echo Chabal and Daloz's 'instrumentalization of disorder'. A notorious example from Africa was the claim by President Mobutu of Zaire (now the Democratic Republic of the Congo): 'Après moi, le déluge' (echoing a remark attributed to King Louis XV of France).[14] Even as Mobutu ruled with an iron fist and actively *stirred up* many kinds of violence within his own borders, he wanted to stress that the country would descend into chaos without him (and in fact levels of violence *did* escalate even further after the luxury-loving dictator's demise as the concentration of power splintered).

In his 2020 campaign, Trump was not only exploiting the impression of chaos and proposing himself as the solution but greatly *inflaming* urban tensions, for example by sending in the national guard and unidentified federal officers[15] and by denouncing angry protesters in Portland as 'a beehive of terrorists'.[16] Insofar as anger spilled or was provoked into violence, that in turn was used to delegitimize the underlying grievances (as we saw in the hugely different context of Syria for example). In Portland, Department of Homeland Security (DHS) paramilitaries fired teargas, projectiles and stun-grenades at demonstrators, while agents in camouflage were snatching protesters from the streets and putting them in unmarked vans.[17] Spencer Ackerman notes that this was 'a taste for native-born whites of what DHS had done to migrants for years',[18] a telling observation that recalls Arendt's and Agamben's concern that the rightlessness of the migrant or 'the camp' may quickly be extended to others. Trump had declared in May 2020 that Antifa, a loosely affiliated group of far-left anti-fascists, was 'a terrorist organization', and Congressman Matt Gaetz said, 'Now that we clearly see Antifa as terrorists, can we hunt them down like we do those in the Middle East?'[19] Attorney General William Barr declared that the Joint Terrorism Task Forces would train their resources on 'extremists, anarchists ... agitators'.[20] Meanwhile, violence was being further stoked by self-declared vigilantes and by those with links to right-wing groups – groups that had themselves drawn significant encouragement from Trump's cocktail of intolerance and xenophobia.

Apparently echoing the way that officials have long talked about terrorism linked to radical Islamism, Trump declared in Kenosha, Wisconsin, that 'To stop the political violence, we must also confront the radical ideology that includes this violence.'[21] He explained that this ideology pushes 'the destructive message that our nation and our law enforcement are oppressive or racist'.[22] In this way, highlighting racism was positioned as encouraging violence (and indeed terrorism) just as official policy in the US (and the UK) had for some time interpreted the highlighting of foreign policy grievances as a sign of dangerous radicalization (and possible future terrorism). The dangerous reflex to criminalize critical opinion as a seedbed of violence, having been imported into the US and UK as a domestic arm of the global 'war on terror', was now sometimes extended to radicalism in general.

Identifying Enemies

After Trump lost the 2020 presidential elections, the working definition of emergency switched from the Black Lives Matter protests to the so-called 'steal'. Trump urged his Vice President, Mike Pence, to reject the state-certified Electoral College results. Then, in an incendiary speech in Washington on 6 January 2021, while this was being considered, Trump painted a picture of catastrophe. He told the assembled crowd that the disasters threatening America included a stolen election, a mendacious media, and a country that was disappearing before their very eyes. These crises were presented as compelling reasons why his listeners should 'fight' for overturning the election result:

> We will never give up. We will never concede. It doesn't happen. You don't concede when there's theft involved. Our country has had enough. We will not take it anymore, and that is what this is all about. And to use a phrase that all of you people really came up with, we will stop the steal … You will have an illegitimate president. That is what you will have, and we can't let that happen. These are the facts that you won't hear from the fake news media. It's all part of the suppression effort … We fight like hell, and if you don't fight like hell, you're not going to have a country any more.[23]

Trump turned his attention specifically to Pence and others who might not join this fight:

> When you catch somebody in a fraud, you are allowed to go by very different rules. So, I hope Mike has the courage to do what he has to do, and I hope he doesn't listen to the RINOs [a term of abuse for those deemed to be 'Republicans in Name Only'] and the stupid people that he's listening to … If Mike Pence does the right thing, we win the election …

Trump then added a characteristic hint of menace, invoking the 'courage' that anyone *failing* to challenge the election result would need: 'I actually think, though, *it takes, again, more courage not to step up* [my emphasis], and I think a lot of those people are going to find that out. And you better start looking at your leadership, because your leadership has led you down the tubes.'[24]

At the 6 January 2021 Capitol riot/insurrection, banners shouted 'Stop the Steal', 'Jail the fraudsters', 'Election fraud – treason', and so on. During the riot and the invasion of the Capitol that followed, some in the crowd chanted 'Hang Mike Pence.' The Republican Party had been rather deeply infused with the impulse to search for an internal enemy within America, not only during Trump's presidency but also going back to many earlier outbreaks of scapegoating and paranoia that had been pushed by Nixon, Goldwater and others. But there was no logical reason why the search for an internal enemy should stop at the borders of the Republican Party itself. This was demonstrated dramatically by Trump's turning on his Vice President and the 'RINOs'. Many Republican Congressmen had previously complained of feeling intimidated by Trump and his supporters, sometimes citing the large proportion of Trump's supporters who have firearms.[25] Another argument was that impeachment could incite more violence.[26] When the Senate subsequently voted against finding Trump guilty of 'incitement to insurrection' (thereby leaving him free to run for president again), Trump's continued sway over his party was evident. Alarmingly, the Republicans have recently been pushing through voter suppression laws in Republican-led states, forming districts to favour Republican candidates and manoeuvring 'stop the steal' Republicans into positions where they will have key roles in future elections.[27]

The turning inwards of Trump's aggression underlines two important points made by Arendt in her discussion of how democracies may be undermined. First, a project of persecution and enemy-creation tends constantly to expand; once the link between crime and punishment is broken, no one is safe. Second, a determination to defend 'big lies' and fictional realities tends itself to promote a rapid and volatile expansion in the 'enemy' category, so as to include and intimidate all of those who dare to affirm the reality that is vehemently being denied. When it came to Trump and the crowd's turning on Pence and the so-called 'RINOs', we may also observe – in line, for example, with Omer Bartov's analysis of fascism and the process of redefining enemies at the end of the First World War[28] – that the *hidden* enemy and the *internal* enemy can often be constructed as more alarming than any others.

Of course, Trump had already demonstrated that the 'enemy category' could be quickly and intimidatingly expanded from its original focus. During his 2016 presidential campaign speech in Phoenix, Arizona, for example, Trump's threat to deport 'illegal aliens' was quickly expanded into a theatrical threat to deport or jail Hillary Clinton, with Trump playing to the crowd and inciting laughter through his transgressive remarks. Trump's 2017 ban on immigration from seven Muslim countries had in effect expanded the working definition of the enemy far beyond the long-reviled category of 'Islamist terrorists'. And, foreshadowing Trump's threats to the 'RINOs' in his 6 January 2021 speech, in 2016 Trump had reacted to criticism of the Hollywood Access sexual aggression revelations by tweeting, 'Disloyal R's [Republicans] are far more difficult than Crooked Hillary. They come at you from all sides.'

In any case, the possibility of a rapid expansion in the 'enemy' category was a constant source of threat and a constant invitation to complicity in the violence and the accompanying 'alternative facts' that were unfolding under Trump. It was logical that this threat was extended to Trump's own Vice President when he did not comply with the officially favoured fictions – and thankfully Pence had the nerve and integrity to resist.

On top of this, we are finding that shame directed at policy-makers is itself being instrumentalized – another dangerously self-reinforcing element in contemporary politics.[29] As policy drifts further from a sense of reality or even from basic consideration for others, condemnation of this trend has often been put to use. A striking example was Trump seizing on Hillary Clinton's (rather reckless) description of half of his supporters as a 'basket of deplorables'. Subsequently, after President Trump drew fire for saying of white supremacists and anti-racist protesters in Charlottesville that there were 'good people on both sides', the US President told a rally in Arizona, 'The media can attack me but where I draw the line is when they attack you, which is what they do when they attack the decency of our supporters.'[30]

Charisma and Self-Reinforcing Cruelty

Part of the problem in the variations of 'emergency politics' that we see today is the construction of 'charisma' not just from individual abuse but from the conspicuous and unapologetic infringement of democratic norms. So behaviour that we might expect to trigger a corrective mechanism, whether legally or in the media or in popular revulsion or electoral defeat, has quite frequently *attracted support*. Again, we can see important elements of a *self-reinforcing* system. At the extreme, it's a system that has elevated cruelty to the ranks of a political virtue and a political asset. One *Financial Times* article picked up on the idea of 'virtue signalling' and pointed to the growing practice of 'vice signalling', announcing cruel policies (like the UK's extraordinary callous and expensive sending of asylum applicants to Rwanda) that signal toughness with little chance of impacting the problem they claim to be addressing.[31]

Norbert Elias famously detected a 'civilizing process' in the history of Europe, with a growing shame around violence playing an important role.[32] Of course, this was always a fairly optimistic view of history, and we know that things can also go in the other direction. In 1990 (a moment of notable optimism when some were even declaring 'the end of history'), Stephen Mennell addressed Elias's work and noted the possibility of a 'decivilizing process', which would include 'the re-emergence of violence into the public sphere and a decline in mutual identification' as well as 'reduced pressures on individuals to restrain the expression of impulses (including the freer expression of aggressiveness)' and 'increasing fantasy content of modes of knowledge'.[33] That looks prophetic today, and we might add that Elias himself linked increasing fantasy content with both a lack of self-control and elevated levels of danger.[34]

It is Hannah Arendt, however, who gives us the most detailed and helpful understanding of a 'decivilizing' process – not least the process by which cruelty is rewarded with support. As part of her analysis of the appeal of totalitarian leaders and ideologies, Arendt emphasized the allure of 'crimes committed in the spirit of play ... the combination of horror and laughter'.[35] She realized that considerable popularity could be found through praising or embodying cruelty in the face of alleged hypocrisy. Hypocrisy awakened a kind of rage,[36] and after the First World War many European intellectuals

> were satisfied with blind partisanship in anything that respectable society had banned, regardless of theory or content, and they elevated cruelty to a major virtue because it contradicted society's humanitarian and liberal hypocrisy ... The point was to do something, heroic or criminal, which was unpredictable and undetermined by anybody else.[37]

In such circumstances, 'Everything hidden, everything passed over in silence, became of major significance', and 'truth was whatever respectable society had hypocritically passed over, or covered up with corruption'.[38]

Sadly, these dangerous reflexes cannot be neatly 'confined' to the twentieth-century totalitarianism with which Arendt was primarily concerned. Nor can the hypocrisy on which they fed. Strikingly, the current politics of cruelty within Western democracies has also included attempts to construct a kind of *charismatic authority* based on conspicuous 'shows of strength' and on a willingness to flout norms and procedures that tend to be rhetorically linked to a 'hypocritical' or 'metropolitan' 'establishment'.[39] Again, there is said to be a hidden truth which a fake media and corrupt elites are obscuring.

In line with Arendt's analysis, Trump positioned his own 'politically incorrect' behaviour, and even his threats and abuses, as some kind of 'refreshing' antidote to the hypocrisy and insincerity of his opponents. Drawing on her study of Louisiana, Hochschild suggested that Trump had been particularly successful in taking a set of 'politically incorrect' attitudes for which people have been made to feel shame and then removing this shame through his own 'politically incorrect' pronouncements and through the shaming of 'outsider' groups.[40] In this way, some kind of *collective* cruelty could be unleashed.

Arendt's varied insights underline the possibility that when Trump won the presidency (and subsequently retained considerable popularity despite an array of scandals), some part of his audience was not so much *forgiving* his transgressions as *rewarding* them. Trump seems to have understood this mechanism rather well himself, noting for example that he'd correctly predicted that Montana Congressman Greg Gianforte's popularity would be helped, not hindered, by Gianforte's assault on a *Guardian* reporter.[41] In a brazenly confident move, Brett Kavanaugh, who had been accused of attempted rape in a distressing testimony at confirmation hearings (an accusation Kavanaugh denied), was appointed as a Supreme Court judge.[42]

Meanwhile, Trump hardly hid his determination to cut taxes for the rich or to strip away regulations for protecting the environment, something that may even have underscored his 'plain speaking' persona. One *New Yorker* cartoon featured sheep staring at a billboard that shows a wolf in suit and tie. The wolf is running for office on the slogan 'I am going to eat you', while one sheep observes, 'He tells it like it is.'[43]

Of course, people may also *recoil* from cruelty, particularly if they think it may be directed *at themselves*.[44] But Arendt's analysis helps us to understand the perils in the current moment. In particular, it highlights the danger that a toxic politics will end up reinforcing itself. In many ways, Trump's bizarre and abusive behaviour revealed a dangerous appetite for illegality and for freedom from restraint. It's an appetite that seems unlikely to disappear whenever Trump himself vanishes from the political scene. And, of course, it extends well beyond the United States.

The Politics of Distraction

Keeping our focus on the US, a strong case can be made that a primary and underlying crisis has been the extreme and rising inequality in the country over the last half-century. As noted, between 1978 and 2012, the share of wealth enjoyed by the richest 0.1 per cent of the population in the United States rose from 7 to 22 per cent.[45] Remember, that is not the top one per cent; it's the top 0.1 per cent. Underpinning this inequality has been a complex array of policies including relatively low taxation for the rich, financial deregulation, anti-union legislation and cuts in welfare. International trade agreements have also played a part, sometimes severely limiting the freedom of national governments and defining some forms of financial regulation as improper barriers to free trade.[46]

Of course, listing economic mechanisms that facilitated inequality doesn't explain why they were adopted and maintained. Important explanatory factors here include fear of socialism as well as adherence to the 'American Dream' that anyone can 'make it' if they work hard enough. Another factor is that plans to tax the corporate sector either at state or national level have often led to threats that businesses and investment will move elsewhere.[47] Also helping to underpin inequality has been *disenfranchisement*, including concerted attempts to discourage voter registration and postal voting, resistance to reforming the Electoral College, and so on.

While all these factors are important, what is generally under-recognized is the extent to which a kind of shifting *emergency politics* has reinforced this inequitable system. This amounts to a politics of distraction that has kept much of the population focused on endless high-profile disasters, or the possibility thereof, even as economic policies have rather systematically been steered towards the interests of a small privileged group.

While Trump has been especially adept at the politics of distraction, he is very far from being an isolated example. This brings us back to the possibility that Trump-as-the-enemy may *itself* be a kind of politics of distraction, not least from the underlying inequality and socio-economic processes that helped to *give rise* to Trump.

We have noted from our discussion of many conflicts around the world in Chapter 2 that the enemy may be useful, for example in legitimizing repression, delegitimizing dissent and distracting from class grievances. Of course, every context is different. But the endless reinvention of enemies, whether external or internal or both, is a striking feature of American politics over a long period; and, while again the definition of the enemy may shift quite rapidly, the underlying functions of *having* an enemy often change less quickly.

In the case of the United States, many of the dangers highlighted in America's long-standing politics of distraction are not actually imaginary, from the Soviet Union to terrorism and crime and drugs. But these dangers have routinely been highlighted and hyped in ways that distract attention away from other crises and from extreme and rising inequality in particular. We have also seen a focus on the disaster that is *about to happen*, with strong measures said to be necessary to prevent it (a habit explored further in Chapter 10). High inequality creates incentives to construct enemies in ways that defuse and redirect frustrations that might otherwise be directed at those who are most privileged and powerful. The politics of distraction frequently involves strategically advancing very particular definitions of the enemy, as well as instrumentalizing blowback from a range of crises.

The Cold War itself was a particularly useful distraction; at once an existential threat, a focus for aggression and a way of delegitimizing socialism at home. Defeat in Vietnam fed into an escalating 'war on drugs' (as we discuss a little more in Chapter 8). Then there was the 'war on terror' from 2001, another shift in the enemy category; while the causes of this shift were complex (and the 9/11 attacks were of course a key factor), comedian and activist Michael Moore put his finger on something important when he wrote that 'the war on terror' was a useful distraction from 'the war on us'.

We can get a better sense of the politics of distraction when we put together the varied insights of such writers as Thomas Frank, George Akerlof, Robert Shiller, Arlie Russell Hochschild and Timothy Snyder. In his landmark 2004 book *What's the Matter with Kansas?*, Frank suggested that large numbers of poorer people have been persuaded to vote against their own interests in a context where a range of emotionally charged issues (like abortion, immigration and terrorism) have tended to loom larger in people's minds than socio-economic issues (such as unionization and anti-oligopolization) that once informed a strong radical populism within the state.[48] Making a related argument in their important 2016 book *Phishing for Phools*, Akerlof and Shiller noted that emotionally charged issues tend to seize voters' attention while policy on complex economic issues is often left to 'insiders' who can understand the boring details and can skew the system to their own advantage.[49] Many kinds of 'threats' are obviously highly charged emotionally, and they will tend to fall into that category of attention-absorbing issues – potentially distracting from taxation, financial regulation, and so on. To the extent that a threat is intrinsically located in the future, moreover, its emotional resonance is in a sense unchallengeable since the absence of a future harm cannot be proved.

Arlie Russell Hochschild's fine 2018 book *Strangers in Their Own Land* helps us to understand how a politics of distraction fed into the rise of Trump and how it has negatively impacted poverty and the environment over a longer period. Hochschild showed how a deep environmental crisis has been affecting people in Louisiana – whether this is pollution, or storms like Hurricane Katrina, or the sinking of flatlands (and correspondingly rising sea levels). Meanwhile, environmental deregulation has significantly increased people's exposure to pollution, notably from chemicals production, while also contributing to global heating via the large oil and gas industry in particular. In general, the legal sanctions for environmental transgressions have fallen much harder on errant individuals than on big corporations. As one 77-year-old Louisiana pipefitter told Hochschild, 'If you shoot an endangered brown pelican, they'll put you in jail. But if a company kills the brown pelican by poisoning the fish he eats? They let it go. I think they overregulate the bottom because it's harder to regulate the top.'[50] At the same time, poor social services and health services have been fuelling vulnerability to a range of disasters. Yet somehow Louisiana has remained a stronghold for Republican sentiment and for politicians (including Trump himself) vehemently opposing environmental regulation.

Emphasizing this paradox, Hochschild suggests it can be resolved with the help of what she calls a 'deep story', one that has been routinely exploited by Republican politicians with Trump in the forefront. By 'deep story', Hochschild means a story that seems to explain much of people's world and a story that is widely subscribed to. The 'deep story' begins with the perception that ordinary people are standing in line and waiting for the American Dream to arrive – a wait that has become increasingly frustrating and, in many cases, hopeless. While waiting, as this popular 'deep story' would have it, people find that a motley collection of immigrants and welfare cheats have been line-jumping on a grand scale, aided and abetted in this unfairness by 'big government' and by liberal politicians in Washington. Hence the remedy to 'unfairness' is to target immigrants and welfare in the way that Republican rhetoric has frequently done. One of the obvious qualities of such a 'deep story' is that it lets a lot of powerful and wealthy people off the hook. It contributes hugely to the politics of distraction. And meanwhile, Hochschild presents us with the further paradox that many of the ordinary Americans exhibiting hostility to 'big government' have actually been chronically and increasingly reliant on federal largesse of many kinds. It is as if the shame associated with this has actually been reduced by *denouncing* 'big government' and by focusing on immigrants in particular. And, insofar as that dependence increases, the impulse to deny it may also be expected to rise.

A related paradox highlighted by Snyder among others is that the antipathy to 'big government' that has frequently been expressed by Republican politicians has tended to co-exist with high federal spending by Republican administrations. Part of the reason is the rise of mass incarceration and high-cost policing that accompanied escalating inequality and associated discontent. Another reason is that wealthy individuals and companies have generally been quite happy to benefit from state spending in cases (including prison spending and defence) where it fuels private profits. Since stocks of capital tend to increase substantially even as poverty proliferates (and effective demand is thereby limited), finding outlets for capital may even *depend* on state spending, including on defence.

Part of Thomas Frank's argument in *What's the Matter with Kansas?* was that the Democratic Party had generally deserted its traditional class analysis as well as class politics more generally. During the twentieth century, there *were* some major progressive redistributions of wealth. Roosevelt's radical New Deal was one. And another, as Keller and Kelly show, came after the Second World War, when there was a significant divergence on financial policy between the Republicans and the Democrats along with significant Democratic strength in national politics. But from the 1980s, the picture has been very different. In particular, Keller and Kelly note that 'After 1982, there is no discernible difference between the two parties with regard to their effect on financial deregulation … it did not matter whether Democrats or Republicans were ascendant in Washington.'[51] This paved the way for much of the burgeoning inequality from the 1980s onwards. Particularly important here was the 1999 repeal of the Glass–Steagall Act, a piece of banking regulatory legislation that had originally been passed in the aftermath of the Great Depression. This is where the shady side of politics begins to come more into the light. Keller and Kelly found that 'members of Congress who receive more donations from the finance sector were much more likely to support repeal'.[52] And when the authors focused only on those representatives who'd received high levels of donations, they found that the Democrats were more likely to support repeal than the Republicans.[53]

In their important 2010 book *Winner-Take-All Politics*, Hacker and Pierson similarly stressed that it is not simply 'the market' that creates inequality; rather, a damaging brand of insider politics has been strongly shaping the market and fuelling inequality. Hacker and Pierson noted:

> If one looks at the 100 biggest contributing firms [to federal campaign finance] since 1989, the financial sector totals more than the contributions of energy, health care, defence, and telecoms *combined* ... On critical economic issues, business interests could often count on a handful of moderate Democrats to complement the expected solid bloc of Republicans ... Leading Democrats supported many of the deregulatory initiatives of the 1990s ... the incentives for resisting the deregulatory wave were meager compared with the financial rewards. Revealingly, for all the talk of unfettered markets Democrats proved more than willing to embrace dubious loopholes and subsidies, and to assist market insiders in hiding what they were doing, when lobbyists pushed hard enough ... On tax policy, the stimulus plan, climate change, and labour law reform – just to name some of the most prominent fights with the greatest long-term stakes – pivotal Senate Democrats generated costly delays, scaled back the more serious reform efforts of the House, or blocked those efforts entirely.[54]

Despite the financial disaster of 2007–8 and the austerity that followed, and despite the reckless lending practices that made all this possible, it is striking that there were no legal recriminations against banks and bankers during the two terms of President Obama. Nor were the banks broken up.[55] Hacker and Pierson suggested, moreover, that when Obama did manage to push through a major healthcare reform, 'the leverage of the most conservative Democrats was used to diminish or eliminate some of the most important reformist impulses'.[56] Obama also pursued policies of austerity that had the effect of protecting tax cuts under Bush as well as protecting defence spending.[57]

A hard look at such failings might bring us back to look a little critically at Hochschild's *Strangers in Their Own Land* and the paradox it highlights – namely that victims of poverty and pollution in Louisiana have often voted for the party (the Republicans) that has done most to help the polluters and least for the poor. As the American sociologist Raka Ray has noted, at least some of this 'paradox' dissolves when we realize that Hochschild's informants in Louisiana actually 'feel more betrayed by the state than by capitalism. The state is not seen as their own.'[58] That analysis tends to shift the focus to what the Democrats have done with the state apparatus when they *have* been in power.

In a landmark 2014 paper in *Perspectives on Politics*, Martin Gilens and Benjamin Page gave the results of a study of 1,779 policy issues in the period 1981 to 2002. After carefully measuring the policy impact of the preferences of economic elites, organized groups and average citizens, the authors found that the preferences of economic elites had 'far more independent impact upon policy change than the preferences of average citizens ... When a majority of citizens disagrees with economic elites or with organized interests, they generally lose.'[59] Significantly, the period studied was *before* the Supreme Court's 2010 *Citizens United* opinion opened the floodgates to a major surge of big money into US politics,[60] a move that one careful 2020 study found had boosted Republican finances disproportionately and increased the percentage of Republican seats in state legislatures by an average of 11.5 per cent.[61]

Such factors mean that it tends to be very difficult even for a reform-minded democratic president to push through far-reaching changes. In 2021, Democratic Senators Joe Manchin and Krysten Sinema got a major surge in corporate donations as they worked to stymie President Biden's ambitious package of social and climate policies within an evenly divided Senate. Major donors were keen to prevent increased personal and corporate tax rises and some warned of the danger of inflation. Billionaire Kenneth Langone, a long-time donor to the Republicans, promised that Manchin would get 'one of the biggest fund-raisers I've ever had'. Sinema, incidentally, did not repeat the view she had expressed as a young politician – that political donations were like 'bribery'.[62]

Corruption in government – whether under the Republicans or the Democrats – has been so far-reaching in the US, in fact, that it's easy to miss. Part of the problem is that corruption tends to be called something else – like 'the lobby system' or (commonly in the UK) 'sleaze'.[63] One advantage of looking at emergency politics in the Global North in the context of emergency politics in the Global South (and of simultaneously questioning the West's sense of *exceptionalism*) is that corruption in the Global North can be revealed more clearly for what it is.

In his book *Capital*, Thomas Piketty showed how the rich have been able to use their wealth to lobby for rules that keep taxes low while protecting wealthy people's relatively unfettered financial activities.[64] This form of corruption has been supplemented by Washington's 'revolving doors' system, which involves influential individuals moving back and forth between high-paying corporate jobs and powerful positions in government. Hacker and Pierson describe how Robert Rubin, having been a major advocate of the repeal of financial services regulations (notably the Glass–Steagall Act) as Secretary of the Treasury under Bill Clinton, became a senior adviser at the newly formed Citigroup (whose very formation in a merger of Citicorp and Travelers is described by Hacker and Pierson as 'a blatant violation of the Glass–Steagall Act'). The authors note that Rubin (who had spent 26 years at Goldman Sachs before joining the Clinton administration) went on to make in excess of 126 million dollars in cash and stock at Citigroup, even as the bank engaged in highly risky lending practices and headed for a major crash and quarterly losses of over 65 million dollars.[65]

Meanwhile, large parts of the United States were effectively being stripped of their industries and their stable employment. Michael McQuarrie has emphasized the receptive audience that this process created for a Republican candidate who promised a radical overhaul of the system and a draining of the 'swamp' in Washington. McQuarrie notes that in 2016 'it was overwhelmingly in Rust Belt territories [the industrial Midwest] that support for the Democratic candidate [Hillary Clinton] collapsed'.[66] The seeds for this were sown, in large part, under Bill Clinton in the 1990s when President Clinton, having campaigned on the promise of labour law reform and state-backed aid to manufacturing, set about financial deregulation and 'shifting America's trade policy decisively in the direction of free trade'.[67] Replacing the old job security with asset-ownership (stocks and homes) proved a chimera when the tech bubble burst in 2000 and then the financial and housing markets crashed in 2007–8.[68] Meanwhile, Bill Clinton had greatly accelerated incarcerations for non-violent drug crimes, affecting people of colour disproportionately.[69]

Millions of Americans are far from blind to the iniquities of this system. Trump and radical Democratic candidate Bernie Sanders surged together and, after a January 2016 book-tour in America's heartlands, Robert Reich reported, firstly, that many were torn between Trump and Sanders (then in a run-off with Hillary Clinton) and, secondly, that they were incensed by big corporate political payoffs, tax loopholes, high drugs prices and the banking bailout of 2008 – and looking for a strong response.[70] Hillary Clinton promised tax credits and job-training programmes for the Rust Belt and tried to stir up outrage that Trump's ties were 'made in China'. But McQuarrie comments acerbically, 'people already went down that road with her husband and learned that those policies are about performance and not about solutions'.[71]

Sanders has done more than any other mainstream politician to articulate the underlying crisis among ordinary Americans, a crisis that has not been effectively addressed by either major party. In a speech at Georgetown University in November 2015, he observed:

> In the last 30 years we have seen a massive redistribution of wealth. Problem is it has gone in the wrong direction … The top one tenth of one per cent today owns nearly as much wealth as the bottom 90 per cent … I go around the country and I see a lot of working people and you can see the stress and exhaustion on their faces. They're working crazy hours … People don't have the quality time for their kids … Older workers are scared to death and they are saying how am I going to retire with dignity … try to survive on 13,000 dollars [social security] a year! … [We have] the highest rate of childhood poverty of almost any major country on earth … 29 million Americans have no health insurance, and even more are underinsured … They got a 5 thousand dollar deductible, 8 thousand dollar deductible, they can't go to the doctor when they need … Our people pay the highest prices in the world for prescription drugs … One out of five Americans cannot afford to fulfil the prescription their doctors write. We have more people in jail than any other country … Countless lives are being destroyed as we spend 80 billion dollars a year locking up our fellow Americans … Real freedom must include economic security.

If compromises made by Democrats have helped to usher in this system, the Republicans have evolved their own techniques for managing discontent. In a helpful analysis, Snyder divided Republicans into the 'gamers' (who try to preserve the status quo, using their money and connections) and the 'breakers' (who emphasize shaking things up in the interest of small government). Snyder noted in January 2021:

> In the four decades since the election of Ronald Reagan, Republicans have overcome the tension between the gamers and the breakers by governing in opposition to government, or by calling elections a revolution (the Tea Party), or by claiming to oppose elites. The breakers in this arrangement provide cover for the gamers, putting forth an ideology that distracts from the basic reality that government

> under Republicans is not made smaller but simply diverted to serve a handful of interests.[72]

We can see here a process of shoring up an inequitable system with a critique that looks much more radical than it turns out to be in practice. It's a cycle that in important respects mirrors the Democrats' cycle of radical hope and then accommodation to vested interests. Radicals on both sides emphasize the slow-burning disasters that have affected 'ordinary Americans' as well as the sharp shock of 2007–8. But this radicalization is constantly defused and deflected in ways that keep an increasingly inequitable system on the road.

This is where the instrumentalization of blowback becomes key. It was Gore Vidal who famously observed that in America there was 'free enterprise for the poor and socialism for the rich'.[73] The latter was starkly in evidence when the big banks were bailed out at a cost of 700 billion dollars in 2007–8.[74] When this process unsurprisingly *deepened* disillusionment in the broader American population, right-wing populism fed on this discontent with its denunciation of 'metropolitan elites'.[75] As Mark Danner noted in the *New York Review of Books*, 'Trumpism is partly the child of the 2008 Wall Street collapse and the vast sense of political corruption and self-dealing it brought in its wake … .'[76] In this political climate, Trump was able to harness anti-elite sentiment and to use it to support a range of *rather traditional* Republican policies, including lower taxes, weaker environmental regulation, and increased spending on defence. In another remarkable trick, Trump instrumentalized his own history of corrupt wheeler-dealing: 'Nobody knows the system better than me', he boasted, 'which is why I alone can fix it.'[77] Former Alaska governor and 'Tea Party' star Sarah Palin said in her endorsement of Trump, 'Only one candidate's record of success proves he is the master of the deal. He is beholden to no one but we the people. How refreshing!'

While it is easy to paint Trump as uniquely damaging and deceptive, his brand of harnessing disillusionment was foreshadowed in the Republicans' 'Tea Party' movement in which Palin played such a prominent part. Notable here was the Tea Party's (understandable) insistence that bailing out the banks under Bush in 2007–8 was a mistake and the more general conclusion that markets should be allowed to operate *more freely*.[78] Thus, after a crisis caused in large part by financial deregulation, Republicanism was invited to adhere more strictly to its rhetorical commitment to *laissez faire*. One of the greatest crises of capitalism and neoliberalism became a way to mobilize people behind *free markets and further deregulation*: a 'hair of the dog' remedy of startling proportions.

Through his record as President, Trump illustrated how right-wing populism, which was often anti-elite in its rhetoric, has tended to be pro-elite when it comes to actually running the country. This is part of a more general pattern that spans the 'Global North' and the 'Global South'. As James Putzel observed in an incisive analysis of ascendant right-wing populists in the US, the Philippines and Brazil in particular. 'In what seems almost a masterful "confidence trick", they have come to power backed by alliances of business interests often promoting greater deregulation of domestic markets than the neoliberals before them.'[79] The Brazilian stock exchange was happy at Bolsonaro's win in 2019, essentially because of his neoliberal economic policies favouring the rich.[80] Bolsonaro said he was going after corruption (an idea probably threatening to business interests) but he seems to have meant primarily the alleged corruption of some of his political opponents. Bearing in mind the close link between some of the emerging right-wing populist leaders, David Harvey goes so far as to discern a 'neoliberal neo-fascist alliance coming to dominance'.[81] Governments on these lines may also ratchet up repression of opposition movements, often embracing elements of a 'big state' amid a rhetorical lauding of the 'small state'. The Kurz government in Austria ramped up rhetoric against migrants while pushing through a rise in the maximum working hours from 40 to 60.[82]

Breaking Bad

The UK, meanwhile, has exhibited its own politics of distraction. Writing in 2011, Owen Jones noted that under the Labour government of 1997–2010 a failure to supply adequate jobs and affordable housing had fed the rise of the far right (first the British National Party and then a resurgent UK Independence Party) amid 'a popular perception that Labour had abandoned the people it was created to represent'.[83] It's true that Labour made a dent in child poverty and put substantial resources into health and education. But diverse discontents over jobs, industrial decline and housing remained. Grievances were exacerbated by the 2007–8 financial crisis and subsequent austerity, and they fed into the rather magical idea that breaking ties with the European Union would bring a solution (an idea that Labour leader Jeremy Corbyn did not challenge).[84] When the referendum went in favour of the Leavers, some Brexit supporters celebrated that at last they had found a 'voice'.

Arendt noted that those who feel lonely, discarded or forgotten might want 'access to history even at the price of destruction'.[85]

Of course, there was also some genuine hope attached to the Brexit vote. Concerns around national sovereignty should not be dismissed, particularly in view of some of the corruption within the European Union.[86] But it is hard to see any plausible mechanism by which Brexit can address key underlying problems like inequality, de-industrialization and the erosion of public services that helped to generate at least part of the groundswell of support for Brexit. Indeed, a range of economic impacts and falling levels of social protection look set to make these underlying problems *worse*. While the Leave campaign claimed that leaving the EU was going to free up 350 million pounds a week for the National Health Service, this claim had no basis in fact and the promised windfall duly failed to materialize.

Meanwhile, a remarkable sense of political crisis and associated norm-breaking came to the fore around Brexit. This was 'emergency politics' writ large. With Leave campaigners having stressed the need to escape 'subordination' to Brussels, the 2016 referendum vote itself ushered in a kind of fever to 'Get Brexit Done.' In this atmosphere, the Hansard political audit for 2019 found 54 per cent of respondents agreeing that 'Britain needs a strong leader willing to break the rules.'[87] In September 2019, Parliament was temporarily and illegally suspended (or 'prorogued').[88] Jonathan Freedland noted that Prime Minister Johnson's chief adviser Dominic Cummings 'reckons a willingness to defy norms wins the devotion of your base',[89] while European politics specialist Jonathan White commented:

> It is as though Dominic Cummings and co want to teach the public that liberal democracy is a charade: that notions of the separation of powers, checks on the executive, procedures and standards of conduct in public life are just so much fluff, that playing dirty is how it must go.[90]

Truth was one casualty of this 'emergency' – not just in the deception over the NHS but also in the Leave campaign's claim that if the UK stayed in the EU, then Turkey would soon be a fellow member, putting British schools and hospitals under more strain. As so often, invoking a *future* disaster and linking it to the present proved politically useful. A notorious Leave poster showed huge numbers of refugees with the slogan 'BREAKING POINT: The EU has failed us all.'

After the Brexit referendum, warnings of future unrest carried heavy overtones of intimidation and even incitement. 'Crush the saboteurs', ran a *Daily Mail* front-page headline after Prime Minister May called for an election to try to overcome objections in the House of Lords and House of Commons. In January 2019 the UK's *Daily Express* ran the headline 'Second Vote Will Lead to Civil Unrest', noting that 'Theresa May last night warned that a second EU referendum could trigger civil disorder and unrest across Britain by destroying trust in Parliament.' In September 2019, the UK's Parliament reconvened after its illegal suspension. Prime Minister Johnson and others used inflammatory language such as 'treason' and 'surrender bill'. After the murder of MP Jo Cox in June 2016 by a white supremacist and amid growing concerns about MPs' safety, Johnson went so far as to tell MPs that the best route to *their own personal safety* was to 'Get Brexit Done'. In saying this, he was himself instrumentalizing the possibility of violence.

In *Twilight of Democracy*, Anne Applebaum recalls working and socializing with many of the most prominent Brexiteers, presenting herself as the serious foil to an increasingly reckless group of jokesters and extremists. 'For some', she notes, 'the potential for constitutional and political chaos was not just a regrettable side effect: it was part of the Brexit appeal .... They wanted disruption.'[91] A 'no deal Brexit' was courted by some, she observes, while disruption 'became, for many Brexiteers, the real goal. And if the institutions of the British state stood in the way, then the institutions would suffer.'[92] Some of the most prominent pro-Brexit Conservative MPs (including Liz Truss who later became Prime Minister) had contributed to a radical policy document that insisted, 'The British are among the worst idlers in the world', and needed a shock. While Labour leader Jeremy Corbyn prevaricated, deputy leader of the Labour Party Tom Watson privately told journalist Nick Cohen that part of the Labour leadership 'absolutely believe that if Brexit brings chaos the voters will turn to the radical left'.[93]

Meanwhile, the danger of erosion of democratic safeguards has been exacerbated by the act of breaking away from the European Union, which imposes certain obligations and an overarching legal framework on its member states (reflecting in part an original intention that the EU be a bulwark against revived authoritarianism in Europe).[94] Authoritarian tendencies in Hungary and Poland still have to manoeuvre within the framework of EU membership, a protection the UK now lacks.[95]

Conclusion

In the context of several conflicts in the Global South, I have found that the declared goal (like winning a war) is sometimes held to justify abuse, infringement of important rights, and suppression of dissent; but at the same time it is sometimes the abuse, the infringement of rights and the suppression of dissent that are mostly highly valued while the declared aim (like waging and winning a war) provides legitimacy for these underlying priorities. This is an important reason why enemies tend to be reinvented even when a war comes to an end. The 'emergency' itself becomes useful.

In the UK, 'Brexit' was commonly presented as a crisis where the 'end' (leaving the EU, respecting the referendum) justified drastic means like suspending Parliament. It was also the 'end' that, in some politicians' and journalists' eyes at least, justified stirring up fears of civil disorder, denigrating judges as 'enemies of the people', distorting the truth, and so on. The idea that 'the end justifies the means' was indeed an important part of the story, and it shows how an obsession with one particular goal or threat or pseudo-threat can open the floodgates to a much broader erosion of democratic rights and norms.

At the same time, we should also keep in mind the possibility that Brexit was in some respects *a useful crisis* and a means to *some more fundamental goals* that went beyond Brexit and continue to animate British politics now that Brexit itself is (largely) a *fait accompli*. Here, we might think of the erosion of democratic authority, a deepening of neoliberalism, and the assertion of a more 'presidential' form of government based on some kind of presumed bond between charismatic leader and the populace.[96] Perhaps the overarching goal was not Brexit at all but *the freedom to do what one likes*, unconstrained by rules and conventions and consideration for others. After all, Johnson himself did not really believe in Brexit: 'Nobody serious wants to leave the EU', he told Anne Applebaum when he was mayor of London.[97] For all the talk of freedom and sovereignty around Brexit, it was often Johnson's ambition and his *personal* sovereignty that held sway. Trump's politics too, as noted, were to a large extent about his personal sovereignty – the thrill of winning and the freedom 'to do whatever the hell he wanted'.[98] And for all of those who *cannot* do whatever they want (which after all is pretty much everybody), the spectacle of someone who *can* may be oddly thrilling (as well, perhaps, as deeply terrifying).

At any rate, in both the UK and the US the transgression of democratic norms, and of norms around telling the truth, was part of the construction of a kind of 'charismatic' authority that fed on a public appetite for transgression, strong leaders, freedom-from-restraint and even 'access to history'. This has taken politics in some very dangerous directions where the normal constraints on the executive, as well as the normal constraints on behaviour, become significantly weakened. Fortunately, these things do not necessarily proceed in one direction: revelations that Johnson felt free to party in the midst of Covid turned his 'thrilling' irresponsibility into something more like a provocative hypocrisy. Anger at elites, having been channelled towards those said to be blocking Brexit, pivoted quickly towards Johnson himself amid a growing sense that there was 'one rule for them and another for us'.

Earlier in the book, we noted Sen and Drèze's (1989) argument that democracies prevent famines, a logic that would seem to extend to other disasters. But we also observed that in practice much depends on the type of disaster and the type of democracy. A lesson from disasters in the Global South is that some groups tend to lack the political muscle with which to protect themselves. A helpful response to disaster will depend on who has political influence, how seriously the disaster is taken, what the media coverage is like, and who thinks they can *benefit*. The same goes for disasters in the Global North.

Focusing primarily on the US and the UK, this chapter has highlighted the salience of a *politics of distraction* that uses high-profile disasters and related definitions of 'emergency' and 'the enemy' to deflect attention from underlying (and often slow-burning) disasters. This is a politics in which cruelty and violence have at times been elevated to the status of political virtues, with politicians sometimes being rewarded rather than punished for transgressing both democratic norms and norms of decent behaviour more generally.

In the case of the US, an especially striking phenomenon has been the *lack of protection*, democracy notwithstanding, that millions of Americans have experienced in the face of a wide range of disasters – from the slow-moving disaster of de-industrialization to the opioid crisis, the Covid crisis, Hurricane Katrina, mass foreclosure, urban decline, and mass poverty (with UN Special Rapporteur Philip Alston noting in 2018 that there were some forty million people living in poverty and 5.3 million living 'in Third World conditions of absolute poverty').[99] Anne Case and Angus Deaton have shown how what they call 'deaths of despair' – whether from suicide, drug overdose, or alcoholism – have risen sharply over the last two decades, resulting in the deaths of hundreds of thousands of Americans every year.[100] Again, such deaths have proven entirely compatible with the existence of a democratic system.

When it comes to democracy's ability or inability to protect from disaster, we need to understand what Henry Giroux has called 'the politics of disposability' in which certain groups of people are deemed in effect to be disposable and not worthy of care or rescue.[101] We have seen this politics playing out in Detroit and Flint, where the infliction of misery by officials and financiers was also greatly assisted by steps that significantly eroded democracy. While the cases of Detroit and Flint underline that actually existing democracies do not necessarily protect against disasters, they also suggest that what is needed is not less democracy but a democracy that is more genuinely democratic.

A *politics of disposability* also played out in the context of Hurricane Katrina, as Giroux himself observed. The contours of disposability became clearer when Katrina itself disproportionately affected Black residents and other people of colour (due partly to greater average poverty and partly to occupying on average, more flood-prone regions).[102] Later, efforts to rebuild the city tended to exacerbate underlying vulnerabilities. Part of the problem was that an overwhelmingly privatized recovery programme greatly impeded *accountability*. This was due in large part to confidentiality clauses,[103] a phenomenon, as Loewenstein has stressed in *Disaster Capitalism*, that itself represents a kind of creeping de-democratization via privatization.[104] In New Orleans, when private contractors proved expensive (and needed expensive bureaucratic oversight), this fed into a fiscal crisis, in parallel to the fiscal crisis in Michigan and elsewhere, and this in turn led to redundancies and pension cuts.[105]

While the 2020 Black Lives Matter protests have rightly been seen as triggered by police violence, they also need to be understood against a broader backdrop of socio-economic neglect and longer-term failings in the US democratic system. Perceptions on whether Black lives matter and, more generally, whether the lives of the poor count for anything, have naturally been profoundly shaped by a politics of abandonment and exploitation that extends to pollution, weather-related disasters, fiscal crisis, mass incarceration and penal systems sometimes explicitly intended to fund struggling municipalities by exacting widespread and escalating fines that frequently end with imprisonment.[106]

When Trump proclaimed in his 2016 presidential campaign that America had 'third world' infrastructure,[107] he was pointing to a genuine problem. The struggles for water, housing and safety in places like Detroit, Flint and New Orleans showed that the most powerful country in the world was not actually providing a minimal level of comfort, dignity and infrastructure for many of its citizens. In the event, Trump did virtually nothing about the defective infrastructure when he became President – and virtually nothing to help the poor either. His main focus, apart from cutting taxes and pushing through further deregulation, was on *security*. And when the Black Lives Matter protests gathered steam, those too were placed within the framework of 'security' – another example of instrumentalizing blowback. In effect, the protesters were added to an expanding list of 'useful enemies' that already included, at various times, 'metropolitan elites', Muslims, and migrants coming into the US from the south. It is to the 'migration crisis' and the rather systematic political exploitation of this particular 'blowback', on both sides of the Atlantic, that we now turn.

5

Hostile Environments

In the swelter of July 2016, the refugee camp seemed rather below the normal standard for Sudan. Improvised tents provided little protection against either the heat or the sudden rains. People were crammed much too close together, a major fire risk. And the toilets were in a terrible state.

But this was not Sudan. Nor was it Bangladesh or Ethiopia. It was a coastal resort in France. When child psychiatrist Lynne Jones visited Calais in October 2015, she asked:

> How is it possible that on the borders of a north European town, there are some 6,000 people living in conditions worse than those I have encountered with Somali refugees on the Ethiopian border, Pakistanis after a devastating earthquake, or Darfuris in the deserts of Northern Chad, one of the poorest countries in the world?[1]

In July 2015, to give one snapshot, aid workers reported 'an undignified and intolerable situation (a single water point for nearly 3,000 persons, no shelters, no toilets accessible from 7pm to noon the following day) … waste and excrement litter the ground'.[2] Calais even added its own industrialized twists to the knife: the stench of a nearby chemical factory was everywhere; and there was a major problem of asbestos strewn across the camp, with all the attendant health hazards.[3]

One night in July 2016, at a dinner with some of those who had fled the war in Syria, everyone in our group suddenly raised their feet and put them on the edge of the table. For a moment, I wondered if this might be some intriguing Syrian ritual I had not yet encountered. But it turned out that a large rat was running round under our feet, and this synchronized foot-lifting had become quite normal. In the Calais 'jungle' camp, you could also hear rats running over the canvas or metal rooves of restaurants. One senior Syrian man said, 'If Bashar Assad can drop barrel bombs on hundreds of thousands of Syrians, the French government can surely get rid of the rats here!' Fires were a constant problem and, indeed, one evening I managed to set my own shoes on fire while still wearing them. (My friend and fellow researcher confided she had noticed the smoke a minute or so earlier and was waiting for a polite moment to mention it.) In general, residents and volunteers at the camp emphasized grave deficiencies in hygiene, shelter, heating and lighting.

We've noted Agamben's conception of 'the camp' as a zone in which crimes do not count as crimes. To a large extent, this applied to the Calais camp. Apart from the neglect of basic human needs, police violence was routine, and complaints fell on stony ground.[4] One volunteer told us: 'Everyone has had experience of teargas or rubber bullets. The head injuries from rubber bullets were terrible.' The lack of access to basic human rights was underlined when people, having been moved to the 'jungle' site on the basis of a promise that they would not be displaced from there, found that half the camp was destroyed by police in early 2016 and the rest in October of that year. After that, conditions for the migrants/refugees *deteriorated*, and they were kept constantly on the move by French police.[5]

One of the tragic ironies in this situation was that the inhuman conditions in Calais were allowed to occur within a well-established democracy that had a strong claim to have *originated* the concept of human rights. That proud history, which of course was flagrantly disregarded in empire, turned out to mean very little even within *La Métropole* (or European France). In fact, the empire's routine suspension of law and rights was 'coming home' in the highly racialized context of Calais.[6] One is strongly reminded of Hannah Arendt's reflections on the precarious situation of those fleeing the Nazis (and she herself was interned in a French camp after fleeing Germany):

> The conception of human rights, based upon the assumed existence of a human being as such, broke down at the very moment when those who professed to believe in it were for the first time confronted with people who had indeed lost all other qualities and specific relationships – except that they were still human. The world found nothing sacred in the abstract nakedness of being human.[7]

Arendt noted, further, that while certain rights had been proclaimed as 'inalienable', it turned out that in the victims' hour of greatest need 'no authority was left to protect them and no institution was willing to guarantee them'.[8] In the case of Calais, we may go further. For a key problem in the 'jungle' camp, and even more so once the camp had been destroyed, was not simply indifference or a lack of willingness to protect the people who were stuck there; rather, this suffering was in many ways *actively functional*.

The Functions of Disaster

If today humanitarian disasters are 'coming home' to Western democracies, we should also recognize that the phenomenon of a *functional* disaster, for some time familiar from many disasters around the world, is also increasingly 'coming home'.

Deterrence

In Calais, suffering and a purposefully hostile environment have served, and have at times been openly deployed, as a deterrent in relation to additional migration. In 2011, with police carrying out almost daily raids on migrants in an abandoned factory, Calais' deputy mayor Philippe Mignonet said the local council was determined to maintain 'a certain level of pressure' on migrants coming into the city. 'We want them to send a message back that it's useless to come to Calais', he added, 'that it's not as easy to come here as their mafias tell them.'[9] The instrumentalization of disaster as a tool of deterrence was also clear in a chilling question posed by Fabienne Buccio, prefect of the Pas-de-Calais, in 2015: 'To what extent can conditions in the "camp" be made human without endangering the local inhabitants' situation through the creation of a magnet effect?'[10]

Unsurprisingly perhaps, we have not witnessed UK politicians spelling out an intention to deepen the suffering in Calais. But such suffering was a predictable and, within a short space of time, a *known* consequence of a range of policy decisions: tightening British border controls inside northern France from 2002; British pressure to restrict humanitarian aid (including the closing of the 'Sangatte' centre in Calais in 2002) and later British pressure to break up and deter settlements, for which funding was provided to the French police. Migrants/refugees in Calais complained bitterly during our research in 2016 that Britain was contributing greatly to the violence there. In effect, a hostile environment on France's northern coast was serving as a vicious complement to the 'hostile environment' that was being fostered – and named as a policy goal – inside the UK. Deterrence was pivotal in both contexts.[11]

Putting on a show

A second function of the disaster in Calais has centred on a kind of *political theatre* aimed at Western audiences. In Orwell's *Nineteen Eighty-Four*, the very first act of rebellion by the central character, Winston Smith, was to write a diary, and in his first entry he recounted his experience watching a movie about bombing refugee boats in the Mediterranean, with the audience laughing at the footage. It was a chilling vision of suffering-as-entertainment and suffering-as-distraction – part of Orwell's broader dystopia in which people follow official guidelines on *who they should hate*.[12]

One might wish to believe that we have not yet reached this level of callousness. But much of the coverage of Calais was well calibrated for whipping up a sense of hatred and fear. After a July 2018 story about a French policeman being injured in Calais by a migrant/refugee who threw a rock, one online reader observed, 'Should have brought in the National Guard and beaten the sense out of them. Chucked them in a boat and dumped them in the sea!' Revealingly, this comment received 177 'likes' from other online contributors, and only one 'dislike'. Yet this was not a fringe far-right website; it was the website of the *Daily Mail*, Britain's biggest selling newspaper. This underlines the extent to which hatred had gone mainstream in the UK.

The spectacular degradation and desperation of migrants was put to use by significant elements of the media and by many politicians. Calais was often on the front-page of the UK press. And those leading the successful campaign for Britain to leave the European Union (or 'Brexit') were able to make significant political capital out of the disaster in Calais.

In particular, Calais proved extremely useful for UK newspapers and politicians seeking to suggest that migrants 'from Europe' were an existential threat to the UK, a threat that leaving the European Union would somehow 'fix'. One study of UK media coverage between December 2013 and March 2014 found that while eight per cent of *Guardian* stories on refugees/migrants were about Calais, almost 40 per cent of refugee/migrant stories in the *Daily Mail* focused on Calais. Just one week before the Brexit referendum, the *Daily Mail* ran the front-page headline 'We're from Europe – Let us in!' above a story about Iraqi and Kuwaiti migrants hiding in a lorry.[13] In general, the image of migrants desperate to 'invade' chimed conveniently with the 'take back control' slogan of the 'Leave' campaign.[14] With fears around immigration to the UK having traditionally centred largely around non-European people,[15] a focus on Calais usefully recast leaving Europe as a way to take control and shut out non-European as well as European people.

Significant deception was involved here, as well as considerable magical thinking among those 'buying' the message. For one thing, leaving or staying in the EU did not actually affect Britain's ability to regulate non-European immigration, especially as the UK was not part of the 'Schengen Area' in which freedom of movement has been facilitated. Strong physical controls on the movement of (mostly non-European) migrants moving through northern France *already existed*, with the UK inside the EU. Third, leaving the EU actually promised to *weaken* these border controls, an added incentive for attempted crossings. In the event, there has indeed been a surge, after Brexit, in attempts to reach the UK by boat. Back in 2016, the *Daily Mail* ran a story with the headline 'Illegal immigrants aiming to cross the Channel say Brexit will make it EASIER to sneak into Britain because France will no longer try to stop them.'[16] But, significantly, the story was published on 24 June, the day *after* the UK's Brexit referendum – a classic case of 'Now they tell us!' as well as an illustration of the *Daily Mail's* determination to *keep the fear going*. French officials expressed scepticism around helping Britain's border control given that Britain was quitting the EU. Amid the subsequent rise in sea-voyages, November 2021 saw at least 27 people die after trying to cross from France to the UK. Refugees in northern France reported that Brexit had indeed had the effect of making it easier and more attractive to set out for the UK in small boats, not least because they could no longer be sent back to other European countries.[17]

As is often the way with propaganda,[18] the UK's feverish popular press saw no particular problem in simultaneously peddling two contradictory messages. One example was that quick about-turn on Brexit – from portraying it as making crossings less likely, to painting it as making crossings *more* likely. Another example was the mixed message on *squalor vs luxury*. The UK popular press tended to emphasize that the Calais migrants/refugees were living in (threatening) squalor. Yet at the same time they were sometimes said to be living in (enraging) luxury. Both stories played into a kind of politics of outrage. When overnight accommodation for a small number of women and children was set up at the 'jungle' site in 2015, UK popular newspapers stressed that a Michelin-rated chef was cooking for those nearby. Invoking the old 'Sangatte' site at Calais that was closed in 2002 under UK pressure, the *Sun* headline asked, 'Anyone for Sangatteau?'[19] Meanwhile, the *Daily Mail* stressed that UK taxpayers' money was contributing to such indulgence.[20] The *Sun* subsequently featured an idyllic picture of lakeside dining at the camp, complete with comfy armchairs and a waiter serving drinks. We went to this particular shack-cum-restaurant in 2016, and it was indeed a strangely tranquil venue looking out over calm water, reeds and the occasional heron. But still, the image conveyed in the picture was *extraordinarily unrepresentative*: leaving this little slice of bliss took you straight back into the tumult and chaos of the camp itself.

Deterrence and Theatre at the Mexican Border

In terms of the political theatre around migration, the drama of Calais was mirrored by the drama of the 'caravan' in North America. Some Trump administration officials seemed to acknowledge that, with elections coming up and the Republicans trying to hold onto majorities in both Houses, truth was less important than the tensions that could be stirred around the caravan. That, in the words of one official, was 'the play'.[21] Children were forcibly separated from their families and held in detention; John Kelly, Trump's secretary of homeland security, said the move was made 'in order to deter movement along this terribly dangerous network'.[22]

Trump's wall, endlessly announced, is really an elaboration of the miles of fortification that have accumulated since the Truman presidency at the end of the Second World War.[23] And while Trump brought his own brand of cruelty and rhetorical flourishes to the US's southern border, it's important to emphasize that the instrumentalization of suffering at the border also long preceded his administration. Amnesty International noted in 2017: 'The border control measures proposed by President Trump will intensify a pre-existing enforcement and deterrence-based strategy that began to take effect as early as the mid-1990s and continued in different degrees throughout the George W. Bush and Barack Obama administrations.'[24] In 2016 (before the Trump presidency), there were over 350,000 individuals in civil immigration detention centres in the US and a great many of them were children.[25]

In a 2015 article, De León noted the humanitarian disaster in the deserts of Arizona and highlighted the US's self-styled 'Prevention Through Deterrence' strategy from 1993, a long-standing endeavour in which 'policy makers were well aware of the role that death [in the desert] would play in this enforcement strategy'.[26] In a detailed 2001 article, Cornelius noted that 'The spatial redistribution of migrant deaths since 1994 is an impressive demonstration of the [US] Border Patrol's capacity to herd unauthorized border-crossers into increasingly inhospitable and dangerous areas.'[27] Cornelius also referred to 'the massive border enforcement buildup since 1993', noting 'a further decline in the never-substantial US government effort to enforce immigration control laws in the workplace'.[28]

Brutality around the US southern border was actually routine in the 1970s, 1980s and 1990s.[29] Federal agents would regularly raid ranches just before payment and deport the workers who had earlier crossed the border, at one point explicitly reminding the migrants that 'In this place you have no rights.'[30] In Texas, police filmed their own brutal interrogations and played them back for entertainment.[31] Greg Grandin documents long-standing hostility towards immigration from the south among many vigilante groups and officials, and links it to US imperialism and expansion southwards as well as westwards, whether in the original land-grab from Mexico or in anti-Communist and anti-drugs interventions in Central America. Over many decades, movements of migrants and refugees in the opposite direction have been instrumentalized in US politics – simultaneously an outlet for racism and frustration and an easy card to play at election time. Grandin notes that vigilantes intimidating migrants at the US's southern border 'often describe themselves as the rear guard of the Mexican American War of 1846–8, standing against an enemy they believe is intent on retaking land they lost at the end of that conflict'.[32] It shows how an intolerant politics can be fuelled by blowback and *fear of* blowback.

If much of this is of long standing, Trump certainly hyped up fears around the southern border with particular virulence. The timing of this was interesting partly because it tended to conceal the reality of a *diminishing* interest in coming to the US as an economic migrant. Amnesty noted: 'While there have been some increases in overall apprehensions along the US–Mexico border since 2014, levels of irregular entries into the USA are much lower than 2008 levels, and even lower compared to earlier decades ... Apprehensions of Mexicans by the US Border Patrol dropped from 1.6 million in 2000 to 192,000 in 2016.[33] Furthermore, 'The idea of the "American dream" has changed significantly over the last few decades. Multiple research findings have provided evidence of a sharp decline in economically motivated immigration from Latin America from 2000 onwards …'.[34] Amnesty noted that the slump in Mexican migration reflected recession in the US as well as demographic changes and economic improvements in Mexico itself. It's worth noting, too, that many Americans have been looking south for cheaper medicines and medical care and perhaps a more comfortable retirement. In this sense at least (and despite the southern neighbour's continuing severe problems on many fronts), America's 'Mexican dream' is alive and well.

Promoting Suffering

Back across the Atlantic, concerns around migrants/refugees in Calais and the surrounding region were one of many factors in an increasingly energetic promotion of suffering in the Mediterranean. In late 2014, Italy put a stop to its well-funded Mediterranean rescue operation known as Mare Nostrum, so that search-and-rescue became confined to the immediate vicinity of the Italian coastline. Drownings rose sharply.[35] Shortly before Mare Nostrum was ended, French Minister of the Interior Bernard Cazeneuve had complained, 'although the Italian navy's rescue operation has enabled the rescuing of numerous migrants at sea, [it] has also resulted in the creation of fixed migrant gathering points in the North of France'. The UK government also stated that it was not in favour of planned search and rescue, which it considered a 'pull factor' encouraging migrants to attempt dangerous sea crossings.[36] Yet in practice sea-crossings continued and became even more dangerous. In the first few months of 2019, for example, an astonishing one in ten people embarking on the Central Mediterranean crossing were dying or missing at sea, a huge rise from 2.6 per cent in 2017.[37] This, too, was a purposefully engineered 'hostile environment'.

Within the *system of suffering* that has emerged around mass migration, we can see that drowning, freezing, dying of thirst, and other forms of harm (while sometimes highlighted amid expressions of regret) have been serving important functions: as deterrence, as political theatre and, indeed, as propaganda for the allegedly 'humanitarian' project of preventing people from making 'dangerous journeys' in the first place.

Considering these functions together, we may say that within the political theatre that is accompanying and fuelling Europe's collective assault on asylum (a theatre whose audience is both the migrants/refugees and the Western electorates), the drowning migrant has become a useful victim to set alongside the useful enemy that is the human smuggler. In the discussion of aid to disasters in the Global South, we referred to the dangers in the 'Do No Harm' framework (including the possibility that rebel areas will be denied assistance in the interests of 'preventing terrorism'). Today the 'Do No Harm' injunction is being harnessed to anti-migrant/refugee initiatives, which are bolstered by the idea that rescue will encourage 'dangerous journeys'.

As part of an increasingly repressive border control system in Europe, large numbers of migrants have been forcibly returned to Libya where they have faced, and been known to face, torture and extreme exploitation in detention centres. The Libyan coastguard has played a key role here, turning people back as they set off northwards, and obtaining funding, equipment, encouragement and information from the European Union.[38] Crucially, part of the motive for such 'outsourcing' of migration control has been maintaining an appearance of 'clean hands' even while violence is being rather ruthlessly facilitated. It illustrates that democracies may sometimes be more interested in hiding or even relocating disasters than in actually preventing them. Part of the emerging system of suffering, indeed, has been an increased outsourcing of migration control to third parties. This also gets around laws designed to prevent the *refoulement* of refugees (or forcible return from countries where they have taken refuge) and has the effect of preventing refugees from claiming asylum in the first place.[39]

One way of exploring the possible functionality of disaster is to explore the incentives that a country receiving migrants/refugees ('recipient country') may have in relation to countries in different zones (the recipient country itself, the countries-of-origin, and the 'transit countries' in between). In this exercise, I assume that the recipient country is determined to limit the 'inflow' of migrants/refugees and I suggest three possible ways of doing this: tackling the root causes of migration; building effective walls that physically prevent migration; and deterring migration by other means. If *tackling the root causes* of migration is the chosen means of immigration control, then the recipient country will have an interest in reducing conflict in countries-of-origin. If the immigration control strategy centres on *building effective walls*, there is likely to be an *indifference* to levels of human rights abuse in countries-of-origin (and indeed in all the relevant zones). If the strategy is to *deter* migration (in ways other than simple physical obstruction), then an especially disturbing set of incentives emerges. First, we may expect an indifference to conflict in countries-of-origin. Second, there is an interest in *promoting or at least tolerating* human rights abuses within transit countries (so as to deter migration from countries-of-origin); when it comes to immigration to Europe, Libya is such a zone. When it comes to immigration to the UK, France is such a 'transit' zone. Third, there is an interest in *promoting human rights abuses* among at least certain sections of the population in the recipient country (a 'hostile environment'). I try to illustrate these incentives in Table 1.

Table 1. Recipient countries' incentives in relation to human rights situation in various zones

Three approaches to migration control	*In recipient country*	*In transit country*	*In country of origin*
1. Addressing root causes	Indifferent	Indifferent	Make it better
2. Walling off	Indifferent	Indifferent	Indifferent
3. Deterrence (through suffering)	Make it worse	Make it worse	Indifferent

This shows how the logic of migration deterrence may help to 'bring disasters home' when it is given a high priority, a process that in the real world is well underway. Certainly, a deterrence paradigm takes us well beyond a framework where recipient countries are either generous (welcoming people) or ungenerous (not welcoming them).

We should note, too, that outsourcing migration control can easily rebound in the longer term. In fact, where repressive governments are supported in the name of migration control, this repression is likely to deepen the underlying emergencies – and ultimately to generate more migrants/refugees. Such governments might be in 'transit zones' or countries-of-origin. When Western democracies promote or tolerate human rights abuses in 'transit' countries as part of a deterrence strategy, this also strongly feeds instability and, in the longer term, will logically fuel more desire to move.

Part of the problem here, as Ruben Andersson has argued, is that an overriding focus on controlling the flow of migrants creates some very perverse incentives: in particular, it may encourage third parties to stoke the threat and to offer to control the flow in search of aid and impunity.[40] This reflects a process that Andersson has documented in several geographical contexts, not least in Libya, where Gaddafi played on international fears of the sub-Saharan migrants within Libya to secure for himself impunity and the lifting of sanctions – at one point threatening to 'turn Europe Black'.[41] Again, when countries in the Global North play along with this game, it encourages such strategies and amounts to outsourcing migration control to others, while creating a false impression of 'clean hands'. Mali is among the African countries to have exploited its 'leverage' on migration. In relation to Syria in particular, Turkey has tried to use its status as a transit country, telling the European Union countries that they would face increased flows of migrants/refugees if they didn't make concessions such as improved access for Turkey to the European Union and increased freedom-of-operation for Turkey's military operations within Syria. Even France has been keen to stress that its cooperation in discouraging migration to the UK cannot be taken for granted and needs to be paid for.

We discussed disaster in Sudan at some length in Chapter 2, and it's worth reflecting on the role of Sudan in contemporary 'migration control'. When it comes to international migration, Sudan is both a country-of-origin and a transit zone (for example for refugees from Eritrea). In the west of Sudan, we saw the *Janjaweed* perpetrators of Darfur's genocide absorbed into a border security force that courted favour with the European Union, even as the EU became increasingly obsessed with migration control and increasingly determined to *outsource* this control. The European Union actually went to the extreme of praising President Bashir (a man indicted for genocide) as a valuable 'partner' in regional migration control. Meanwhile, Bashir's government in Khartoum courted the EU's favour by establishing the Rapid Support Forces, an organization presented as a border security force but also serving counterinsurgency functions as well as engaging in the intimidation of dissenters and in simple predation.[42] At one point, the leadership of the Rapid Support Forces themselves threatened increased migration unless the European Union gave direct support (rather than indirect support through aiding Khartoum). One of the results of the outsourcing of migration control in relation to Sudan is that outmigration from Darfur (which would be better termed *escape* from Darfur as mass displacement and significant levels of violence continue) was to a large extent blocked by the Rapid Support Forces, so that in effect the victims of Darfur's genocide have been penned in (with EU encouragement) by the perpetrators of genocide.[43]

And all this has been done in the name of 'crime prevention' – the prevention of 'illegal migration' and 'human smuggling'.[44] It's also worth thinking back to the discussion in Chapter 2 of Sudan in 1988 (and indeed Nazi-controlled territory in the Second World War), where we noted that genocide can be fuelled by a project of *expulsion* combined with *a refusal to receive those being expelled.*

Within this emerging apparatus of repression, systems for outsourcing migration control begin to resemble a kind of 'mafia' system. Those who offer to control the flow of migrants, like those who offer to reduce the threat of terrorism, often try to extract a high price for doing so. And, as with the 'war on terror', those offering their cooperation in migration-control may even have an interest in stoking the underlying threat so as to extract the maximum price.[45] Another perverse incentive arises within the *recipient* countries, moreover. For the governments of such countries may try to deny asylum, or even to force people back to countries-of-origin, by exaggerating the 'safety' that prevails in countries-of-origin or transit countries or both. Trump described refugees' journeys through Mexico (journeys on which people have faced multiple threats from criminal gangs and abusive officials) as 'like ... walking through Central Park'.

When Helping People is Wrong

Whatever the complexities and the politics of particular disasters, the 1980s and 1990s were a time when governments and populations in the Global North were usually united in their praise for the heroic aid workers who were bringing relief to the victims of far-away disasters.

Today, as 'migration crises' of various kinds have 'come home' to Western democracies, attitudes to aid workers are changing. In many parts of the Global North, we find the routine obstruction, vilification and even persecution of those who are trying to ameliorate the disaster – and this seems to apply particularly to migration 'emergencies'. As in numerous humanitarian emergencies that have afflicted the Global South over many decades (from Sudan and Ethiopia to Syria and Sri Lanka), the functionality of many unfolding disasters within the West has been revealed most clearly by hostility towards those who are trying hardest to relieve or prevent these disasters.

Coming on top of a routine contempt for asylum, the stigmatization of those supporting the human rights of migrants represents a second significant attack on human rights themselves. It also shows an important mechanism through which Agamben's concept of the 'the camp' (where crimes do not count as crimes) may be extended, as Agamben himself warned was always possible, into a paradigm for governance more generally. Agamben suggested that terrorism pushed societies closer to this nightmare, offering abundant opportunities for governments to set aside constitutional 'safeguards' that turned out not to be safeguards at all. Today, if we look at a variety of migration crises around the world, we find another sphere of rightlessness that can expand with frightening speed – in this case from migrants/refugees to a variety of others.

Consider Calais again. In March 2017, local authorities barred humanitarian groups in Calais from distributing food, water, blankets and clothing; and when French courts objected, assistance resumed only in a very restricted form.[46] A British aid worker was imprisoned for photographing the police and then resisting arrest.[47] In July 2019, Amnesty noted, 'Providing food to the hungry and warmth to the homeless have become increasingly risky activities in northern France, as the authorities regularly target people offering help to migrants and refugees.' Given all the violence in Calais and given all the official hostility directed at aid workers themselves, some aid organizations began to offer these workers periods of 'rest and recuperation' away from France – a practice that is well established in relation to emergencies in Africa and Asia for example. With mainstream NGOs relatively scarce in Calais, the task of speaking up for migrants/refugees has often been left to those who were more inexperienced, more unaccustomed to advocacy, and more vulnerable to retaliation.[48]

Restrictions on humanitarian assistance in Calais have counterparts in restrictions on humanitarian aid in, for example, Greek islands like Lesbos as well as in restrictions placed on aid agencies that have tried to rescue refugees/migrants at risk of drowning in the Mediterranean. Many aid workers have been severely criticized (including by various European governments) for 'colluding' with human smugglers.[49] Meanwhile, dilemmas that have for some time been highlighted by academics and aid workers in relation to 'far away' disasters are now being replicated in relation to Europe.[50] Should one cooperate, for example, with modes of assistance that themselves embody significant violence? Is it better to 'speak out' or to prioritize 'access'? Should one try to address the root causes of suffering?

This last question should remind us that the systemic focus on consequences rather than causes in our disaster-producing system is not just a 'mistake' but has important political motives and roots.

Another dilemma is whether one should sign a silencing 'memorandum of understanding' (MOU) such as those imposed on NGOs by the Italian government, an echo of the silencing MOUs imposed by the Sri Lankan government in 2008–9. Paulo Cuttitta has highlighted the search for an elusive 'humanitarian space' in the Mediterranean Sea itself, with agencies aware that being too vocal may make it hard do their rescue work. Rescuing lives even became subject to legal prosecution from the Italian authorities, with NGOs being accused by public prosecutor Carmelo Zuccaro of colluding with smugglers and of trying to destabilize the Italian economy through an influx of migrants.[51] In 2017, the London-based Institute of Race Relations documented 45 prosecutions of humanitarian workers under anti-smuggling or immigration laws across Europe.[52]

Expansions in rightlessness tend to track a *de facto* expansion in the 'enemy' category – and here we might consider the 'caravan' of refugees/migrants moving up towards the US–Mexico border in 2018. In this case, it was clear that once fear had been whipped up to fever-pitch, the 'object' of fear could shift very rapidly.[53] To a notable extent, indeed, a heightened level of emotion had the effect of freeing the choice of targets from the constraints of reason. A relatively narrow definition of the threat or 'the enemy' centred on criminals: the Trump regime said gang members were hiding among the caravan refugees (though it did not back up this claim with evidence). In terms of 'enemy' definition and 'threat' definition, the category broadened very quickly into the caravan as a whole, so that suddenly even the elderly and families with small children were being re-imagined as a mortal threat.

Sometimes Hispanic immigration in general was portrayed as deeply threatening. The idea that 'Middle Eastern' terrorists were somehow being imported along with the migrants represented a further mutation of the enemy definition. And the fascistic overtones of this rapid expansion of the 'enemy' came even more clearly into focus when the idea emerged (and was widely circulated on the internet) that the ultimate responsibility for this existential threat was not actually the Hispanic gang member or the exhausted and frightened civilian population or even the classic bogeyman of the 'Middle Eastern' terrorist but the archetypical figure of Nazi propaganda – *the powerful Jew*.

Vice President Mike Pence told Fox News that the President of Honduras had informed him that the caravan was being funded 'by outside groups'.[54] Some kind of Jewish involvement was sometimes alleged, with George Soros as a kind of stand-in hate figure. Republican representative Matt Gaetz popularized a video of a man handing money to some women and speculated that George Soros was paying caravan members to migrate to the US. Trump tweeted the video, spreading the idea that caravan members were getting paid (but without

Gaetz's speculations on who was paying).[55] National Rifle Association Television correspondent Chuck Holton said Soros was sending the caravan to the US so the migrants could vote in the mid-term elections, while CNN conservative commentator Matt Schlapp said, 'Because of the liberal judges and other people that intercede, including George Soros, we have too much chaos at our southern border.'[56] Perhaps worst of all, Chris Farrell, head of a conservative activist organization Judicial Watch, said on Fox Business that the caravan was being funded/directed by the 'Soros-occupied State Department'.[57] The situation was all the more incendiary as open expressions of anti-Semitism were rising under Trump, proving integral for example to the neo-Nazi/white supremacist demonstrations in Charlottesville, Virginia (a clash that prompted Trump's notorious remark that there were 'fine people on both sides'). Robert Bowers, charged with killing eleven people at a Pittsburgh synagogue in October 2018 and at the centre of a long-delayed case, explicitly condemned the Maryland non-profit organization HIAS, which helps refugees (and says on its website that it is 'guided by Jewish values and history').[58]

Significantly, we also saw Trump rounding on four female Democratic Congresswomen of colour (sometimes known as 'the squad') who had drawn attention to suffering at the US/Mexico border and were calling for the abolition of Immigration and Customs Enforcement (ICE) because of its mistreatment of migrant families and children. All of the women were US citizens, with all but one having been born in the US. But Trump pronounced that the women should not be expressing critical views on government policy, adding 'Why don't they go back and help fix the totally broken and crime infested places from which they came?'[59]

The Expanding Enemy

Arendt gives us a chilling and illuminating window on many of the less obvious perils and pitfalls arising within an exclusionary system of migration control, whether this is in the 1930s and 1940s or in the contemporary era. Rather central here was her observation (noted earlier) that once the link between crime and punishment has been severed, no one is safe. This severed link was key to the rapid expansion in the category of 'enemy'. When it comes to imposing suffering on refugees, that link between crime and punishment tends to be severed at least twice: first, when people are punished in the countries-of-origin (despite generally not being guilty of anything) and then when these people are punished after managing to escape. When hostility is then extended to others (such as those helping them or speaking up for them), the link between crime and punishment is weakened still further and the whole idea of human rights is put more deeply into jeopardy.

Of course, a hostile attitude to the relief of migrants goes back a very long way. It's been documented, for example, in relation to the Middle Ages in Europe, where it often reflected residents' fears for their own safety, health and so on.[60] One might fondly imagine that such concerns would be set aside for the victims of something as extreme as the Nazi genocide. But this was not the case. Arendt noted that mass migration from Nazi territories actually led democratic and would-be recipient governments to remind the UN's forerunner, the League of Nations, 'that [its] Refugee work must be liquidated with the utmost rapidity'.[61] As so often today, the main aim in withholding aid was deterrence: it was feared that supplying aid would lead to a greater outflow of people.[62] More generally, Arendt showed how widespread was hostility towards migrants/refugees in Europe between the two world wars, most notably towards the Jews. Even in these extreme circumstances, the human right to asylum,[63] which was seen by Arendt as a fundamental symbol of 'the Rights of Man', did not count for much. Indeed, the extremity of the circumstances may even have *hardened* the impulse to exclude since the scale of the crisis and the potential migration was clearly very large. Arendt's own experience of being interned in France in 1940 led her towards the startling view that countries receiving refugees may end up imitating (perhaps in watered-down form) the practices of countries that are generating refugees. As Arendt put it: '... if the Nazis put a person in a concentration camp and if he made a successful escape say, to Holland, the Dutch would put him in an internment camp'.[64] Since many were deported from internment camps to the Nazi concentration camps, the boundary here was hardly rigid.

Arendt also stressed the tendency of the police in many 'receiving' countries to acquire special powers and special status in the context of a 'migrant crisis':

> ... in one sphere of public life it [the police] was no longer an instrument to carry out and enforce the law, but had become a ruling authority independent of government and ministries. Its strength and its emancipation from law and government grew in direct proportion to the influx of refugees.[65]

Arendt referred to close connections between police in potential recipient countries, on the one hand, and the Gestapo and Soviet secret police on the other.[66] She even saw this elevated role as feeding the 'disgracefully little resistance from the police' in countries occupied by the Nazis.[67]

Today, as in the era of Nazi persecutions, relationships between security services can grow up amid a shared interest in 'national security', 'crime prevention', 'migration control', and so on, with a sense of 'emergency' serving to limit transparency and accountability.[68] For example, abusive activities by the French police in Calais have not only gone unpunished but have been met with silence from the UK government in the context of cooperation, much of it covert, between the British Home Office and the French Interior Ministry. Requests for information (for example, on British funding of the French police carrying out abuses in Calais) have sometimes been met within the UK with the response that openness on such issues would jeopardize both anti-crime initiatives (like the task of stopping 'human smuggling') and even Anglo-French relations.[69]

Today, it is also clear that many Western governments have been cooperating with the security services in authoritarian countries, not least when it comes to the forcible repatriation of refugees/migrants. For example, Emma Larking notes that 'There is ... evidence in Australia of officers from the departments of immigration and foreign affairs engaging in identity fraud and conspiring with officials in autocratic countries to facilitate the deportation of asylum seekers.'[70]

More generally, while we do have both an international refugee regime (administered by UNHCR) and an international human rights regime that are more sophisticated than in the 1920s, 1930s and 1940s, nevertheless Arendt's 'right to have rights' still does not extend in practice to millions of asylum seekers or undocumented migrants. In fact, it has usually been impossible for asylum-seekers to *get to a country* in the Global North where they can make a claim to asylum.[71] Crucially, the right to seek and enjoy asylum (granted under the 1948 Universal Declaration of Human Rights) does not translate into an equivalent and enforceable obligation to accept asylum-seekers. The UK government even went to the extreme of trying to get asylum seekers deported to Rwanda for 'processing' there.

A further problem highlighted by Arendt was that 'the arrival of great masses of newcomers actually changed the always precarious position of naturalized citizens of the same origin'.[72] In fact, the latter were 'frequently deprived of important civil rights and threatened at any moment' with the fate of the newcomers.[73] Part of the problem here was that when a particular community of 'stateless' people within a country was deprived of rights, those state actors who had, in Arendt's view, a taste for unaccountable power could easily extend their domination to other spheres and other groups, not least to those whose claim to citizenship had now become increasingly fragile. Meanwhile, putting refugees outside the protection of the law threatened the institution of law itself, which rests on being universally applicable.[74] As Arendt put it, 'the nation-state cannot exist once its principle of equality before the law has broken down'.[75]

Again, the resonances with today are very disturbing: under the Trump administration many people who had already been granted citizenship in the US were threatened with de-naturalization.[76] Trump also said he would move to end the right to American citizenship for the children of non-citizens born in the US, a right that is actually part of the US constitution.[77] In the UK, a growing number of people have been deprived of citizenship in recent years.[78] Ben O'Loughlin and Marie Gillespie commented in 2012 that 'Citizenship in the UK since the 2002 Nationality, Immigration and Asylum Act is a privilege, not a right; it not only has to be "earned" but protected and maintained.'[79]

A further and in many ways non-obvious problem highlighted by Arendt was that a very dangerous *signal* is sent to autocratic or fascist regimes by not accepting refugees. In her discussion of the plight of Jews seeking to escape the Nazis, Arendt described entirely stateless people as 'undeportable',[80] and she observed further 'Only in the last stage of a rather lengthy process is their right to live threatened; only if they remain perfectly "superfluous", if nobody can be found to "claim" them, may their lives be in danger.'[81] The Nazis deprived the Jews of all legal status before forcing them into ghettos and camps. And Arendt noted that before the Nazis set the gas chambers into motion, 'they had carefully tested the ground and found out to their satisfaction that no country would claim these people. The point is that a condition of complete rightlessness was created before the right to live was challenged.'[82]

In *The Abandonment of the Jews*, David Wyman's analysis supports some of Arendt's points. Wyman showed the failure of the UK and the US to prioritize the rescue of the Jews both during and before the Second World War, with rescue initiatives generally weak and late and sometimes non-existent. In early 1943, with the UK government under growing pressure to provide sanctuary for those who could get out of Nazi Europe, the British Foreign Office sent a memo to the US State Department proposing an informal UN conference to consider evacuating a proportion of the refugees who had reached neutral European countries, a move that it was thought would encourage those countries to allow more refugees in from Nazi territory. However, the British Foreign Office pointed out that 'certain complicating factors' made the matter very difficult. One was the danger of stimulating anti-Semitism in areas to which the Jews were transferred. Another was that

> There is a real possibility that the Germans or their satellites may *change over from the policy of extermination to one of extrusion*, and aim as they did before the war at embarrassing other countries by flooding them with alien immigrants.[83] [Emphasis added]

Of course, Britain was at war with Germany and in this sense was hardly standing idly by as the Holocaust unfolded. But Wyman questions the primacy of *saving the Jews* as a war aim; and the fact that the possibility of such a switch between killing and expelling was presented in this instance as a *problem* should remind us of the potentially contaminating effects that a focus on preventing migration can have. Today, it is quite common for Western democracies to claim that particular countries-of-origin or transit countries are 'safe' when they are actually not safe, and this impulse, coming largely from the Home Office or other interior ministries, may encourage a misrepresentation of human rights abuses and a corresponding weakening of international pressures. When that regime is courted as an ally in *stemming the migration* (as in the case of Sudan or indeed France), then the danger of promoting impunity is redoubled. More generally, the widespread neglect of the right to asylum today is not simply a failure to help, but something that sends a very dangerous signal to abusive regimes.

Conclusion

Although we tend to imagine that Western immigration systems are based on careful discrimination between 'refugees' and 'economic migrants', we need to face the fact that the right to asylum, regarded by Arendt as the most fundamental of human rights, is to a large extent *unavailable* within Western democracies: for the great majority of those fleeing persecution, the opportunities for claiming asylum via legal pathways are vanishingly small. So the would-be refugee is effectively forced into breaking the law if that person wishes to claim his or her rights according to international law, and the physical obstacles to doing so have escalated.

The violence and neglect in Calais is part of a wider *outsourcing* of violence and immigration control. In the course of this outsourcing, the right to asylum is being radically undermined, while the causes of outmigration are being stoked through various kinds of accommodation with authoritarian regimes and abusive militias – from Turkey to Libya and Sudan.

An egregious instrumentalization of suffering increasingly characterizes Western democracies' approach to migration control. Whether in France, Italy, Libya, Greece, Turkey, the Mediterranean Sea, Mexico or the US deserts of Arizona, suffering has been tolerated and often actively promoted as part of a strategy of deterrence and indeed as part of a *theatre* of deterrence. This process has helped to nurture a growing disaster both within Western democracies and on their immediate geographical doorstep.

Deterrence – when taken to its logical conclusion – involves fostering human rights violations both in 'transit' countries and in 'recipient' countries (as with the so-called 'hostile' environment in the UK). Meanwhile, the belief that one can 'build a wall' to keep out immigrants logically implies an indifference to the *causes* of outmigration, including conflict and poverty. The response becomes part of a wider collective focus on instrumentalizing consequences rather than tackling root causes.

As one element of her attempt to understand the Nazi concentration camps, Arendt referred to 'holes of oblivion', which were zones of lawlessness from which neither people nor information could escape. While the concentration camps have of course been dismantled, we are today seeing the re-emergence of various kinds of 'holes of oblivion'.[84] Crucially, the current Western obsession with curbing migration flows seems to be encouraging the creation of a set of geographical zones-of-impunity from which it is increasingly difficult for either people or good information to escape. These zones include Mexico's southern borderlands, Honduras, Libya, Sudan, the Sahara, Turkey, Greek islands and even France and the Mediterranean Sea itself. Part of the problem is that Western officials do not wish to acknowledge, or perhaps even to *know*, the full extent of the abuses that are being encouraged within these zones. This amounts to the manufacture of disaster within the West and its immediate environs.

In the twelfth century, the English King Henry II is said to have incited the murder of Archbishop Thomas-à-Becket by asking his knights 'Who will rid me of this troublesome priest?' Today, a number of Western governments have effectively been asking abusive governments and militias, whether within Sudan or a number of other countries, 'Who will rid us of these troublesome migrants?'

If we go back to Sen and Drèze's argument that democracies prevent the disaster of famine, we may observe, first, that democracies are not protecting migrants/refugees from disasters. Particularly when disaster has been implicitly or explicitly redefined as *a good thing*, it is rash to assume that a government, whether elected or not, will be interested in preventing it. To the extent that a politics of scapegoating has entered into the heart of Western politics (and into the fast-pumping blood of an excitable media), we need to be sceptical about Sen and Drèze's claim that democracy and a free press will prevent disaster.

A second observation in relation to Sen and Drèze's optimism is that a variety of disasters unfolding in Western democracies are feeding back into these democracies' vulnerability to *other* disasters, including the disaster of a drift or lurch towards authoritarianism.

In the case of the 'migration crisis', an increasingly common message is that if you are critical of governments that are nurturing a migration 'disaster' or if you are seen to collude with the 'criminals' who are said to be behind international migration, then you, like the migrants within the ever-encroaching disaster zone, may be deemed undeserving of key basic human rights such as free speech, safety and liberty. At the extreme, your residency and citizenship may be called into question. We can see here that what is being deterred can spread quickly from *migration* and begin also to embrace *assistance* as well as *free speech*. In this way, the rightlessness of the home-grown disaster zone is always threatening to spread, while the possibility that *you yourself* will be incorporated into the enemy category serves to protect an abusive system and to police the delusions that (in Foucault's telling phrase) are being 'made to function as true'. Meanwhile, the conspicuous rightlessness of a relatively small or minority group is itself an implied threat to much larger groups.

In line with emergencies further afield, very particular definitions or framings of crises affecting Western democracies have also been policed through a conveniently expandable 'enemy' category. The suffering in Calais represents a kind of canary in the mine. It should alert us to a wider project that centres on manipulating and instrumentalizing the side-effects of disasters. Calais should also warn us about the tendency of violence to spread beyond the initial target group, underlining Arendt's and Agamben's warning that the exception is always threatening to become the rule. Where rights become conditional, they are not really rights at all; and once you accept that some people within your borders can be deprived of rights, you may be tempted to expand that 'hostile environment' to any critics. If the functionality of disaster was once thought to reside in lands far from Western democracies, today we must face the fact that the manufacture of suffering has 'come home', or at least has 'come back home' – and with it the vilification of those who try to relieve the suffering.

6

Welcoming Infection

As of February 2022 the total number of people who had died from Covid in the US was the highest in the world and edging closer to one million people, while in the UK the figure for deaths per capita was only a little less than in the US.[1] In July 2021 (after the first two main 'waves' of Covid infections), Professor of Global Health at University College London Anthony Costello noted that when the relative death rates from China, Vietnam, the US and the UK were plotted on the same graph, 'you cannot see the death curves for those two Asian states because they are so low'.[2] Of course, China implemented some pretty draconian controls that would be unacceptable in a democracy (and eventually in China too). But we still need to ask how two of the world's proudest democracies and two of the world's richest countries have fared so badly.

The story of Covid in the US and UK illustrates that while Sen and Drèze are correct that democratic accountability creates a significant incentive to prevent disasters, this incentive may not be decisive. Indeed, the prospect of being held accountable may also have more perverse effects. We have noted that there may be an incentive to *cover up or downplay* a disaster, that democracy may create a related incentive to *exaggerate the effectiveness* of a response, and that elected governments may *instrumentalize* disasters for political purposes. We will need to keep all of these perverse incentives in mind when looking at the US and UK Covid responses.

This chapter focuses primarily on the earlier part of the pandemic in 2020 in the US and UK. It finds that an important source of vulnerability, particularly in the UK, was reconceptualizing infection (and, in the short term at least, disaster) as *a good thing*. Democracy proved an extremely uncertain protection against this manoeuvre. I look at these dynamics in the section called 'embracing disaster'. A second important source of vulnerability was attachment to growth, to the economy and more generally to neoliberalism. I look at this in the second section on 'public health and the economy'. The concluding section looks at possible implications of the Covid crisis for democracy itself – not least at the possibility that it could reinforce a drift towards authoritarianism and disaster-producing politics.

Several caveats to the argument in this chapter should be stressed at the outset. First, it's important to note that the US and UK are hardly alone in their highly problematic responses. Many other countries from Brazil to India to Poland have had a bad record on Covid. Secondly, Covid responses fluctuated over time. Having downplayed the crisis for several crucial weeks in February and March 2020, the UK went into a hard lockdown and oscillated between lockdowns and 'opening up' thereafter. The vaccination performance of the UK proved to be a strong one, while incoming US President Biden also pushed strongly on vaccinations (though vaccination and booster rates in America remained damagingly behind most high-income countries).[3] Third, this was a rapidly evolving crisis and it was not easy to get things right. For example, as the pandemic evolved and as vaccines became more widely available, a different balance between locking down and 'opening up' became appropriate, and the need to take proper account of the many social, psychological and economic costs of lockdown became increasingly evident.[4] Having said all that, the paradox of the US and UK's vulnerability and high death rates remains.

Embracing Disaster

While we've emphasized that there is much to learn from experience with disasters in Africa, Asia and Latin America, a particularly telling point of reference for London's response to the arrival of the coronavirus was a disaster much closer to home.

When the Great Famine devastated Ireland in the 1840s, the island was part of the United Kingdom of Great Britain and Ireland. It was also part of the UK's emerging parliamentary democracy, which enjoyed a lively press. But none of this protected the victims. In London, a peculiar combination of callousness, self-interest, science and fatalism produced a calamitous response. Generally, the famine was framed as the result of the failure of the potato crop: it was a natural disaster, the responsibility of God, perhaps, but not of the British government. At the same time, the dominant political and economic science of the day, often known as 'political economy' and strongly influenced by the Anglican clergyman Thomas Malthus, held that famines could be a natural corrective to overpopulation. Many even saw disasters as a way that God induced moral behaviour: humanitarian disasters deterred laziness, dependency, promiscuity, and so on. In this way, a famine might even *avert* a disaster, whether this was a moral disaster or a population disaster. More prosaically, given the felt need to transform Irish agriculture into a pastoral economy (meeting the growing demand for meat on the rapidly industrializing mainland), famine offered the opportunity to get rid of 'unproductive' tenants (whether through emigration or mass deaths). In short, many elements of current thinking were *pro-famine*. Since the famine itself was seen to a large extent as *functional*, effective relief would actually have been 'counterproductive' while delay became a silent ally. Despite reforms in 1832, the franchise in the UK remained extremely restricted, with most of those suffering famine not having the vote, while those who owned large amounts of land in Ireland were much better represented. British government adviser Nassau Senior, who shared the vision of an economically transformed Ireland, notoriously said that he feared the famine would not kill more than a million people, which would scarcely be enough *to do any good*.

If we fast-forward to 2020 and some more decision-makers in London, it is pretty obvious that the context was hugely different. Nevertheless, when 'herd immunity' was articulated by UK government officials as a strategy in response to the coronavirus in February and March 2020 (and subsequently only partially and unconvincingly disavowed), it was once again as if the disaster was being conceived of as *a natural disaster* with its own laws, a disaster to which the population must dutifully submit. Even as predictions of mass mortality from an unmitigated epidemic were disseminated within UK government circles, strategies that were working for other countries like Germany and South Korea were quickly deemed impractical. As with the crisis more than 170 years earlier, a very particular kind of science was again legitimizing delay. Wary of interfering in the economy and expressing reluctance to interfere with the 'freedoms' of the British population, the British government also projected itself as dutifully following 'the science' (a kind of in-built alibi).[5] Strikingly, the science that prevailed (particularly in the critical period January to mid-March 2020) frequently framed infection as *a good thing*: it was good in the long run because it would promote 'herd immunity'. Yet since infection was actually causing the disaster, this manoeuvre came alarmingly close to framing the disaster itself as positive. Once again, the *functionality* of the underlying disaster (in this case, mass infection) was being stressed by powerful officials and a kind of fatalistic magical thinking, allied both to 'science' and to a substantial dose of self-interest, was once again integral to the process. Living through this was certainly a strange and disturbing experience.

Consider this statement in a 13 March 2020 article in the UK's *Guardian* newspaper: 'The government is concerned that if not enough people catch the virus now, it will re-emerge in the winter, when the NHS (National Health Service) is already overstretched.'[6] For all the epidemiological complexities of the coronavirus, this simple statement tells us a lot. The startling point being made was that the government actually *wanted* infections. The UK government's chief scientific adviser Patrick Vallance had said in mid-March that a figure of 60 per cent infection would be required to get herd immunity, noting 'If you suppress something very, very hard, when you release those measures it bounces back and it bounces back at the wrong time.'[7] Vallance spelled out the objective here:

> Our aim is to try to reduce the peak, broaden the peak, not suppress it completely; also, because the vast majority of people get a mild illness, to build up some kind of herd immunity so more people are immune to this disease and we reduce the transmission, at the same time we protect those who are most vulnerable to it.[8]

With the possibility of all-out *suppression* of the virus being rejected, the strategy of *mitigation*[9] was bolstered by graphs reproduced in the press that were said to show the danger of a winter resurgence of the virus if suppression was too vigorous. In line with Vallance's comments on 'herd immunity', David Halpern, head of the UK government's Behavioural Insights Team (or 'nudge' unit), told the BBC's Mark Easton:

> … there's going to be a point, assuming the epidemic flows and grows as we think it probably will do, where you'll want to cocoon, you'll want to protect those at-risk groups so that they basically don't catch the disease, and by the time they, you know, come out of their cocooning, herd immunity's been achieved in the rest of the population.[10]

Nobody explained how or when this 'cocooning' would be done or how many would die in the meantime. Graham Medley, one of the UK government's expert advisers on pandemics, said in a 13 March 2020 *Newsnight* broadcast 'We are going to have to generate what we call herd immunity ... And the only way of developing that, in the absence of a vaccine, is for the majority of the population to become infected.'[11] Medley said ideally one could put all the more vulnerable people in the north of Scotland and the rest in Kent and then have 'a nice big epidemic' in Kent. He acknowledged, however, that this would not be possible in practice.[12] On 5 March 2020, Prime Minister Johnson had himself said:

> One of the theories is, that perhaps you could take it on the chin, take it all in one go and allow the disease, as it were, to move through the population, without taking as many draconian measures. I think we need to strike a balance, I think it is very important.[13]

Johnson did go on to say that he favoured reducing the peak of the disease and that there were things the government 'may be able to do'. But on the whole the idea of 'striking a balance' meant, in practice, striking a balance between tackling and not tackling the virus.

As noted, decision-making in a rapidly changing situation was difficult. It is fair to point out that the costs of lockdowns – economically, educationally and in terms of many aspects of public health – were very large. Moreover, the case for building up immunity became stronger once the availability of a vaccine reduced the severity of the illness for most people, reducing also the risk of death. Indeed, the UK population did go on to acquire a degree of immunity based on a combination of vaccination and large numbers having had the disease. So there was a lot to consider.

But in early 2020 there was no sign of a vaccine, and it is revealing that the idea of letting the virus rip was repeatedly voiced in the context of some very dire predictions about mortality. One of these came in a 26 February 2020 paper by the government's own scientific advisory group known as SAGE: commenting on 'the proportion of deaths within a designated population due to an epidemiological outbreak', the SAGE advisers noted: 'Uncertain but planning on the assumption 2–3%.'[14] But, on the basis of the predicted 52,480,000 people who would be infected in an unmitigated epidemic, this gave a total of 1,049,600 deaths (using the two per cent figure) and 1,574,400 million deaths (using the three per cent figure).[15] These are huge numbers (not spelled out in the report but the maths is not difficult). Some have argued that these predictions were too pessimistic,[16] but they were the most authoritative available; one common fallacy, moreover, was retrospectively interpreting lower mortality figures *that resulted from social distancing* as evidence that predictions were too pessimistic and 'the scientists were wrong'.[17] Significantly, the early SAGE meetings were not actually published until the end of May 2020,[18] and public pressure for a quicker lockdown would almost certainly have been significantly greater if they had been.

In any event, the SAGE private predictions did not prompt an immediate government response. More figures were given in a 2 March SAGE report (still around two weeks from any major UK government reaction), which stated that 'Current estimates are that mortality rates are 12% for hospitalized people ... with 50% mortality in those hospitalized who require invasive ventilation.'[19] Since 3,608,000 people were expected to be hospitalized in an unmitigated epidemic, that gave an expected death toll of 396,880[20] – a much lower figure than the one we have extrapolated from the 26 February paper, but still a massive disaster.[21] On top of all this, when it came to the goal of 'herd immunity', we should also note that the 'immunity' arising from catching Covid was at this point extremely uncertain in terms of its strength and duration (and indeed remained a grey area for a long time).[22] And, crucially, there was always the possibility that relatively lax restrictions would open the path for mutations that were more infectious or more severe in their effects, or both; and several threatening mutations did indeed emerge.

Of course, 'herd immunity' is an established term in epidemiology and it generally refers to the effects of vaccinations. But again when Covid hit, *there was no vaccine*. Harvard epidemiologist William Hanage noted on 15 March 2020: 'We talk *about vaccines generating* herd immunity, so why is this different? Because this is not a vaccine. This is an actual pandemic that will make a very large number of people sick, and some of them will die.'[23]

In general, the favoured approach in the UK was strangely fatalistic. WHO had repeatedly warned Europe to respect its guidelines, urging 'Do not let this fire burn.'[24] With Covid, even a few days make a big difference. A key problem, as David McCoy (Professor of Global Public Health at Queen Mary University London) pointed out, was that the UK's expert modelling around the coronavirus did not account for 'the potential role of testing and contact tracing in mitigating the epidemic'.[25] This was the strategy advocated by WHO[26] and successfully implemented in Germany and South Korea.[27] At the beginning of April, Germany was carrying out up to 100,000 tests a day while the UK was carrying out only about a tenth of that.[28] A 28 February 2020 study in *The Lancet* noted: 'In most scenarios, highly effective contact tracing and case isolation is enough to control a new outbreak of Covid-19 within three months.'[29] Yet on 12 March, the UK government decided to stop community testing and contact tracing, and this decision was not reversed even when Health Secretary Matt Hancock said the government was not pursuing 'herd immunity'.[30] When contact tracing was eventually re-established, the effort was weak. For example, as of mid-May 2020, the government had recruited only 1,500 out of the 18,000 contact tracers that it said it wanted to recruit.[31]

Meanwhile, science was in many ways being harnessed to the project of delay. For one thing, SAGE behavioural scientists said that bringing in 'social distancing' too early could make the public 'fatigued'. In line with this, Chris Whitty, England's Chief Medical Officer, said on 12 March 2020 that he expected the peak of the outbreak in 10 to 14 weeks and 'If you move too early, people get fatigued.'[32]

It's clear that large sporting events played a significant role in spreading the virus.[33] But reading the 11 February 2020 SAGE document on public gatherings, one has the impression that the experts' intelligence was rather working against them. The opening statement is that 'The direct impact of stopping large public gatherings on the population-level spread of the epidemic is low, because they make up only a small proportion of the attendee's contacts with other people.'[34] Also, 'stopping some public gatherings could mean people replace this with other activities (i.e. playing football behind closed doors could mean fans watch the match in the pub), potentially slightly *accelerating* epidemic spread'.[35] Again: 'contacts tend to be less intimate and shorter at public gatherings than in other settings such as contacts with family members and coworkers. The risk to an individual from attending large events is generally no higher than in smaller events.'[36] After Prime Minister Johnson attended a rugby international in London on 7 March, some 250,000 attended a packed Cheltenham horseracing festival that began three days later.[37] In addition to spreading the virus, these things sent their own signals.

It was not until a 16 March 2020 paper from Imperial College predicted an overwhelmed National Health Service that the UK government (a week later) imposed strict social distancing as well as a 'lockdown' of schools and inessential businesses.

While contact tracing is complicated and expensive, neglecting this was a false economy. At the beginning of April, Annelies Wilder-Smith, an epidemiology professor at the London School of Hygiene and

Tropical Medicine, noted, 'To anyone who tells me that contact tracing is too expensive or not do-able, I just say, rubbish. We are now basically quarantining 68 million people. That is so much more expensive.'[38] By the beginning of May 2020 the UK had already overtaken Italy as the European country with the highest death toll from Covid and the highest deaths per million.[39]

After talking with ministers, with special advisers, and with Downing Street staff and civil servants, *Sunday Times* journalists noted:

> At a private engagement at the end of February, [Dominic] Cummings [Johnson's senior aide] outlined the government's strategy. Those present say it was 'herd immunity, protect the economy and if that means some pensioners die, too bad'.[40]

While this was later denied by Downing Street,[41] Cummings himself said later that herd immunity 'was literally the official plan in all docs/graphs/meetings until it was ditched'.[42]

There were several other telling hints of a rather ruthless attitude to those who were predicted to die. A whiteboard for a Downing Street meeting on Covid in March 2020 displayed the sentence 'Who do we not save?'[43] One of the 'the more thoughtful' Conservative MPs (in the *Sunday Times*' telling phrase) observed: 'It is unsustainable to have people in their youth put their whole life on hold for months while the economy tanks to save a 91-year-old who would have died six months later anyway.'[44] Jeremy Warner, a columnist in Britain's bestselling broadsheet newspaper *The Daily Telegraph*, suggested that 'from an entirely disinterested economic perspective, Covid might even prove mildly beneficial in the long term by disproportionately culling elderly dependants'.[45] While it might be tempting to dismiss such sentiments as outliers, UK government policy was itself callous in relation to care homes, as we shall see.

As for the US, the 'herd immunity' strategy was not highlighted in the same way as in the UK. More prominent in America was the simple insistence, spearheaded by Trump, that the virus was not a grave threat and that businesses should be either kept open or reopened very quickly. This was an example of a democratically elected government responding to disaster by minimizing it. In September 2020 Trump did tell an ABC journalist that, given time, the virus would go away even without a vaccine, adding 'And you'll develop – you'll develop herd – like a herd mentality.'[46] So the concept had clearly percolated to the President, albeit in bizarrely mangled form. In that same month, the

Washington Post calculated that in the absence of a vaccine and assuming a fatality rate that stayed at 2.1 per cent and herd immunity at 60 per cent saturation, achieving 'herd immunity' would mean 3.8 million total deaths in the US.[47] Meanwhile, there were many examples of the kind of ruthlessness (in relation to likely victims) that had been voiced in the UK. As one woman at an April 2020 anti-lockdown protest in the US state of Arizona put it: 'The people that are getting sick are the people that are already compromised in the first place. They're usually older. They're unhealthy!'[48]

Public Health and the Economy

The severe impact of Covid in the UK and US is difficult to separate from underlying vulnerabilities that themselves owed a great deal to neoliberal ideology. At key moments, business was elevated above health so that Covid became (in Trump's eyes, for example) a 'lesser evil' compared to damaging business.

Protecting business and protecting the economy was a key reason for weak measures to control the virus, not only when the virus hit but also in the repeated rush to end lockdowns in both the US and the UK when proper track-and-trace measures had not been put in place. Of course, protecting the economy is one important goal that governments have and should have. Lockdown's negative impact on the economy was very significant (as noted) and managing the pandemic was undoubtedly not easy. But particularly when there was no vaccine, the priority given to reopening or keeping open tended strongly to undermine a public-health response that could have protected the economy much better. A leaked recording of a Home Office Deputy Science Adviser has him noting on 7 April 2020: 'So carrying on with your normal work is not putting you in harm's way any more so than staying at home or going out shopping.'[49]

In the context of Britain's much trumpeted exit from the EU, government officials expressed the idea that Britain had a special relationship with freedom and 'could not be expected to submit to the Covid restrictions favoured by those in Continental Europe'.[50] The summer of 2021 saw the UK government subsidizing diners in its 'eat out to help out' scheme, against much of the scientific advice at the time. Before Boris Johnson became UK Prime Minister, he had routinely railed against 'health and safety' in his *Daily Telegraph* column. He once said that his political hero was the mayor in the film *Jaws*, a character he praised for defying mass hysteria to keep beaches open after a shark killed a constituent.[51] *The Times* reported that in September 2020 (when coronavirus infections in the UK were rising rapidly and many experts were pushing for a second lockdown) Johnson brought up the *Jaws* comparison and 'allegedly told aides in Downing Street that he would rather let coronavirus "rip" than impose a second lockdown because of the economic harm further restrictions would cause'.[52] Again, we should stress that this was well before any vaccines had become available. In the US, there were also strong pressures to keep things open. After the initial lockdown, 'most states felt compelled to reopen without accruing enough tests or contact tracers'.[53]

In the context of prioritizing business opening, a commonplace claim to be 'at war' with the virus, whether by politicians or in the media, may have lent itself to an acceptance of 'casualties'. UK Health Secretary Matt Hancock declared 'we are at war against an invisible killer',[54] while *The Lancet* was critical of 'war' language, noting that 'A war means that sacrifices have to be made' and that such metaphors 'encourage the view that criticizing government strategy is somehow unpatriotic'.[55] Trump told reporters on 5 May, 'The people of our country are warriors. I'm not saying anything is perfect, and will some people be affected? Yes. Will some people be affected badly? Yes. But we have to get our country open and we have to get it open soon.'[56] Adam Serwer observed in *The Atlantic*:

> The frame of war allows the [US] president to call for the collective sacrifice of laborers without taking the measures necessary to ensure their safety, while the upper classes remain secure at home. But the workers who signed up to harvest food, deliver packages, stack groceries, drive trains and buses, and care for the sick did not sign up for war, and the unwillingness of America's political leadership to protect them is a policy decision, not an inevitability.[57]

In both the UK and the US, the push to keep people working on 'essential' jobs had a disproportionate effect on non-white sectors of the population. In the UK, one 2020 study found that there had been 56 deaths from coronavirus for every 100,000 black people compared with 36 for every 100,000 white people.[58] Among those badly affected were members of the Somali community in Brent, London, among whom Covid infection was promoted by a combination of 'front-line' jobs and crowded living conditions. These conditions themselves reflected broader political policies, not least the sale of public housing and the extreme difficulty of affording private accommodation.[59] We've noted that a well-known lesson from so-called 'natural disasters' around the world is that the problem is not simply the flood or the storm or the earthquake; it's the underlying vulnerability of the population, especially the poor, to that specific event. This played out strongly in the Covid disaster.

Since richer people tended to have more opportunities to work at home, the push to reopen the American and British economies compounded the uneven exposure to the virus. In the US, with the 'essential workers' being disproportionately non-white,[60] *The Lancet* noted on 19 April 2020:

> Across the country, deaths due to COVID-19 are disproportionately high among African Americans compared with the population overall. In Milwaukee [Wisconsin], three quarters of all COVID-19 related deaths are African American, and in St Louis, [Missouri], all but three people who have died as a result of COVID-19 were African American. Minorities often don't have the privilege of staying home and working; they tend to live in more crowded areas; and they often suffer disproportionately from pre-existing medical conditions.[61]

In New York City, the zip codes with the highest rates of Covid-19 infection were in the boroughs of the Bronx, Brooklyn and Queens, which have the majority of African Americans and Hispanics living in the city.[62]

Particularly in the US, democracy had not protected the population to the extent of creating a strong social security system, a shortcoming that greatly exacerbated the impact of Covid. Ed Yong noted in *The Atlantic*, 'The decades-long process of shredding the nation's social safety net forced millions of essential workers in low-paying jobs to risk their life for their livelihood.'[63] Lack of sick leave was also making it hard or impossible to take time off work even when symptomatic.[64] Over 33 million Americans, amounting to almost a quarter of the civilian workforce, lacked any paid sick leave at all.[65]

A related problem, harder to pin down but hovering over much of the Covid response, was that neoliberal ideology suggested that if you left things unregulated, some variation of Adam Smith's 'invisible hand' would somehow ensure the long-term good of the public. Again, this presumption suited the virus. In the past, free-market ideologists have sometimes combined a rather far-reaching ruthlessness with an expressed intention to 'protect the vulnerable'. In development policy for the Global South, this was part of the thinking behind 'structural adjustment with a human face', for example. In the context of Covid, the 'herd immunity' strategy – with its rather theoretical 'cocooning' alongside a more general *laissez faire* – mirrored this template rather precisely.

Markets depend on confidence, and Trump's denialism reflected in part a desire to maintain business confidence. Pinning hopes of re-election on a strong economy, Trump himself admitted to journalist Bob Woodward in March 2020 that he was downplaying the virus to avoid 'panic'.[66] In effect, a health disaster was being weighed against a combined economic and *political* disaster, and the very thing that Sen and Drèze saw as protecting against disaster (or at least famine), namely, the desire to be re-elected, was serving as an incentive to *deny* the disaster. Explaining in May 2020 the extreme slowness in rolling out testing in the US, Trump said 'When you test, you find something is wrong with people. If we didn't do any testing, we would have very few cases.'[67] Other elements of denial were Trump's claim that Covid would one day disappear 'like a miracle',[68] his claim in March 2020 that a vaccine would be available in months,[69] and his suggestion that injecting oneself with disinfectant could be a good remedy.

There was also something cultural in the push against lockdown in the US. Following the 9/11 attacks, President Bush famously observed, 'They want us to stop flying and they want us to stop buying, but this great nation will not be intimidated by the evildoers.'[70] As anti-lockdown protesters in Michigan urged onlookers to 'Live free or die',[71] Ed Yong noted in *The Atlantic*:

> Many of the country's values seemed to work against it during the pandemic. Its individualism, exceptionalism, and tendency to equate doing whatever you want with an act of resistance meant that when it came time to save lives and stay indoors some people flocked to bars and clubs. Having internalized years of anti-terrorism messaging following 9/11, Americans resolved to not live in fear.[72]

From April 2020 cases in the European Union came down sharply while cases in the US came down only slightly before shooting up in June. Anthony Fauci, a key scientist on the White House's Coronavirus Task Force under Trump, explained that while Europe 'shut down 95%', 'we shut down only about 50%' and 'when we reopened, we started from a high baseline' with some states not following national guidelines.[73]

Democratic systems were ineffective in protecting many people from the virus in part because these systems had failed to provide an adequate system of public health in advance of the pandemic. The inadequacy of public-health provision was most striking in the US but also very relevant in the UK. In America, the huge number of people without health insurance created extreme vulnerability to the virus. A detailed report on the US in *The Lancet* noted:

> 14 US states (mostly in the south and the Plains) have refused to accept [Obama's] Affordable Care Act Medicaid expansion, leaving millions of the poorest and sickest Americans without access to health care, with the added effect of leaving many regional and local hospitals across the US closed or in danger of closing because of the high cost of medical care and a high proportion of rural uninsured and underinsured people. People with COVID-19 in those states will have poor access to the kind of emergency and intensive care they will need.[74]

More than half of those employed in the hospitality, leisure and travel industries had no health insurance.[75] Since health insurance in the US is usually linked to people's employment, it followed that unemployment, some of it linked to the impact of Covid, was doubly dangerous, exposing people to crippling medical bills. Meanwhile, millions of undocumented migrants feared seeking medical attention.[76]

In the US, with Trump intent on running down the civil service, a pandemic preparedness office within the National Security Council was dissolved in 2018.[77] Then Trump failed to heed the warnings of the pandemic preparedness exercise, Crimson Contagion, which identified major gaps in October 2019.[78] The inability of the federal government to take charge of responses to the virus meant that states and cities were in effect forced into a bidding war, leaving them exposed to corporate profiteering.[79]

While the UK had a much better functioning public-health system, neglect had nevertheless created very considerable vulnerability. The UK's pandemic planning was hit by austerity as well as by time-consuming preparations for a 'no deal' Brexit.[80] A *Guardian* investigation also found that major public-health responsibilities, including those on pandemic preparedness, had been loaded onto local authorities at precisely the time when they were being subjected to massive cuts in central government funding under the policy of 'austerity'.[81] In terms of the NHS itself, the UK had the second-fewest hospital beds per capita in Europe.[82] The proportion of intensive care units before the crisis was also among the lowest in Europe.[83] Shortages of personal protective equipment became notorious and, for a long time, testing of NHS workers was gravely neglected.[84]

Importantly, the consequences of the neglect of the NHS lay not only in greatly increased vulnerability to the virus among staff and patients but also in the way this fragility helped to foster the dangerous 'herd immunity' idea. A key justification for the 'herd immunity' approach, as we've seen, was the idea that the NHS would be overwhelmed in the winter of 2020/21. Remember the 13 March 2020 comment in the *Guardian*: 'The government is concerned that if not enough people catch the virus now, it will re-emerge in the winter, when the NHS (National Health Service) is *already* overstretched [emphasis added].'[85] What different policy options might have been adopted if the NHS had not been considered already overextended, even in a normal year?

Many would naturally assume that the responsibility of a government health service is to protect the health of the population. But in the UK the chronic neglect of the National Health Service (NHS) had contributed to a strange, upside-down world in which the proclaimed responsibility of the population was to *protect the health service*. UK Health Secretary Matt Hancock exemplified this way of speaking when he announced on 15 March, 'Our strategy is to protect the most vulnerable and protect the NHS through contain, delay, research and mitigate ... We must all work together and play our own part in protecting ourselves and each other, as well as our NHS, from this disease.'[86] Of course, much of this was eminently sensible: public-health systems across the world were under huge strain (including in the UK), and responsible individual behaviour has been essential for tackling Covid. But 'mitigating' the virus was very different from 'suppressing' it (which means getting the 'R' or reproduction number below 1). And the reversal of responsibilities was remarkable. It brings us back once more to the embrace of mass mortality (in 'herd immunity') to protect the NHS from a 'winter resurgence'.

It also seems revealing that while the 16 March 2020 Imperial College paper's prediction about an *overwhelmed health service* did belatedly have a major effect on UK policy, SAGE predictions of mass mortality from an unmitigated epidemic were not in themselves enough to spur the government into vigorous suppression of the virus, or indeed to dent the hope-cum-policy of 'herd immunity'. Again, it was as if the protecting the health service was more important than protecting the people the health service was supposed to protect.

Meanwhile, blaming individual health behaviours ran the risk of distracting attention from *government* behaviour. In this connection, we should note that in many emergencies around the world (as Mark Duffield and Susanne Jaspars have shown) the grave neglect of official protection and assistance often exists alongside a growing insistence that individuals must be responsible and resilient and must adopt a range of health-producing behaviours, another reversal of responsibilities.

On top of all this, the NHS was in some respects being protected at the expense of elderly people in care homes. By May 2021, at least 42,000 care-home residents in England and Wales had died of Covid.[87] A May 2020 *Guardian* investigation of care-home deaths found:

> To protect the NHS from the devastating situation that emerged in Italy – with the near collapse of hospitals – UK ministers ordered 15,000 hospital beds to be vacated by 27 March [2020]. Making beds available was part of the 'national effort' and 'will help to save thousands of lives' they told care homes. Guidelines said there was no need to test discharged patients because Covid-19 sufferers 'can be safely cared for in a care home'… It wasn't until 16 April that the government announced NHS patients being discharged into care homes would be first tested for Covid-19 – by which time almost 1,000 homes in England had suffered outbreaks.[88]

A survey of more than one hundred care homes by the Alzheimer's Society found that one-third had taken in Covid-positive patients discharged from hospital.[89] On 3 March, England's chief medical officer Chris Whitty defended a lack of specific measures to protect care homes, saying 'One of the things we are keen to avoid is doing things too early.'[90] Public Health England advised in March that care-home residents were 'very unlikely' to become infected by Covid-19.[91] The government also neglected the testing of staff and residents in care homes. Moreover, there is evidence of a desire to *keep* elderly patients in care homes rather than hospitals. Robert Kilgour, owner of Renaissance Care, which ran fifteen care homes in Scotland, said there had been a 'huge discouragement by the authorities to hospitalize, a wish to keep them where they are and look after them where they are'.[92] All this takes us back to Giroux's 'politics of disposability'. While some people were so 'essential' that they could not be allowed to shelter at home, others were so 'inessential' that their safety was undermined by other means.

Strikingly, NHS staff were praised as 'heroes', and the UK government was again keen to evoke the comparison with wartime, for example, through repeated references to 'front-line workers'. But a growing number of doctors and nurses expressed their unease with all the praise and the clapping for 'their sacrifice', insisting very often that *this is not a war*.

In some respects, the invocation of wartime 'sacrifice' was perhaps more apt than the government realized. I once had the chance to interview former soldiers who were part of the American pressure group Iraq Veterans Against the War. These veterans expressed a profound unease with being praised for their 'sacrifice' in circumstances where their needs as veterans were routinely neglected and where a combination of a dubious war, dishonest recruitment, forcible retention and a shortage of protective equipment had sometimes induced a feeling of *being sacrificed*. In the UK in March 2020, one doctor said:

> We know that the infection rate for doctors working in this pandemic is high; in Lombardy [Italy] it is 20%. We will be exposed to an extraordinary viral load. How is it that healthcare workers in China and the rest of East Asia are equipped with hazmat suits and respirators, while the government of one of the richest countries in the world cannot even issue us basic masks? We are not being treated with the dignity and care due to frontline workers. Instead, it feels like we are being treated as cannon fodder.[93]

Despite being heavily pregnant, Meenal Viz, a hospital doctor, decided to protest outside No 10 Downing St. 'It's not a "war"', she said. 'This is systematic negligence. I'm not a warrior. And none of us should have to "sacrifice" ourselves to do our jobs.'[94] Quite apart from the notorious shortages of personal protective equipment (PPE), as of 2 April only 7,000 of 550,000 NHS workers dealing directly with patients had been tested for Covid-19.[95]

In the US, Trump mined the war analogy for all it was worth, while blatantly instrumentalizing the dedication and bravery of health workers. In mid-April, CNN reporter Jeremy Diamond asked Trump if it was right to show video clips of self-praise at a point when more than 40,000 people had died from the coronavirus in the US, and Trump turned furiously on the journalist: 'You don't have the brains you were born with! You should be praising the people who have done a good job ... It's dangerous, it's going to a battlefield.'[96] In effect, Trump was invoking the old chestnut that criticism of a war equates to criticism of the soldiers who are fighting it.

Sensitive to accusations that they didn't care about the NHS, Conservative politicians were promising an NHS windfall from Brexit and now, perhaps, underlining their 'love' for the NHS by telling everyone to protect it. Yet with an aging population and escalating demand, the Conservatives had failed to maintain the substantial spending increases on the NHS under Labour[97] and shortages of nurses had grown significantly worse.

Meanwhile, democracy appeared to be no obstacle to a far-reaching contamination of official responses by private profiteering. Lucrative contracts (with minimal oversight or competition) were awarded to a number of firms and individuals with dubious credentials and some personal connection to those in power.[98] In the UK, the contrast between the efficient vaccination programme (run by the NHS) and the ineffective thirty-nine-billion-pound track-and-trace programme (relying on outsourcing to private contractors and with the lowest financial compensation for isolation in any OECD country) was striking.[99]

Covid relief legislation in the US, while eventually offering substantial support to millions of ordinary people, was subject to extreme manipulation by special interests seeking to ensure major tax relief for big business in particular. In last-minute amendments to the CARES Act (economic stimulus to compensate for Covid), Republican Senators slipped in 160 million dollars of tax benefits that were mostly headed for 40,000 of the richest people in the country.[100]

At the same time, some major corporations were using the crisis to insist on high-tech solutions for matters of health, education, distribution, and so on, with important business leaders suggesting that only such a course would prevent global dominance by China.[101] Naomi Klein argues that for some companies the disease represented a chance to push through technological and organizational changes that they favoured in any case.

Conclusion

We've noted already that some processes may push encouragingly against the logic of today's disaster-creating system. The election of President Biden was one such, and a Cambridge University study suggested voters' enthusiasm for (mostly right-wing) populist politics had actually waned since the start of the pandemic, in part as voters turned away from leaders who downplayed the crisis.[102] That might give some support to Sen and Drèze's optimism on democracy's ability to protect against disasters. But Covid had already wreaked much of its havoc by Biden's victory. And there appear to be at least five important respects in which the coronavirus disaster has *reinforced* a disaster-producing politics: through fuelling nationalism; through fuelling 'conspiracy' theory and a search for 'internal enemies'; through fuelling economic hardship; through encouraging an increase in surveillance and control; and through encouraging attempts to discredit democracy.

The risk of fuelling nationalism was perhaps clearest when Trump repeatedly referred to 'the Chinese virus' and explicitly blamed China for the pandemic. One of the heaviest blows to *inter*nationalism came on 14 April 2020 when, in the midst of the worst global pandemic since 1918, Trump announced that he was suspending US contributions to the World Health Organization,[103] which he accused of being a 'puppet of China'.[104] This was part of Trump's more general policy of scapegoating and it also reflected a longer-standing antipathy within the Republican Party in particular towards UN interference with US autonomy.

As for the UK, when the government turned its back on the WHO guidelines, it was hard not to see in this 'go it alone' strategy a reflection of the overconfidence and isolationism that helped to shape the almost-completed process of leaving the European Union. As the 'herd immunity' idea took hold, it was almost as if a long-standing British sense of immunity and exceptionalism was being rescued from the jaws of failure by shamelessly recasting disaster as *a good thing*. The very phrase 'herd immunity' acquired in this context (and in the absence of a vaccine) some oddly nationalistic overtones. Revealingly, amid all the official concern for strengthening the British 'herd', no one in the Brexit-oriented UK government seems to have considered the need to develop a coordinated European response that might help to protect other 'herds' on the Continent. Perhaps if Chancellor Merkel had spoken of the need to protect the German 'herd', alarm bells would have rung.

More broadly, the dangers of assuming immunity to disaster, perhaps *literal* immunity, had been underlined by the early stages of the coronavirus crisis. Historian Andrew Liu said of the slow reactions and the weak preparations in the UK and the US in particular, 'This inactivity was partly the product of western exceptionalism that believed viruses and epidemics only happen "over there", in poor and non-white countries.'[105] The 2019 Global Health Security Index (from the Johns Hopkins School of Public Health and the US-based Nuclear Threat Initiative) rated 195 countries' capacity to face infectious disease outbreaks. The US ranked as the best, with UK second. South Korea was ninth and China 51st. This must have been reassuring. But it proved dangerously misleading.[106] At the risk of understatement, these rankings may now need some adjustment. (Incidentally, the 2021 rankings still had the US at number 1 with the UK falling to number 7; China had slipped to number 52.) The Johns Hopkins 2021 report observed:

> Despite its ranking, the United States has reported the greatest number of COVID-19 cases, and its response to the pandemic has generally been viewed as extremely poor. The result highlights that although the GHS Index can identify preparedness resources and capacities available in a country, it cannot predict whether or how well a country will use them in a crisis.[107]

As the Covid crisis unfolded, the risk of fuelling nationalism was underlined when countries started competing for protective equipment and when various versions of 'vaccine nationalism' emerged, with many governments taking steps to ensure that vaccines were reserved as much as possible for their own populations. For many, the virus seemed to speak of the need for self-sufficiency.

A second major worry is that with the Covid crisis having been worsened by a kind of flight from the truth, the pandemic also seems in many ways to have *fuelled* a flight from truth, including the embrace of conspiracy theories. This is potentially another dangerously self-reinforcing mechanism within a disaster-producing system.

In the UK, far-right groups often blamed immigrants for the virus crisis as part of a worldwide narrative positioning migrants as an existential threat.[108] Anti-Asian violence increased. And, at a time when internet connectivity was becoming more important than ever, telecommunications engineers were repeatedly threatened after baseless conspiracy theories linked the coronavirus to the roll-out of 5G technology.[109]

In the US, right-wing journalists, pressure groups and anti-vaxxers seized on the crisis as evidence that the government was determined to take away their freedoms, as well as evidence that the media was feeding them lies. If the idea of a 'fake media' fed Covid scepticism, those who were determined to deny the necessity of strong measures saw in Covid a further proof of just how 'fake' the media was. Banners at 'right to move' protests in the US ('COVID is a lie', 'Jesus is my vaccine') were one window on a widespread resort to magical thinking. More generally, the internet became choc-full of conspiracy theories, including the idea that the virus is part of a 'Big Pharma' conspiracy. As in the UK, anti-Asian violence increased. Meanwhile, Russia supported some of the disinformation around Covid-19, according to the EU's European External Action service.[110]

As in so many other ways, Trump stoked these conspiratorial reflexes, not least with the magical view that the virus was about to disappear or with his crazy treatment-with-disinfectant idea. Trump also used the virus and the alleged danger to 'public health' to ramp up the impediments to seeking asylum.[111] Having narrowly avoided being removed from office over charges that he improperly sought help from the Ukraine to discredit Biden and boost his own chances of re-election, Trump was keen to suggest that the virus was the Democratic Party's 'new hoax' designed to bring him down.[112] Responding to protests against stay-at-home measures in three states led by Democratic governors, Trump tweeted that people should 'LIBERATE MINNESOTA!', 'LIBERATE MICHIGAN!' and 'LIBERATE VIRGINIA, and save your great 2nd amendment [a reference to new gun-control measures in Virginia]. It is under siege.'[113] Bizarrely, Trump seemed to be campaigning against his own lockdown policies, encouraging 'rebels' to rise up against the quarantine, and roping guns into the equation.[114]

In April 2020, David Weigel noted in the *Washington Post*, 'Uncertainty and fear over the economic impact of stay-at-home orders is fuelling a sort of culture war between conservatives, whose political strength now comes from rural America, right now less affected by the virus, and liberals, whose urban strongholds have been most affected by it.'[115] No doubt those disparities contributed to the sharp divergence in perspectives. But, as the virus spread, the culture war did not seem to get any less intense.

A third significant political danger today is that the *economic* hardship arising from the coronavirus crisis will end up fuelling the toxic, xenophobic and populist politics that helped to generate the crisis in the first place. Since deprivation fed into right-wing populism (not least when charismatic leaders promised to turn shame into pride), impoverishment arising from the virus could easily do likewise. In the UK under Prime Minister Truss an escalating public debt combined with heating subsidies and proposed tax cuts to generate a major economic crisis with uncertain political implications.

A fourth danger resides in the stepping up of surveillance and control in the Covid crisis. The same Cambridge University study that found a waning of support for populist leaders during the pandemic also drew attention to a 'disturbing erosion of support for core democratic beliefs and principles, including less liberal attitudes with respect to basic civil rights and liberties'.[116] So that is a distinctly mixed picture. Covid has encouraged a range of governments around the world to relabel dissent as disloyalty, to step up surveillance of the population and to claim emergency powers that threaten to outlast the virus emergency itself.[117] An April 2020 United Nations report suggested, 'what is justified during an emergency now may become normalized once the crisis has passed'.[118] Hungary's Viktor Orbán said he needed emergency powers to fight the disease, but these lacked a time-limit and looked set to extend beyond the crisis.[119] Journalists in Hungary risked being jailed for five years for criticizing Orbán's Covid response.[120]

The coronavirus crisis may also feed the toxic and disaster-producing elements in politics if it contributes to the discrediting of *democracy itself*. Some have suggested that the authoritarian nature of China's government helped to control the virus. In the UK, far-right groups have sometimes stressed that authoritarian regimes have outperformed Western liberal regimes in tackling the health crisis, with some even claiming that liberal states are on the verge of collapse.[121] (Of course, the limits to the protection provided by democracy have also been stressed in the current book.)

Yet disasters surely call for a *reinvigoration* of democracy rather than a knee-jerk invocation or imitation of autocratic 'emergency' rule.[122] We saw how human suffering, including mass water cut-offs, in Detroit was facilitated when democracy at the local level was effectively suspended by 'emergency management'. Relatedly, a key problem in relation to Covid in the UK and US has been that these countries are *not democratic enough*: too secretive about their 'science'; too intimidatory towards critics; too ready to protect some constituents rather than others; too excluding when it comes to the voices of healthcare professionals, manual workers, minorities, prisoners, the elderly and so on; too ready to sacrifice those regarded as either 'useless' or 'essential'; and generally too much in awe of individual 'charismatic' leaders, who have themselves proven woefully out of touch with reality. A House of Commons report noted in January 2021 that 'It is disappointing that the details of SAGE's preliminary meetings were not made public for over two months, leading to unnecessary concern and confusion over what advice the Government had been receiving'. The report added that 'SAGE has yet to publish any papers that might have been considered in the first two meetings.'[123] In general, disaster prevention depends not just on the existence of democracy but the *quality*.

As the Covid crisis deepened in the UK, doctors and nurses were warned by hospitals and other NHS bodies not to raise their concerns publicly when it came to the shortage of personal protective equipment and the consequent danger to their lives (and, by extension, to patients). Some staff received threatening emails and warnings of disciplinary action, according to evidence from the Doctors' Association UK (DAUK).[124] One doctor wrote to *The Lancet*, 'I never thought I lived in a country where freedom of speech is discouraged.'[125] Meenal Viz, the hospital doctor protesting in Downing St, said 'We are being silenced. In our own hospitals. By our own managers. A lot of people are afraid for their own safety but they're also afraid of losing their jobs. Some of them have visas tied to their work or families to feed …'.

While this kind of intimidation is certainly shocking, it can also be seen in some ways as simply an exaggeration of normality. Even in those (increasingly scarce) times when we are not inhabiting some kind of 'emergency', a perverse general law arguably limits the efficacy of free speech in democracies: 'Where we know little, we are free to speak; where we are knowledgeable (notably from our work), we must remain silent.' Here, one need perhaps look no further than my own world of academia, where the *Guardian*'s collection of articles by 'anonymous academics' reveals significant levels of fear within a profession ostensibly committed to free thought and free speech.

It's clear that a crisis can bring to the fore some of these underlying problems, while organizational reforms can strongly affect the degree to which free speech exists. Professor McCoy at Queen Mary noted in May 2020 that Public Health England 'has remained conspicuously quiet during the pandemic, and it has fallen to independent public-health experts to point out the errors of the government's approach'.[126] Public Health England relied on local authority budgets, which themselves have been undergoing a significant financial squeeze as part of the government's austerity policies.[127] *The Lancet* reported that when Public Health England was abolished, inadequate consideration was given to ensuring replacement organizations would be able to speak with a greater sense of independence from ministers.[128]

Compounding the obstacles to speaking freely during the coronavirus crisis was a habit of media hounding of individual scientists, which seemed to be part of a dangerous disrespect in much of the press and among many politicians for science that they don't like.[129]

In Trump's America, selectively giving and withholding assistance became an integral part of trying to control dissent, a phenomenon that mirrored some 'far away' disaster zones in Sudan, Syria and elsewhere. State governors friendly to Trump tended to get the full measure of protective equipment, while opponents (often attacked on Twitter) got only a fraction. When CARES (stimulus bill) funds were distributed, New York got $12,000 per patient, while less-affected, Trump-voting states got up to $470,000 per patient.[130] This is the kind of striking disparity between regional need and relief response – and the punitive attitude to dissent – that has sometimes been observed during famines in Africa. A shamelessly partisan approach to the pandemic was also exemplified when the HEROES Act (intended to provide one trillion dollars of assistance to state and local governments) ran into stiff opposition in the Senate. With Covid initially hitting urban (and disproportionately Democrat) areas much more severely, Republican Senate majority leader Mitch McConnell said it was time to end 'blue state bailouts'.[131]

Again, the incentives within a democracy were more complicated than the Sen/Drèze model implies. Far from instilling into politicians the fear that they would not be re-elected if they failed to relieve the suffering, the Covid emergency was often interpreted as a chance to punish those who voted for the wrong party. It was in this context that American journalist and author George Packer referred to the US as a 'failed state'.[132] But, as with the 'failed states' in Sudan and elsewhere in Africa and Asia, many were pushing their political and economic agendas with considerable efficiency.

More generally, we may say that in the absence of a vaccine the idea of 'herd immunity' was a kind of pseudoscience in which senior officials ignored their own (huge) numbers on predicted deaths, while all the time claiming to be 'following the science'. Significantly, the UK's code for modelling control measures against Covid-19 was written thirteen years previously to model flu pandemics, as Neil Ferguson acknowledged.[133] In these circumstances, perhaps it is little wonder that the UK government was so sensitive to criticism, particularly to criticism from within the medical profession. Yet this dangerously constrained debate. Nobel laureate Sir Paul Nurse said of the UK system: 'It sometimes seems like a "black box" made up of scientists, civil servants and politicians are coming up with the decisions ... We need greater transparency.'[134]

Among the voices that need to be heard are also those highlighting the social and health costs of lockdowns themselves, costs that need to be better understood if they are to be better mitigated. In a highly charged political environment, those trying to draw attention to the negative public-health effects of lockdown risked being attacked as 'Covid deniers'. Some have argued that the UK government overreacted to Covid and the risks to all but the elderly were exaggerated.[135]

In her bestselling book *A State of Fear*, for example, Laura Dodsworth claimed that the UK government 'weaponized fear' in order to clamp down hard on personal freedoms. While this is not my view, it is clear that there were many voices and many opinions that struggled to find a hearing amid a general official lauding – and often misuse – of 'the science'.

More broadly, without the active facilitation of dissent, we are in grave danger of reconstructing the causes of the problem. As Aditya Chakrabortty put it in the *Guardian* on 13 May 2020, 'in England this week we begin the slow and risky stagger right back to the broken social settlement that landed us in this catastrophe'.[136]

There is still the possibility that the severity of the Covid disaster will be a useful prompt for change more generally. For one thing, Covid-19 adds weight to the possibility that problems commonly dismissed as affecting 'only' the Global South will now be taken more seriously and proper protection put in place. As George Packer put it, 'If 9/11 and 2008 wore out trust in the old political establishment, 2020 should kill off the idea that anti-politics is our salvation.'[137] At the same time, we have noted several important reasons for suggesting that Covid might give such 'anti-politics' another 'shot in the arm'.

7

Magical Thinking

If we are to understand our current disaster-producing system, we need to understand its functions as well as its causes and consequences. But, as we saw in Chapter 2's discussion of disasters in poorer countries, we also need to understand how disasters are being *legitimized*. More broadly, we should be asking how our disaster-producing system, with all the suffering that is involved, is being rendered somewhat acceptable, whether to the politicians and senior officials who disproportionately shape it or to the wider electorate.

While there are many ways to address this issue, in the chapters that follow I find myself drawn back repeatedly to Arendt. Her writings show an extraordinary ability to illuminate the human propensity for embracing fictional realities and she can help us to understand how this feeds into political catastrophe. This chapter looks at the role of magical thinking – essentially, believing in causal processes that lack basis in reality – in fuelling and legitimizing the current disaster-producing system. To understand magical thinking, we need to look at the allure of false certainties, as well as the flight from shame and responsibility. After this, Chapter 8 examines the way alternative realities have been defended through the intimidation of critics and potential critics. The chapter has a special focus on the 'war on terror', and it shows how magical thinking and the *defence* of magical thinking have for some time been fuelling a variety of related disasters. Chapter 9 makes use of Arendt's concept of 'action as propaganda' in seeking to deepen the investigation of how our overlapping disasters are being legitimized, while Chapter 10 looks at the role in this legitimizing process of 'lesser evil' arguments (arguments of which Arendt was deeply, and rightly, suspicious).

On top of the many types of political, economic, epidemiological and 'natural' disaster discussed in this book, a mass contemporary flight from reality can plausibly be depicted as *a disaster in itself*. In particular, the rise of right-wing populism has often involved a substantial break with the truth – and even a break with the notion that the truth is important. Such a flight has already been feeding into a wide range of other disasters, impeding both their recognition and their prevention; in terms of climate change, the negative impact of such a flight is already catastrophic.

Trump

At the risk of stating what is 'obvious' to millions and 'claptrap' to millions of others, a lurch into magical thinking was strongly evident in the case of Donald Trump, who was elected on the basis of a set of attitudes and policies that had wide appeal but did not actually represent realistic means to the stated policy goals. Famously, a wall was going to be built to cut crime and poverty. Infrastructure was going to be rebuilt alongside sharp cuts in taxation. And there would be 'great health care at a tiny fraction of the cost, and it's going to be so easy'.[1] If nothing else, the US's inability to cope with Covid was a devastating illustration that the last of these promises did not come to fruition. In fact, the Covid pandemic saw Trump trying to prop up his own crumbling, magical system with ever more fanciful statements and ever more destructive instructions to 'get back to normal' – even when there was no vaccine.

More generally, Trump and his acolytes have tended to laud intuition rather than evidence. Thus, Trump told *Time* magazine in 2017, 'I'm a very instinctual person, but my instinct turns out to be right.'[2] Trump's officials sometimes dutifully echoed this way of speaking, as when Peter Navarro, head of the White House National Trade Council, affirmed 'My function, really, as an economist is to try to provide the underlying analytics that confirm his [Trump's] intuition. And his intuition is always right in these matters.'[3] Such subservience was part of a gathering sense of unreality and unquestioning loyalty within parts of the US administration.[4] Significantly, Trump had started his administration by (literally) binning 30 binders of plans for an orderly transition that had taken 140 people nearly six months to prepare.[5] Meanwhile, Trump's senior counsellor Kellyanne Conway advised that people should not focus on his words, but on the truth 'in his heart'.[6] In this way, Trump was positioned as infallible, his honesty and good intentions as incontestable.

At the same time, pinning too much of our contemporary madness and magical thinking on Trump may represent its *own kind* of magical thinking. Even if we confine ourselves to American politics, we can see that magical thinking extends much more widely than Trump. Whether in the US or more widely, a key problem has been the focus on symptoms of crisis rather than underlying causes. As part of this, we have seen a concentration on *hyped up* disasters alongside a neglect of several that are more serious and far-reaching. The latter (the economic, ecological and longer-term political crises noted in earlier chapters) can properly be seen as fundamental disasters that underpin many of the more immediate and essentially symptomatic disasters.

Meanwhile, the legitimacy of this dysfunctional, disaster-producing system has been maintained, in large part, through continuously defining and redefining 'the enemy' in ways that encourage the pursuit of magical solutions while simultaneously stifling the dissent of those who try to criticize or change this system.

Popular Affinity for Fictional Realities

We often assume that people want the truth from their politicians, and we know that one of the most common complaints against politicians is that they are *liars*. But Trump's various delusions have been bought as well as sold. The same goes for many other delusions pushed by right-wing populists in other parts of the world.

Arendt flagged the possibility that large elements of a country's population are more interested in certainty than truth. Embracing certain kinds of fiction can not only provide a sense of certainty but also an escape from shame and responsibility.

One problem with certainties that are too readily embraced is that when you think about things in any measured or sustained way, the certainty collapses. But the pushers of magical thinking have their own solutions to this problem. At the extreme, Hitler once observed that 'A mass rally is designed to switch off the thinking process. Only then will people be ready to accept the magical simplifications before which resistance crumbles.'[7] On this model, group-think becomes, conveniently, a kind of no-think. As noted, we should always be wary of superficial comparisons between the Nazis and present-day phenomena. But one of the reasons why many people found Trump so frightening – and many so thrilling – was precisely the sense of collective elation at his political rallies. Arlie Russell Hochschild captured some of this in her study of Louisiana, with participants expressing a determination to hold onto the profound exhilaration that they had experienced as part of a crowd that validated some of their deepest feelings and beliefs, while explicitly rejecting 'PC' attitudes.[8] Part of the thrill was that the crowd would sometimes turn collectively against any journalists or protesters that Trump himself was highlighting as a problem, so that scapegoating was not only advocated but *enacted*.[9] It's notable that Trump maintained his campaign-style rallies even after becoming President.

If groupthink was sometimes a collective release, Arendt's work (and especially *The Origins of Totalitarianism*) can also help us to understand why false certainties and false explanations have particular allure in uncertain times. In addition, she illuminates the attractions of relentless oversimplification in circumstances where 'facts' and 'opinions' are proliferating at a bewildering rate. Arendt suggested that in times of upheaval (for example the combination of war, military defeat, hyperinflation and then mass unemployment that Germany experienced from 1914) people would tend to look for ideologies that gave them an explanation for their troubles. They would look for a way of interpreting the world that freed them from the extreme anxiety of incomprehension and unpredictability. Ideologies could also provide explanations that helped to avoid the painful business of blaming oneself, particularly given the common view that impoverishment was the fault of the individual rather than the system.[10]

Arendt suggested, further, that a lonely or isolated person will 'think everything to the worst', and that the 'ice-cold reasoning' of totalitarian ideology appeared to vast numbers of people as both 'a suicidal escape' and a precious source of 'self-respect' in the face of atomization and loss of old identities that were themselves the result of modernization and rapid urbanization.[11] Pluralism, in Arendt's view, was becoming unbearable to those who had lost their place and their orientation within a world of upheaval.[12] Today, there is a rather terrifying ring to Arendt's observation in 1951 that

> The ideal subject of totalitarian rule is not the convinced Nazi or the convinced Communist, but people for whom the distinction between fact and fiction (i.e. the reality of experience) and the distinction between true and false (i.e. the standards of thought) no longer exist.[13]

Arendt also noted that '... ideologies are systems of explanation of life and world that claim to explain everything, past and future, without further concurrence with actual experience ...'.[14] She stressed that the *accuracy* of ideological explanations was often surprisingly irrelevant. In fact, when asserting particular positions became part of one's *identity*, then the speaker had actually moved beyond the world of weighing facts and opinions. Arendt noted that 'Nazi propaganda was ingenious enough to transform antisemitism into a principle of self-definition, and thus to eliminate it from the fluctuation of mere opinion.'[15]

A key reason why today's disaster-producing politics may be dangerously self-reinforcing, we have noted, is that a flight from reality becomes more and more tempting as reality itself becomes more frightening. Again, Arendt can help us to understand this phenomenon. We've noted that what she called the non-totalitarian population would often indulge in 'wishful thinking' that 'shirks reality' and systematically disbelieves the monstrous.[16] Arendt saw this propensity for denial as particularly important in helping totalitarian fictions to gain a hold. Indeed, her writings suggest that the horrors of Nazism thrived on the combination of the *lies that people wanted to believe* (for example about the Jews' responsibility for Germany's ills) and *the truth that people did not want to believe* (for example about the existence of concentration camps).[17] Arendt reminded her readers that even those confined to the camps (and she herself was confined to a camp in Gurs, France, before escaping to America via Portugal) sometimes had to convince themselves that what was happening was real and not just a nightmare.[18]

Of course, the Nazis' central themes were not just false but ludicrous, and most notable here was that idea that the Jews were undermining the wellbeing of Germany. Arendt highlighted the remarkable ease with which a group that posed *no* security threat was elevated into *the ultimate* security threat. The Jews in Germany were not engaged in rebellion and, unlike minorities in many countries, had no history of rebellion or agitation for autonomy. Nor were the Jews under-represented in the German army that fought in the First World War, despite repeated Nazi allegations to the contrary. Yet, crucially, the absence of any threat to Germany's health or security proved absolutely no impediment to a Nazi discourse – to a large extent a *convincing* discourse – that centred on the mortal threat allegedly posed by the Jews.[19] Of course, many beyond Arendt have tried to contribute explanations for this bizarre and destructive disjuncture. For example, Omer Bartov showed that the Nazis even turned around the fact that Jewish people were generally rather well integrated into German society by redefining this as 'pollution'.[20] More generally, French philosopher René Girard noted that the targets of violent scapegoating tend to be those who are vulnerable and close at hand – people who can be attacked without provoking an endless cycle of retaliation; from this perspective, scapegoats are not targeted because they pose a threat but because they don't.[21]

As for Arendt, even when writing about an era as distant as the 1920s and 1930s, she understood that the very proliferation of opinions in the media was feeding a desire for certainty, however false such certainty might be.[22] In her article 'At table with Hitler', Arendt referred to Hitler's view that 'in the modern world's chaos of opinion the normal mortal is yanked about from one opinion to another without the slightest understanding of what distinguishes the one from the other'.[23] She added:

> Hitler knew from his own most personal experience what the maelstrom was like into which modern man is drawn and in which he changes his political or other 'philosophy' from day to day on the basis of whatever options are offered to him as he whirls helplessly about. He [Hitler] is himself that newspaper reader of whom he says that 'in a city [in which] twelve newspapers each report the same event differently … he will finally come to the conclusion that it is all nonsense'.[24]

Hitler thought that by sticking rigidly to one viewpoint, you could cut through this bewildering proliferation of perspectives and sell the public an alluring certainty. Arendt wrote that Hitler, unlike this newspaper reader, understood that 'if you really hang onto any one of the current opinions and develop it with (as he was fond of saying) "ice-cold" consistency, then everything would somehow fall back into place again'.[25]

Arendt's analysis is helpful when we try to understand why arguing with a committed conspiracy theorist is so difficult, not least today. The system of thought adhered to by such an individual may seem crazy. It probably *is* crazy, at least in the sense that it constantly misreads the causes of things, fleeing from facts into fantasy, and directing the individual's energy towards magical solutions. But Arendt helps us to see *what is at stake* for the deluded individual in terms of their identity and in terms of avoiding uncertainty, anxiety, and shame. Conspiratorial views, moreover, tend to have an internal consistency, while the believer (who may be surprisingly keen on 'research') sometimes displays a sense that everything has fallen into place. There is also likely to be a 'fit' of some kind between the ideas being embraced and the believer's own experiences – another reason why simply labelling particular ideas as crazy or magical is likely to be ineffective or actively counterproductive. This 'fit' with individual experience represents part of an idea's *conditions of plausibility*, and these conditions need investigating.

Now if some of the appeal of false certainties lay in the proliferation of news and opinions during the 1920s (as Arendt suggests), then it is not hard to imagine that false certainties might today even be *more* tempting amid the potentially endless supply of views and largely unverified 'facts' that pours out of the internet. Even back in 2008, Farhad Manjoo suggested in his book *True Enough* that America had become a country that could not agree over basic facts.[26] And again, where opinion is polarizing, the temptation to 'pick a lane' is likely to be reinforced by the growing tendency (as Arendt put it earlier) to 'report the same event differently'.

False certainties are today spectacularly evident in the conspiracies of QAnon. Conspiracy theorists have often homed in on disasters such as Covid and migration – and again the refugee/migrant caravan moving north from Mexico was a focus for many conspiracies. The fact that fears around the 'caravan' were dramatically out of proportion to any objective threat was well conveyed by former President Obama: 'They're trying to convince everybody to be afraid of a bunch of impoverished, malnourished refugees a thousand miles away', he said.[27] But the key, in this case as so often with orchestrated panic, was not the size of the threat but what the targeted group was made to symbolize or represent. Media stories hyped up not just the threat of 'crime' but also the alleged threat of disease (including smallpox, certified as eradicated in 1980).[28] Alongside their 'research' (at least on the internet), conspiracy theorists are often 'skilled' in the art of deduction – and Arendt, significantly, was deeply suspicious of the art of deduction when it was divorced from human experience. If those who were lonely might dangerously 'think everything through to the worst', the conspiracy theorist may combine a certain distance from organizations rooted in politics (unions, cooperatives and so on) with the presence of a virtual community of 'fellow believers'. Meanwhile, part of deductive reasoning is seizing on, and extrapolating from, small details. Again, the 'caravan' offered revealing examples. After a Fox News story on the caravan, someone picked out a Star of David symbol on the side of a truck that many people were climbing into. The image was posted and reposted on right-wing websites, including by Robert Bowers (the man arrested at the scene of the 2018 Pittsburgh synagogue massacre).[29] At least according to one way of looking at the world, 'everything was falling into place'.

Elite Magical Thinking

Again, there has been an understandable tendency to portray Trump as uniquely out of touch with reality – a crazy idiot with crazy hair who hijacked political life and took it to 'la la land'. But the politics of magical thinking has a long history, not least within the US itself. It has often involved flights from reality among senior officials. And it has frequently contributed to disasters of one kind or another. From this perspective, Trump's magical thinking might be compared to a disease like shingles in which an underlying condition is activated when the body is weakened or stressed. And the truth crisis of recent years, far-reaching within the US but certainly not confined to it, is not something completely new but a kind of *flare-up* within a much longer-standing tendency to drift into alternative realities.

More than four decades before Donald Trump entered the political scene, Arendt herself showed how systematically American politicians and officials could set their face against reality. More specifically, she argued that during the Vietnam War American policy-makers' relationship with the truth became systematically distorted by an obsession with image, by a preoccupation with avoiding the impression of a humiliating defeat, and by a concern with winning the next election.[30] Arendt showed how these obsessions led even democratically elected officials to make a radical leap into a world of fantasy, adopting and then adhering to 'solutions' (like the catastrophic bombing of North Vietnam) that were not only morally abhorrent but also predictably counterproductive when it came to winning the war – not least because they unsurprisingly created additional enemies by multiplying antipathy to the US.

Arendt went so far as to say that the problem in relation to Vietnam was 'the wilful, deliberate disregard of all facts, historical, political, geographical, for more than twenty-five years'.[31] She highlighted US officials' basic lack of curiosity about Vietnamese society so that, for example, 'no one at the top knew or considered it important that the Vietnamese had been fighting foreign invaders for almost 2,000 years'.[32]

Arendt also observed that the officials working on US policy towards Vietnam 'prided themselves on being "rational", and they were indeed to a rather frightening degree above "sentimentality" and in love with "theory", the world of sheer mental effort'.[33] This involved finding formulas, usually 'expressed in a pseudo-mathematical language' that would give the illusion that the world was predictable, bringing social science more into line with the sense of predictability that the natural sciences had often aimed at.[34] Influenced also by Adolf Eichmann's robotic persona when she saw him on trial in Jerusalem, Arendt reminded her readers that even coldly calculating officials could embrace highly irrational policies, and she argued that reason is frequently undermined, rather than reinforced, by a lack of emotion.

Arendt's analysis here is interesting partly because it shakes up one of the most influential binaries of today – the idea that there are on the one hand a set of calm, rational and educated people who carefully weigh the evidence and model the future, while on the other hand there are the 'crazies' who like to veer off into a world of conspiracy and emotion. By showing the sheer craziness of some of the most highly educated people in America, she shifts the sociological focus in helpful ways.

Importantly, Arendt saw the embrace of irrational and disaster-producing policies as perfectly possible in democracies as well as in totalitarian systems. She argued that the modern elected official differed from the majority of statesmen in past eras, who had a better grasp of whatever truth they were concealing.[35] Stressing that democracy made it necessary to *convince* people, she suggested that 'under fully democratic conditions deception without self-deception is well-nigh impossible'.[36] Thus, modern political liars tended to fall victim to their own falsehoods. So rather than banishing delusions, democracy was in many ways encouraging them, even among its leaders.

Many people have been condemned for their ignorance and prejudice – and for 'voting irrationally'. Relevant stereotypes here have included the impoverished Trump supporter who gets little or no benefit from Trump's policies of deregulation and cutting taxes[37] as well as the working-class Brexit supporter who gets nothing from leaving the European Union. Of course, self-defeating voting behaviour *is* important to understand. But Arendt's work, and her analysis of American policy-making in Vietnam in particular, is a reminder that we need to take a critical look at relatively privileged and powerful decision-makers who may inhabit delusions and 'alternative realities' of their own. We might even call this 'elite magical thinking'. A magical belief in 'the free market' has often been manifest – and powerful Democrats' reverence for 'the free market' has contributed to an extraordinary escalation of inequality in the last 40 years.

At any rate, it's important to look at wider propensities for magical thinking, moving beyond our favourite targets or 'deplorables'. In his extended 2017 article 'How America lost its mind', Kurt Andersen pointed to a popular belief that 'being American means we can believe anything we want'. He traced the current 'post-truth' moment back to the 1960s and to what he presented as the dangerous idea, particularly popular on the left, that the truth was 'socially constructed' and somehow 'all relative'. Andersen noted:

> Neither side has noticed but large factions of the elite left and the populist right have been on the same team ... more and more people on both sides would come to believe that an extraordinarily powerful cabal – international organizations and think tanks and big businesses and politicians – secretly ran America.

One problem with Andersen's analysis is that, in many respects, a rather tiny elite actually *has* been running America and we saw plenty of evidence of this in Chapter 4. Nevertheless, presenting reality as 'constructed' does have its dangers.

In his influential 1965 book *The Paranoid Style in American Politics* Richard Hofstadter had already observed that a conspiratorial mindset has roots within the Left as well as the Right. Nevertheless, Hofstadter's analysis of 1960s politics emphasized the particular dangers of right-wing conspiracy theory – notably in the (ultimately unsuccessful) 1964 campaign for the presidency by the Republican Barry Goldwater. There is more than a hint of today's political atmosphere in Hofstadter's observation that

> ... Goldwater's zealots were moved more by the desire to dominate the party than to win the country, concerned more to express resentments and punish 'traitors', to justify a set of values and assert grandiose, militant visions, than to solve actual problems of state.[38]

Like Trump, Goldwater put great emphasis on the need to restore pride and dignity. He also proclaimed that 'status politics' was far superior to 'interest politics'. Since politics was increasingly centred on expressing your identity and self-worth, according to Hofstadter, the actual impact of policies was in a sense secondary.[39] Within a magical mindset, for Goldwater (as later for Reagan), even a nuclear war was winnable, underlining the extent to which euphoria around winning had shifted beyond the world of facts. Hofstadter stressed that what Goldwater prefigured was not exactly fascism or totalitarianism as these things have been known in European history, but rather a persistent and dangerous strand of politics that was very American and strongly related to the frontier experience. Thus:

> The American frame of mind was created by a long history that encouraged our belief that we have an almost magical capacity to have our way in the world. From the beginning of our national life, our power to attain national goals on which we were determined was in effect irresistible within our chosen, limited continental theater of action. Our chief foes – Indians, Mexicans, the decaying Spanish empire – were on the whole easily vanquished.[40]

When Joseph McCarthy went looking for the Communist 'fifth column' or when Goldwater's more ardent followers attributed America's setbacks to 'treason', the assumption of omnipotence came back to bite the domestic polity through the desperate hunt for internal enemies, a reflex that at least maintained the fiction of history being *determined by 'us'*. The fall of Saigon was to trigger some related paranoia. When the 'war on terror' also proved unwinnable (as we shall see in Chapter 8), the search for internal enemies was again a notable and destructive part of responding to setbacks.

Violence Coming Home

In an insightful and disturbing book that focuses more on society than on individual leaders, historian Greg Grandin has highlighted the American reflex to expand – a reflex nurtured and indulged at the ever-shifting frontier within the North American continent. But again expansion ran into obstacles, and some of the violence and frustration 'came home'. Changing fortunes in foreign wars could significantly shape the nature and extent of violence against migrants and refugees. Grandin notes that in 1970s California 'Anti-migrant violence was fuelled by angry veterans returning from Vietnam, who carried out what they called "beaner raids" to break up migrant camps.'[41] Snipers took aim at Mexicans coming over the border, and federal agents were finding pitfall traps modelled on those that the Viet Cong would set for US soldiers.[42] More generally, increasing numbers of radicalized veterans were filling the ranks of white supremacist organizations, some of them involved in 'policing' the southern border.[43] Grandin argues that this radical energy was appeased with President Reagan's revival of the Cold War, especially Reagan's support for covert actions and anti-Communism rebels in Nicaragua and Afghanistan, with radical veterans also becoming involved in funding, weapons supplies and training.[44] Yet this proved to be a self-fuelling system of abuse, with support for the Nicaraguan Contras and for death squads in El Salvador, Guatemala and Honduras helping to create millions of refugees (of whom a large proportion fled to the US). Grandin comments, 'As they came over the border, they inflamed the same constituencies that Reagan had mobilized to wage the wars that had turned them into refugees in the first place.'[45] This is another striking example of instrumentalizing blowback.

Vigilantism at the US's southern border was growing at the turn of the twenty-first century but went into reverse when the nation mobilized for war in Afghanistan and then Iraq.[46] Grandin observed:

> Had the occupations of Afghanistan and Iraq not gone so wrong, perhaps Bush might have been able to contain the growing racism within his party's rank and file by channelling it into his Middle East crusade, the way Ronald Reagan broke up the most nativist vigilantes in the 1980s by focusing their attention on Central America.[47]

As it happened, 2005 saw the establishment of the Minutemen Project, which not only helped to organize vigilante patrols of the desert in search of undocumented migrants but also encouraged vigilantes to seek them out all over the US. Again, the project absorbed a great many veterans, some them returning from the new 'war on terror' and some being veterans of older wars. By the end of 2006, 140 Minutemen branches had been set up in 34 states, and violence against Latinos within the US was rising rapidly.[48] Agents from Immigration and Customs Enforcement (or ICE) were pulling children off school buses and tracking undocumented residents in New York state and Massachusetts. Some two million people were deported in Bush's eight years as President.[49] In the last years of the Obama administration, vigilante groups were surging as the Iraq War worsened and growing numbers arrived from conflict in Central America. Grandin notes that these groups were 'obsessed equally with ISIS, Central American gangs, Mexican cartels, and Black Lives Matter. Most have done multiple stints in Afghanistan and Iraq.'[50] By 2015 the border Minutemen were claiming to be keeping ISIS out of the US and saying they often spotted 'Middle Eastern guys with beards' and found 'Arabic–English dictionaries in the sand'. [51] Here was some of the wider social context for Trump's dangerous expansion of the 'enemy' category. As so often with Trump, it was a reflex that did not come out of nowhere.

Grandin suggests that the US is 'founded on a mythical belief in a kind of species immunity ... an insistence that the nation was exempt from nature, society, history, even death'.[52] In these circumstances, 'the realization that it can't go on forever is bound to be traumatic'.[53] Anything that signals that you will not submit to limits becomes attractive, from pulling out of the Paris Climate Accords to a rebellious truck that's rejigged to burn extra diesel and spew out spectacular black smoke. To this we might add not wearing a Covid mask, voting for Trump, and refusing to accept Trump's electoral defeat in 2020.

Grandin argues that the US is a nation that still thinks 'freedom' means freedom from restraint, but no longer pretends that *everyone* can be free. And given the limits to expansion, 'displays of freedom become increasingly cruel'. Much of that cruelty, as so often, has been directed southwards: 'Trump's cruelty takes many such forms, but it is most consistent in its targeting of Mexicans and Central American migrants.'[54]

A key point, more broadly, is that when expansion runs into its limits, the diverse blowback that results has repeatedly been incorporated into a cruel and delusional politics, so that magical thinking ends up feeding itself.

In Search of a 'Golden Age'

Wherever they occur, major disasters call for some kind of *explanation*; and very frequently explanations have been couched in moral or explicitly religious terms. In these circumstances, interpretations of disaster have frequently been harnessed to some kind of project of 'moral reform'; indeed, part of the *function* of the disaster may be to underwrite such a project. This in turn points towards another self-reinforcing tendency in our disaster-producing system: the explanations to which disasters give rise are very often disaster-producing in themselves.

The perennial impulse towards 'moral reform' is illuminated in Clifford Longley's book *Chosen People*, which showed how Protestants in Britain and America repeatedly drew on Old Testament accounts of the ancient Israelites as a model for how a 'chosen people' should react to misfortune. A notable influence was the Israelites' habit – when disaster gave a sense of losing God's protection – of finding a remedy, and the prospect of renewed favour, in moral renewal; at times, the search for renewed purity among the Israelites even spilled over into the massacre of 'idolators'.

In America, setbacks abroad have repeatedly helped to energize religiously influenced projects of 'moral reform' based on 'family values'. Thus, Kathleen Belew notes in her book *Bring the War Home*, 'In the wake of military failure in Southeast Asia, masculinity provided an ideological frame for the New Right [and] challenged antiwar sentiment'; at the same time, there was a renewed idealization of the family and 'traditional' gender relations.[55] Some 25 years later, American evangelist Jerry Falwell portrayed the 9/11 attacks as God's retribution for abortion, homosexuality and secularization.[56] Meanwhile, President George W. Bush explicitly said after 9/11 that Americans needed some kind of moral renewal (and a forceful response) if the terrorists were not to continue to view the country as weak, hedonistic and 'not very tough'.[57]

We have noted Thomas Frank's argument in 2004 that millions of Americans were voting against their own interests on emotionally charged issues like abortion, immigration and terrorism. Part of Frank's explanation was that the Democratic Party had failed to articulate or protect the interests of poorer people – and we've already seen how far-reaching this failure was. But we can also read Frank's book in the light of the human inclination to see safety in ritual and in a return to some kind of 'moral order'.

Here we might remember Jason Hickel's anthropological work in South Africa, and his suggestion that many Zulu people reacted to socio-economic disruption and deprivation by trying to reassert the 'traditional' homestead, not least through restrictions on women's freedom and sexual behaviour.

In the face of major social and economic disruption, many Americans have similarly expressed great anxiety about the breaking of taboos that centre on sexuality and the family. As in South Africa and indeed many other parts of the world, a desire to return to some kind of 'golden age' (often not specified) has been associated with the call for greater adherence to the taboos that are associated with this lost era, a time that is held to be more stable, more pious, more honest and more predictable than the modern mixed-up world. Beyond the sphere of private morality, there was a variation of this in the Tea Party's vigorous criticism of the bank bailouts that accompanied the 2007–8 financial crisis, with the movement's leaders suggesting a need to adhere much more firmly to a taboo that was seen as having made America great and kept Americans safe. This was the taboo

– sometimes more honoured in words than deeds, incidentally – on state interference in the market.

We have seen that the invocation of a Golden Age can quickly morph into aggression against those whose behaviour is seen as transgressive. But again, it may be useful to go beyond condemnation, a reflex that has energized our current highly polarized politics.

The perennial instinct to call for moral reform in the face of disaster found a particularly odd figurehead in 2016. But many Christian evangelicals emphasized that they were willing to look beyond Trump's dubious personal morality because he was supporting policies they liked and because he was ready to bring back a Golden Age in which they had felt more comfortable and more dominant.[58]

Going forward, as fears for the future increase, the search for a Golden Age and the perennial call for adherence to taboos associated with feeling safe in this lost era can be expected to intensify, perhaps further infringing the rights of women, minorities and others who find themselves on the wrong side of such a 'moral' agenda. In countries like Hungary and Poland, this kind of a 'revived morality' has sometimes been preferred to democratic safeguards, or at least has helped to justify their severe erosion. Meanwhile, whether in Washington or Warsaw or Budapest, the template for reformers of this ilk is not the 'small state' of neoliberal theory but a state that wants (in the 'moral' sphere at least) to be big and tough and actively interfering.

In these circumstances, Hungary and Poland may properly be seen in 'the West' as a *warning* and not simply an example of *what can happen to others*.[59] We are seeing a strong affinity between self-styled moral reformers in a variety of countries; indeed, international alliances between right-wing groups with related agendas are part of the current political crisis.[60] A notable example is the affinity between Orbán's government in Hungary and parts of the American Right, something that was underlined when America's Conservative Political Action Conference hosted an event in Budapest in May 2022. Panels at this cozy get-together included 'Western civilization under attack', with speakers including Orbán himself, Fox media star and 'great replacement theory' promoter Tucker Carlson (beaming in), and a range of conspiracist and anti-Semitic speakers.[61] Orbán's assault on Hungarian democracy did not seem to bother anyone; arguably, it was precisely the point.[62] Historian Andrew Gawthorpe commented in the *Guardian*, 'Among the terrifying implications of the American right's embrace of Orbán is that it shows that the right would be willing to dismantle American democracy in exchange for cultural and racial hegemony.'[63]

It's also another sign of moving away from the vision of a minimal state to the idea that the state should energetically legislate on morality, particularly on LGBTQ rights, on teaching race and gender issues in schools, and on abortion (a concern reflected in the Supreme Court's reversal of 'Roe v. Wade' on abortion in June 2022). Anne Applebaum suggests that while America's Founding Fathers were very concerned with how to prevent a democracy from becoming a tyranny, the new Right is not concerned to preserve institutions in a Burkean manner but instead 'to overthrow, bypass or undermine existing institutions'.

It is striking that anti-democratic tendencies from the old Cold War 'East', for so long condemned and indeed used to justify astronomical spending on the military, are today being actively welcomed as a shining inspiration. Of course, this extends well beyond Hungary and embraces the strange 'love affair' between Putin and elements of the American Right. In 2013, Conservative commentator Patrick Buchanan noted approvingly that Putin was speaking out against the destruction of traditional values by those at the top of the political system, adding that 'Putin may be seeing the future with more clarity than Americans still caught up in a Cold War paradigm', a future where 'conservatives and traditionalists in every country [are] arrayed against the militant secularism of a multicultural and transnational elite'.[64]

The Magical and the Mundane

Behind a favoured programme of 'moral reform' we can often detect substantial elements of self-interest. Indeed, in highlighting magical thinking here, my aim is not to marginalize analysis of the role of self-interest in politics but to get a better idea of how the magical and the mundane interact. The politics of 'moral reform' was brilliantly discussed in relation to Germany and the First World War in Paul Lerner's *Hysterical Men*, not least when it came to the dangerous and proto-Nazi idea that war could heal political divisions (and defuse radical politics) as well as remedying individual psychological weakness.[65]

While not giving sustained attention to the mundane political functions of selling and buying delusions, Arendt was herself aware that even the craziest persecutions could bring significant economic benefits – for example, in terms of jobs that were vacated or possessions stolen. Others, as noted, have stressed the *political* functions that Nazism (which received significant backing from big business) seems to have served in derailing class politics within Germany and in channelling frustration into persecution rather than revolution.[66] But even the concrete political benefits that sometimes accrue to those who stir up a sense of emergency would not arise unless a significant portion of the public bought into the combination of 'problem' and 'solution' that relevant politicians are offering. In this way, too, the magical can be said to underpin the mundane. When relevant delusions are sold (by politicians) and bought (by the electorate), politicians may or not buy into the delusions themselves.

In the case of Trump, his more magical ideas (and their strong popular appeal) helped to usher in a government with economic policies that were were geared strongly towards the interests of richer Americans. Given the levels of anger in America towards the political class (particularly after the 2007–8 financial crisis) and given the surge of popular support for Bernie Sanders with his explicit support for 'democratic socialism', there were significant threats to wealthy interests and to a profoundly unequal system. But the Tea Party managed to harness anti-establishment feeling to support regressive economic policies – and Trump followed suit.

In the case of Hungary, the rise of Orbán and his Fidesz party meant that a 'moral reform' agenda became intimately entwined with the construction of a fictional reality that has also served identifiable material interests. This fictional reality has been constructed both through lies and through magical thinking (which are often hard to disentangle). Central to this fictional reality (and mirroring similar claims on the far right in the US) has been the idea that Hungarian Jewish billionaire George Soros is plotting to destroy the country by importing migrants and replacing the white, Christian population with Muslims.[67] As Applebaum among others has emphasized, the fact that there are relatively few immigrants in Hungary (with large numbers of Syrians having left for Germany, for example) has not been a major obstacle to the embrace of this 'big lie'. One result of the official embrace of untruths was that the government forced the Central European University, founded by Soros, out of the country. Another has been the use of anti-Soros sentiment to intimidate civil society, including NGOs. Meanwhile, Orbán's government has undermined the independence of the press and the judiciary, helping to skew elections in favour of Orbán's Fidesz party.[68] Like Poland, Hungary also illustrates how those who sign up to relevant conspiracy theories may put themselves in a position to benefit economically – for example when friends and party hacks were brought into the state bureaucracy and when right-wing journalists were given senior positions in public broadcasting stations.[69]

While Hungary had its Soros conspiracy theory, Poland had its Smolensk conspiracy theory – the view that a nefarious plot (perhaps the Russian government, perhaps the former ruling party) brought down the President's plane in April 2010. Applebaum comments that 'Anyone who professes belief in the Smolensk lie is by definition a true patriot and thus qualified for a government job.'[70] An important part of the conspiracy is the view that Poland is, firstly, under siege and always vulnerable to treachery and hostile neighbours and, secondly, being undermined by corrupt interests who are still loyal to Communism and to Russia (and perhaps Germany too).[71] A key charge is that a 'deep state' has never been reformed since the Communist era.[72]

The point is that such conspiratorial thinking will always attract some very hard-headed individuals who see the possibility of a rapid rise on the back of a 'solution' that may be profoundly magical and indeed extremely damaging. Perhaps it is a solution (as we saw with Brexit in the UK) that key facilitators like Johnson and then May do not actually believe in themselves. Former UK Prime Minister Liz Truss voted against Brexit but later was strongly for it. Here it is as if an alleged devotion to the 'will of the British people' (which apparently can only be expressed once) has erased the importance of past beliefs and nurtured the peculiar fanaticism of those who do not actually believe in what they are doing. Signing up to high-profile political projects and beliefs – in this instance we might call it 'the Brussels conspiracy' – can yield substantial power as well as fame and money irrespective of core beliefs. And today, even as more and more people in the UK begin to feel the very practical adverse consequences of Brexit (such as loss of trade and loss of vital staff in hospitals and businesses), some of the strongest supporters of Brexit remain resolutely in power.

Blue Magic?

If we return to Hofstadter's idea of a frustrated sense of omnipotence, we may wonder how the politicians of today are coping with the challenge to their omnipotence that comes with losing an election. In Trump's case, we know the answer is 'not very well'; a more specific answer would be 'by attempting to subvert the democratic process itself'.

If we consider Trump and his most 'loyal' Republican representatives on the one hand and the Democrats on the other, a key difference is that the Democrats did not try to overturn defeat at the polls through inciting mob rule. But there were perhaps some elements of similarity too. Both showed a tendency to label electoral defeat as *illegitimate* – the Democrats in 2016 and the Republicans in 2020. And both appear to have been concerned to ward off shame and responsibility, whether through denying defeat altogether (Republicans) or through denying and downplaying the connection between defeat and past actions (Democrats). For Trump, a defeat will always be someone else's fault. But the Democrats, too, have exhibited some of this reflex, which is after all a common human failing rather than a vice specifically invented by 'the orange monster'. We might remember, too, that Hofstadter, in pointing to paranoia and conspiracy theories, was himself highlighting a tendency within American culture and not just a characteristic of specific Republicans like Goldwater.

How did the Democrats manage to lose in 2016 to a narcissistic and misogynistic reality-show host with a poor grasp of policies and zero political experience? One useful response to this question would have been for senior Democrats to look at the significant role that they and their party had played in deepening America's extraordinary inequality, not least in the de-industrialization of large swathes of the country and in the financial deregulation that laid the conditions for boom-and-bust and for an extraordinary escalation in inequality.[73] But, with some notable exceptions,[74] the path of critical introspection was generally spurned. In the event, it proved much more tempting to blame defeat on three other factors. The first was Trump himself, a feat readily accomplished through focusing on his many aggressions, deceptions and manipulations. The focus on Trump's personality became a morbid fascination of the media, shared by millions around the world (and I have to include myself). A second target for blame were the 'idiots' and 'racists' who *voted for* Trump. Of course, the matter was not always put this starkly but the undertow was there, and these voters had famously been condemned in advance, or half of them at least, in the form of Hillary's 'basket of deplorables'. At times, there was reassurance to be had from finding particular groups of people (on various accounts, southerners, rural 'hicks', racists, the heartlands, the Red States, the uneducated or just 'Trumpies') who could be denounced as ignorant (often tapping into old prejudices) and whose ignorance could be held responsible for defeat. At times, this resembled *its own* version of moral reform – an attempt to bring back, through collective denunciation, an age of tolerance before *half the country lost its mind*.

A third target for Democratic blame, as it turned out, was Russia, a feared and hated entity for more than forty years of the Cold War which now made a major comeback as chief villain, along with the old, old game of seeking out Moscow's secret collaborators. In an increasingly fevered atmosphere, David Fogleson suggested, anyone questioning the relentless focus on Russian interference ran the risk of being accused of *conspiring with* Russia.[75]

All of this is not to say that Russia did not interfere in the 2016 elections. It did. Indeed, the Mueller report found that the Russian government interfered in the 2016 presidential election 'in a sweeping and systematic fashion'.[76] There is strong evidence of Russian intelligence hacking the Democratic National Committee. There were multiple contacts between Trump associates and Russians inside or close to Putin's government, and Trump's associates clearly lied about this.[77] It's clear, too, that Putin has stepped up his attempts to interfere in the political processes of a *number* of Western democracies (as is evident from Catherine Belton's excellent *Putin's People*).

While Democrats pointed the finger at Trump–Putin collusion, under the Trump regime a record 40-plus rounds of sanctions were imposed on Russia. This might suggest that Trump and Putin were not as close as the Democrats suggested. Another possibility is that Russiagate prompted Trump into an elaborate overcompensation. While Trump's statements certainly gave Putin himself an easy ride, Trump declared 'there's never been a president as tough on Russia as I have been'.[78] Fyodor Lukyanov at the Carnegie Moscow Center went so far as to refer to 'a vicious circle, as the presidential administration and Congress vied to see who could be tougher on Russia'.[79]

Of course, the Russian interference was extremely disturbing, and in a tight election it could conceivably have made a difference. But, in a carefully worded statement, the Mueller report itself noted that 'the investigation did not establish that the [Trump] Campaign coordinated or conspired with the Russian government in its election-interference activities'.[80] The long-running Trump–Putin story (and associated hopes that Trump would be impeached) relied heavily on leaks from US intelligence agencies, making it hard to corroborate; we know too that intelligence agencies had often been publicly denigrated by Trump, perhaps eroding their objectivity.[81] Masha Gessen has noted that 'Hacking, releasing email and spreading disinformation has been a standard Russian strategy for a number of years', not only in the US but also in Europe.[82] (And, with suitable adjustments for changing technologies, such meddling has also been pretty standard CIA fare over many decades.) So, while Russiagate reflected some extremely disturbing events, it is also notable that Russia became a pretty *useful enemy* for Democrats reeling from defeat. In turn, this appears to have fed into consistent and vehement denunciations of Russia, a paranoid and in many ways humiliated country that retains the power to destroy the world many times over.

In March 2017, Masha Gessen observed in the *New York Review of Books* that 'Russia has served as a crutch for the American imagination. It is used to explain how Trump could have happened to us.' Richard Sakwa, a former international relations professor at Kent University in the UK, noted that:

> Russia became the scapegoat not only for the failure of the Clinton campaign in 2016, but also for the larger crisis of the American polity. Russia was accused of exacerbating the polarization of American politics by 'sowing discord'. However, the best way of dealing with domestic problems is to resolve them ... Democrats believed that the election had been 'stolen', but it was lost in the most profound sense. The conditions that gave rise to Trump remain, and only when they are addressed will the crisis be resolved.[83]

Of course, we know that Trump erroneously claimed that the 2020 presidential elections were 'stolen'. We know that Trump hates to lose. And we know he will always find someone else to blame. But again he is not the only one with these (very human) reflexes.

Richard Sakwa goes so far as to charge that 'Democrats and liberals sought to build their opposition to Trump on the back of stoking a new Cold War: anti-Soviet sentiment from the 1950s rallied the right, and now anti-Russian sentiment was mobilizing the liberal left.'[84] Sakwa commented in 2021 that 'interventionist Democrats if anything are more militaristic than traditional Republicans'.[85] We might counter, first, that there was plenty to mobilize the liberal Left that had nothing to do with Russia and, second, that Putin did more to stoke the new Cold War by twice invading Ukraine than the Democrats with their anti-Russian discourse. Nevertheless, all the rhetorical focus on Russian villainy in relation to Trump's election has surely contributed significantly to today's strategic tensions, particularly as the Democrats are now in government. President Biden is saying we are closer to nuclear war than at any time since the 1962 Cuban missile crisis. Meanwhile 'Russiagate' consumed a huge amount of political and media attention, leaving less room for reporting on the adverse effects of Trump's domestic politics[86] or on the complex socio-economic and policy issues that helped to put Trump in power in the first place. Whatever self-awareness might look like, this was not it.

In addition, a huge *underlying* problem that has impacted negatively on US domestic politics and on the international sphere has been the bipartisan failure – over a long period that includes the Obama presidency and the Clinton presidency as well as the George W. Bush administration in between – substantially to cut the huge budget of a military machine that for more than thirty years after the official end of the Cold War has continued to be directed, to a large extent, at Moscow.

It is not entirely surprising that the Democrats failed to dismantle this machine since they had played such a huge role – for example under Kennedy – in building it up. On top of this (and again with considerable bipartisan support, including under President Clinton), the end of the Cold War saw NATO retained and then repeatedly expanded. In a series of actions – the bombing of Serbia, the invasion of Iraq, the US's unilateral exit from the anti-ballistic missile treaty and so on – America proclaimed rather loudly its right to do as it pleased and the corresponding powerlessness of a Russia where large numbers of ordinary people as well as the establishment have still clung to their own dreams of greatness.

When it comes to magical thinking among the Democrats, there are long-term domestic issues that also need considering. Nancy Fraser, a Professor of Politics and Philosophy at New York's New School for Social Research, argues that a certain kind of identity politics acquired notably magical aspects. Fraser suggests that this mode of politics raised a kind of false hope while leaving people's increasingly precarious material position largely unaddressed. Shortly after Hillary Clinton's defeat in 2016, Fraser put a heavy emphasis on Bill Clinton's enabling of de-industrialization, financial deregulation and the precarity of the average worker:

> Clintonism bears a heavy share of responsibility for the weakening of unions, the decline of real wages, the increasing precarity of work, and the rise of the two-earner family in place of the defunct family wage. As that last point suggests, the assault on social security was glossed by a veneer of emancipatory charisma borrowed from the new social movements. Throughout the years when manufacturing cratered, the country buzzed with talk of 'diversity', 'empowerment' and 'non-discrimination'. Identifying 'progress' with meritocracy instead of equality, these terms equated 'emancipation' with the rise of a small elite of 'talented' women, minorities and gays in the winner-takes-all corporate hierarchy instead of with the latter's abolition.[87]

The fight against discrimination has, of course, been hugely important and helpful. It's also important to emphasize that a very wide range of progressive and anti-racist activists have fought not only for the rights of those subject to discrimination but against the policies that have led to a massive redistribution of wealth in favour of the rich in the United States.[88] The idea of the 'hegemony' of neoliberalism risks underplaying these struggles. A second concern with Fraser's analysis centres in her emphasis on the need to build a politics around the protection of the working class. Given the drastic de-industrialization in the US and given the spread of precarious employment, it is not clear that an old-style working class is sufficiently large to build a politics around.[89]

Nevertheless, Fraser provides an interesting insight into some of the more magical aspects of a version of 'liberation' that was embraced by privileged market-oriented liberals and by much of Hollywood (as part of what she calls 'progressive neoliberalism') but that left many others out of the benefits. Picking up on Fraser, Michael McQuarrie (whose work on the Democratic Party's neglect of the industrial working class was discussed earlier) has suggested:

> To the extent that the Democratic Party is interested in the protection of minorities, they are interested in the legal protection of abstract citizenship, not the economic protections that would facilitate broader social inclusion. The benefits fall to minorities with good jobs, while most people of colour are ritually sacrificed on a market fundamentalist and carceral pyre.[90]

In a powerful phrase, Walter Benn Michaels warned against 'a commitment to justice that has no argument with inequality as long as its beneficiaries are as racially and sexually diverse as its victims'.[91] Such dangers arise, too, in relation to the universities in the US and UK, for example, where a concern with 'promoting diversity' exists alongside an escalating fee structure that increasingly shuts out those (of whatever ethnicity or nationality) who are not comfortably off. At any rate, we need to explore further the extent to which the magical thinking that has been rather prominently visible in Trump and in some of his supporters (and indeed among many Republican voters in the earlier eras analysed by Hofstadter in 1965 and Frank in 2004) has actually been matched by a different kind of magical thinking among the Democrats, which includes its own versions of scapegoating as well as the belief that pushing 'identity politics' and celebrating the spectacular success of individuals from groups previously shut out of power will radically transform the lives of others within a profoundly unequal society that continues to lock people up in their millions.

Of course, not everyone was hoodwinked by those pushing neoliberal policies (whether those doing the pushing were Republicans or Democrats). Far from it. But hegemony – the Gramscian concept invoked by Fraser – is about convincing enough of the people enough of the time (or at least making them sufficiently uncertain) to allow a particular political and economic order to prevail. The politics of distraction has played an important part in this emerging system. And this politics turns out to be a coat of many colours, some of them blue.

Whose Magical Thinking?

Shortly after Trump became President, Nancy Fraser made an additional analysis that chimed with Hochschild's Louisiana research in particular. Fraser urged the importance of avoiding 'a doubling down on progressive-neoliberalism's definition of "us" (progressives) versus "them" (Trump's "deplorable" supporters)'.[92] She also emphasized the need to forge a common cause 'among *all* whom his administration is set to betray: not just the immigrants, feminists and people of colour who voted against him, but also the rust-belt and Southern working-class strata who voted for him'.[93] After noting that progressive neoliberalism 'mixed together truncated ideals of emancipation and lethal forms of financialization', Fraser suggested that it was precisely

> this mix that was rejected *in toto* by Trump's voters. Prominent among those left behind in this brave new cosmopolitan world were industrial workers, to be sure, but also managers, small businessmen, and all who relied on industry in the Rust Belt and the South, as well as rural populations devastated by unemployment and drugs. For these populations, the injury of deindustrialization was compounded by the insult of progressive moralism.[94]

Some analysts have pointed to an important underlying tension between those whose work involves dealing directly with some kind of physical reality and those who have removed themselves into a world of words and numbers.[95] In some ways, this distinction hardened during Covid when the so-called 'laptop' classes were often able to insulate themselves physically from going to work.

Oddly, many of those who *have* removed themselves into a world of words and numbers claim to be particularly in touch with reality. When it comes to climate change, those on top of scientific data have a decent claim to be more grounded in 'the real world' than most other people. But the division between the physical world and the onscreen world still sets the tone, often a conflictual tone, for much of the debate. And climate-change initiatives can easily look like one more act of indifference or even aggression in the face of the harsh physical reality faced by ordinary people.

In this context, attempts to take climate change seriously have sometimes been met with the accusation that 'elites' are out of touch with ordinary people along with counteraccusations that dissenters are uneducated and do not realize the seriousness of the current predicament. Such tensions are potentially another self-reinforcing element in a disaster-producing system, both because they make it harder to tackle climate change and because they can easily exacerbate political polarization. We have seen these climate change tensions in Australia, France, and the US, for example. How does enlightened messaging look from the other end? If your industries have been dismantled and shipped to China, how does it feel to be told that we must all stop growing and stop pumping filthy pollution into the sky? When the French government put increased taxes on fuel, the *gilets jaunes* reminded officials in Paris that those officials had alternatives to driving while people on lower incomes away from big cities generally did not. In Oxford, where I live, proposed charges on traffic in the city centre have been quite widely seen as disrupting social and economic life while exacerbating a cost-of-living crisis that is already severe.

Today, rising fuel prices (spurred in part by the Ukraine war) are putting a squeeze on farmers in many countries, and many farmers have been among those pushing back strongly against environmental regulations. In Sri Lanka, farmers' protests at a government ban on nitrogen fertilizer were part of a broader popular protest that ended up forcing the resignation of President Gotobaya Rajapaksa. In the Netherlands, new regulations have put a limit on the amount of nitrogen oxide and ammonia that livestock farmers can produce, focusing on 'nature areas' where there are endangered plants and wildlife. In response, farmers have protested the threat to themselves by blocking traffic and setting fire to hay bales.[96] Mary Harrington at the British online magazine *Unherd* observed:

> ... the people who make or grow things, build things, or move things around are both heavily reliant on cheap energy to do their jobs, and easy targets for well-meaning green regulations. From

> farming regulations that strangle small producers to rocketing fuel costs and travel restrictions for logistics firms unable to invest in low-emission vehicles, environmental rules take the heaviest toll on smaller businesses, adding pressure to living standards already squeezed by inflation and the pandemic.[97]

Where people's immediate economic concerns are not addressed and where they see themselves being preached at or labelled irrational by those who are much more privileged, it becomes much more difficult to garner public support for strong measures to tackle climate change. Thus, a political failure to give people a sense that their immediate needs can be met is helping to create the seeds for a wider political crisis in which addressing the existential threat of climate change is sometimes seen as a luxury and an imposition. Again, this shows how overlapping disasters may reinforce each other. And again, it's worth looking at other experiences around the world. As we saw with the Covid research in South Sudan, millions of people are today facing *multiple* disasters – big and small, personal and global. In the absence of *trust* and *a record of care* on the part of the government, as Robinson and her colleagues found in South Sudan, telling people which disaster they are *supposed* to worry about is unlikely to go well.[98]

More broadly, if you ask people to state the most important underlying crises in society and to name the crises that are *secondary* (whether in the sense of less important or in the sense that they *arise from* the most important crises), then you can be sure that different people will produce some very different lists. Such disagreements may constitute a natural and indeed desirable element of pluralism: why, after all, should everyone agree? Nevertheless, the current *very sharp* divergence in people's conceptions of the most important crises in many Western countries would seem to represent an important and perhaps even a defining element of the crisis itself. In this sense, a 'truth crisis' is shaping all the others. Certainly, it has stood firmly in the way of concerted responses to escalating inequality, Covid and global heating.

There is of course something deeply disturbing about the denunciation of 'experts' by right-wing populist politicians in the US and the UK. But the selfishness and magical thinking of experts in the past is not to be underestimated, as Arendt reminds us. Again, sometimes politics looks more like a clash of delusions than a confrontation between 'those who know' and 'those who don't'; and the relevant delusions may easily feed each other.

Magical thinking has been evident in the persistent delusion – frequently manifest among policy-makers as well as some members of the wider public – that complex social problems like crime, drug-addiction, mass migration and terrorism can be resolved by excluding, eliminating or disabling a finite group of 'threatening' individuals rather than through looking seriously at the causes and functions of these social problems. These causes frequently include counterproductive and self-righteous 'wars' or 'fights' that end up fuelling underlying problems like inequality, anger, conflict and global warming. Some of those targeted in these heavily securitized operations are warlords, drug-lords, human smugglers and terrorists; and even as evidence mounts that the responses are not working, it seems to be very difficult to learn lessons that go against well-entrenched and often self-serving paradigms.[99]

Today, as in the context of the Vietnam War, magical thinking is frequently bolstered by the trappings of 'science'. In the financial markets, a highly dysfunctional and dangerous system was endorsed and legitimized by some of the smartest people around. What emerged in the 1990s and early 2000s was an increasingly reckless and profitable financial system based on escalating private and public debt, with bankers lending out of all proportion to either borrowers' incomes or the banks' own reserves, while repackaging risky debt and selling it on. So long as markets were heading upwards, neither the seller nor the buyer of these often-complex products needed fully to understand them. Meanwhile, financial regulators tended to see themselves as working for the banks rather than for the public. The system was underpinned by a kind of reckless optimism. In many ways, this too was a kind of magical thinking, except that the profits made were real enough and often the escape routes when things went bad turned out to be equally real. Risk-taking was encouraged by systems for passing risk to others. And as with a range of other looming disasters, sceptical voices were not welcome. Robert Wade has commented that

> remarkably, no contingency plans had been made in central banks, finance ministries, or banks, because just about the whole financial industry and mainstream economics had a strongly vested interest in denying the dangers of being where we were on the trend line ... Almost everyone was in the grip of something like an addiction – the excitement-dopamine mechanism – and those who tried to draw attention to the growing dangers were squashed or derided.[100]

For the countries that were doing most to fuel (and benefit from) this reckless system, there was a strange sense of immunity (one that was soon to be mirrored in the idea that Covid was something that only happened 'far away'). 'How was it', Jean and John Comaroff have asked, 'that the over-analysed Asian and Latin American financial crises, or the ill-effects of structural adjustment in Africa, sounded no warning bells for the future of the Global North? Could it be because these things occurred outside Euro-America?'[101] As so often, magic and the mundane were combining in dangerous ways, while science was in effect *selected* so as to bolster a fragile (but profitable) system. Wade noted that influential economic models 'predicted a Lehman Brothers collapse once in a million years, even though two similar events (the collapse of the hedge fund Long Term Capital Management in 1998 and the 1987 stock market crash) had occurred in the previous fifteen years'.[102]

So there are many different brands of magical thinking. Some are embraced by those with a lot of education, and many work very well for those who are pushing them (and perhaps even believing in them). It is difficult to think one's way through these systems since many of the risks are being generated within spheres that are either so complex (finance) or so secret (the 'war on terror') that understanding them would be difficult even if dissent were not being rather systematically deterred.

In these circumstances, we often grasp at the most immediate and visible threat, and this may include (as René Girard saw) picking on those who are vulnerable and close at hand. When it comes to right-wing populism in particular, a magical approach to solving problems often focuses on the visible, the tangible and the spectacular, whereas a more genuinely scientific approach may invoke relatively invisible forces like viruses, gases and emotions.[103] Where there is a focus on the seen and the tangible, the corresponding solutions also tend to be physical: destroying smugglers' boats, building walls, bombing rebels and terrorists and so on. These have the 'advantage' that they can be filmed and circulated as evidence of 'tough and decisive' action by government. But they tend to involve a focus on consequences not causes. A more genuinely scientific approach would take more seriously the unseen, the emotional, the difficult-to-measure, the pluralistic, and the hard-to-resolve. This would mean taking seriously the complex social, political and psychological processes feeding into particular policies, including the various addictions that are sometimes driving them. It would also take seriously the concerns of those who are sceptical (often with good reason) about those who claim to be 'following the science'. Turning one's back on those who reject 'the science' is itself profoundly unscientific: it ignores the real world.

Even apparently sophisticated models may lead us rather quickly into a world of magic and a world where we are constantly being taken by surprise. The impulse to focus on visible consequences rather than causes is very familiar to me in terms of some of the more dysfunctional aspects of humanitarian interventions in the Global South – for example the tendency to focus aid on a finite and visible population of displaced people in particular locations, rather than asking about the harder-to-see processes that caused them to *be* displaced. Since these harder-to-see processes tend to be politically and diplomatically inconvenient or embarrassing, we have seen many times in the Global South that a hidden alliance is formed between a markedly technical and self-consciously 'scientific' analysis and the parties who are actively manipulating and benefiting from disaster. In these circumstances, relevant parties (including aid agencies) may 'agree to agree' on a version of reality that is unhelpfully far from the truth.

Conclusion

The many functions of magical thinking, whether political, economic or psychological, mean that it is not helpfully dismissed as madness (and again, for Freud even madness had identifiable functions). In addition to highlighting the *presence* of magical thinking, we have looked at how and why magical thinking arises, how it is put to use, how it relates to contemporary disasters. The functions of magical thinking turn out, very often, to be closely related to the functions of disasters. We have looked at both the political and economic functions of magical thinking.

We also need to understand its psychological functions. Here, we may suggest that magical thinking, in line with Freud's interpretation of neurosis, is a coping strategy that ends up getting us in deeper trouble than before. The allure of certainty in uncertain times stands out as a central attraction, as Arendt shows. And, insofar as these times become *more* uncertain, we may expect that important strands of magical thinking will become more attractive – another hazardous feedback loop.

While we have focused on the allure of certainty as a key contributor to magical thinking, the magical thinking that infuses our contemporary politics of emergency is also infused by other emotional factors.

For example, we have sometimes seen a focus on the emergencies that are *not especially frightening* (including the US's 'caravan' and the UK's terrifying-but-not-terrifying 'subordination' to Brussels)[104] or on the emergencies that can be construed as *oddly flattering* (as when terrorists are said to 'hate our freedom' or, as disillusionment with life in Western democracies increases, when migrants are said to be desperate to partake).

We have highlighted some of the magical thinking of Trump and other right-wing populists, and we've seen that Arendt can help us to understand the conditions that help to make magical thinking and weird conspiracies *plausible* and even *useful*. At the same time, we would ourselves be deluded if we imagined that delusions could somehow be neatly and conveniently packaged up and labelled the exclusive property of those on the political right. Nor does magical thinking emerge from nowhere. Instead, it frequently springs from *other kinds* of magical thinking. Alongside the magical thinking of those with less education we have highlighted (via Arendt in particular) the magical thinking of those with more education; indeed, the two would seem to be strongly connected. Elite magical thinking tends to foster a popular attraction to scapegoating, while scapegoating may in turn reinforce elites in the belief that they are more enlightened!

While pointing to magical thinking has its place (and even criticizing magical thinking can be helpful), we need also to consider the conditions that make magical thinking possible and plausible – and the relationship between different and sometimes 'opposing' sets of fantasies. Probably one of the craziest and most dangerous conspiracy theories, which has gained ground in a wide range of countries, is the idea that there is a plot to replace native-born people, generally glossed as white people, with immigrants. A poll in May 2022 found that *one in three* adults in the US subscribe to this false idea.[105] But rather than simply pointing the finger, we should also be asking what *makes* this conspiracy theory plausible. Racism is part of the answer, but only part. In the *New York Review of Books*, Adam Hochschild commended Farah Stockman's account in *American Made* of the closure of a ball-bearing factory in Indianapolis (a factory that not only moved all its operations to Mexico but also got the existing employees to train their Mexican successors). Noting the audience that Tucker Carlson and his ilk have found for the idea of a 'Great Replacement', Hochschild observed that American workers 'are indeed being replaced'. They are being replaced by workers in Mexico, 'by low-paid laborers in China and other countries, and, perhaps most of all, by machines. The black workers at Rexnord [the ball-bearing factory], 40 per cent of the total, are being replaced as well.'[106]

Commenting on anti-migrant feeling in Central and Eastern Europe, Bulgarian political scientist Ivan Krastev suggested, 'Alarm over "ethnic disappearance" can be felt in these small nations. For them, the arrival of migrants signals their exit from history, and the popular argument that an aging Europe needs migrants only strengthens a gathering sense of existential melancholy.'[107] On top of this, 'integration with Europe and "structural adjustment" meant that major economic decisions such as the size of the budget deficit were effectively removed from the arena of electoral competition. What remained was identity politics.'[108] While the conditions in which xenophobia grows and in which wild ideas become credible will always vary with time and place, it seems more constructive to investigate and tackle these conditions than simply to load opprobrium onto those who give credence to such ideas.

As for Trump himself, we may say that to a significant degree his craziness is everybody's craziness. All that magical thinking does not magically appear from nowhere. And if we focus only on Trump's 'flights from reality', we may not see our own. The ideas and behaviour of relatively privileged people can help us understand how Trumpian politics with its many 'flights from reality' *became possible*. And it is always dangerous, as Arendt herself emphasized, to be so mesmerized by something that we forget to ask what made it possible. Whether Trump is President or not, the forces and delusions that elevated him have not gone away, and the popular reflex to flee from complexity and uncertainty into simplistic solutions and simplistic denunciations has not gone away either. Even the popular pastime of denouncing a Trump or a Putin, understandable but often all-consuming, suggests the longevity of this strongly simplifying reflex.

8

Policing Delusions

We have seen how magical thinking infuses our disaster-producing system, and how magical thinking has been fed by the allure of certainty, by the appeal of an escape from responsibility, and by a range of more mundane and material interests. But *preserving* an illusion is rarely easy. In the real world (if we can still find such a thing), we may expect a significant and growing body of evidence suggesting that magical solutions are indeed magical. If you have a magical refuse collection system, for example, the garbage piles up.

In her discussion of totalitarianism, Arendt noted that when totalitarian regimes enforce and adhere to a set of fictions, they tend to fear 'every bit of factual information that leaks through the iron curtain, set up against the ever-threatening flood of reality from the other, nontotalitarian side ...'.[1] She also stressed that factual information is more threatening to totalitarians-in-power than to totalitarian movements that are *seeking* power. The lies of the latter, she explained, do not have to withstand the day-to-day business of government, whereas totalitarians-in-power will face rather directly a widening gulf between the world as they have portrayed it and the world as it actually is. From a practical point of view, a delusional leader's unrealistic and destructive policies, whether under totalitarianism or not, will tend visibly to unravel.

So how is magical thinking defended and legitimized as time goes by? How does it survive the lessons of experience and the rather specific challenge of being in power? And what are the consequences?

Here we need to understand the *policing* of delusions. In practice, leaders favouring some kind of persecution or scapegoating, or some other violent and magical solutions to social problems, have tended to exhibit a strong hostility to critics of these policies. This process in effect widens the circle of 'enemies' while shoring up the relevant delusions. As so often, a key lesson here comes from outside Western democracies, and we have seen a particularly vicious variation of this process during famines and persecutions under Communist regimes in China, Cambodia and the Soviet Union.[2]

In her insightful essay 'Truth and politics', Arendt quoted the Dutch scholar Hugo Grotius to the effect that 'Even God cannot cause two times two not to make four.'[3] Arendt went on to observe:

> Seen from the viewpoint of politics, truth has a despotic character. It is therefore hated by tyrants, who rightly fear the competition of a coercive force they cannot monopolize, and it enjoys a rather precarious status in the eyes of governments that rest on consent and abhor coercion.[4]

Defending the Big Lie

In the *New York Times* of 6 January 2021, on the morning of the crowd's invasion of the Capitol, Timothy Snyder, influenced by Arendt, wrote that 'Post-truth is pre-fascism and Trump has been our post-truth President.'[5] A key mechanism here, Snyder noted, was that a big lie, such as Trump's claim to have won the 'election by a landslide', 'brings with it, of necessity a conspiracy theory: Imagine all the people who must have been in on such a plot and all the people who would have had to work on the cover-up'.[6]

Of course, this is not an isolated example of contemporary lies fuelling the search for all those who are said to be obscuring 'the truth'. One might think back, for instance, to that claim by Hungarian Prime Minister Viktor Orbán that there was a 'Soros Plan' to flood Hungary with non-Christian migrants, a claim that prompted Yale University philosopher Jason Stanley to observe:

> There is of course no evidence whatsoever that the Jewish financier has any sort of plan to flood Hungary with non-Christian migrants, but the lack of evidence in the mainstream media is taken, by the Orbán government, to be evidence of Soros's control over it, when in fact it is Orbán who is manipulating reality.[7]

Sustaining the big lie demands a search for those, notably in the media, who are displaying their disloyalty by failing to endorse it. Crucially, it is the very ridiculousness of the allegation (and here we might think again of the *lack of threat* that the Jews posed to Germany) that in some sense 'demands' an all-embracing intimidation to 'make it true'. Whether in democracies or more authoritarian or totalitarian rule, a system of 'alternative facts', usually some combination of magical thinking and lying, is likely to feed into a growing paranoia centring on the fear that truth will intrude into an elaborately constructed world of fiction. Preserving a fiction, meanwhile, creates a powerful incentive not only to intimidate and discredit critics but also, at the extreme, to widen the definition of 'the enemy'.

Hostility towards any potential truth-tellers may help to preserve an increasingly fragile image of 'success' in the midst of what may be abject policy failure (as with those Communist famines). And as the definition of the enemy widens or morphs, it often shifts from an external enemy to an internal one. Again, this process may help to spread disaster from the foreign to the domestic sphere, as Arendt showed in relation to the Vietnam War and as we have seen with the 'war on terror'.

Particularly after Trump became President, his determination to be proven 'right' tended to produce a progressive expansion in the category of 'enemy' (which rather quickly embraced the 'fake media', for example). This was not just madness, aggression or narcissism but also *a mode of discipline*. As in the 'war on terror' from 2001 and as so often in wars that have unfolded in the Global South, a potential or actual expansion in the 'enemy' category was used to *police* fictional realities. More specifically, conforming to an officially endorsed lie or distortion was routinely encouraged by the possibility of being incorporated into the enemy category.

Even at a micro-level, Trump seems to have instinctively embraced the value of an enemy, whether as a mode of discipline, a way of uniting a crowd, or both. We've noted how Trump, at his campaign rallies, would repeatedly direct the crowd's anger at protesters or dissenters – a kind of *immediate* enemy within. In October 2018, at a meeting for young African American leaders, Trump praised his son-in-law Jared Kushner for improving the job prospects of ex-prisoners, adding that former prisoners were 'incredible' workers and then noting, 'And I don't mean everyone because there's no – even in this room we probably have a couple of bad ones, right? What do you think? Are there any bad ones?'[8]

Arendt argued that the insecurities and paranoia of the liar-in-power, already fuelled by the gap between alternative realities and the real world, are redoubled when the leader can no longer deploy the kind of anti-establishment rhetoric that helped with acquiring power in the first place. Such a leader cannot denounce the status quo because he or she now *is* the status quo. Again, this insight seems to speak directly to the paranoid insecurities of Trump, which appear only to have worsened in office. Power not only brought the threat of a substantial reality check but also made it harder to rail against the establishment. In these circumstances, it became common for Trump and some of his supporters to denounce an internal enemy, sometimes called the 'deep state', that was said to be undermining Trump's presidency and blocking the easy transformations that he'd promised. Since he had no realistic plan for these transformations, a widening search for scapegoats was in this sense *baked into* his presidency. While Trump did his best to hold onto that sense of being an 'outsider' and a 'movement' (notably with his mass rallies as President), there was no escaping the fact that he was now in power.

Another problem for Trump-as-President was that his populist claim to be speaking for the American people was in some sense challenged by every single act of opposition. In his prescient 2016 book *What Is Populism?*, Jan Werner Müller noted that populist politicians have a dangerous habit of presenting themselves as embodying 'the will of the people' – a claim that Müller saw as fuelling hostility to criticism when these politicians moved into government. In fact, the populist claim that a leader somehow embodies the will of the people against 'the establishment' can easily spill over into the claim, firstly, that any political opponents are somehow 'enemies of the people' and, secondly, that civil servants are failing to implement the 'popular will' with sufficient enthusiasm.[9] Looked at in this way, Trump's railing against the 'fake media' and the 'deep state' was much more than a personal foible; they fitted squarely within a dangerous and pre-existing template.

If the assertion of 'alternative realities' and the associated intimidation of critics came frighteningly to the fore in the US under Trump, this mode of governance (like the magical thinking we looked at in Chapter 7) was also an extension and exacerbation, and perhaps also a product, of habits long evident in US politics.

That takes us back to Hofstadter's acclaimed 1965 book *The Paranoid Style in American Politics*. Given the assumption that America will always win, it was always tempting to blame major setbacks in foreign policy on some kind of *betrayal from within* rather than on the simple fact that there was a complex world out there that did not simply bend to America's will.[10]

Hofstadter's emphasis on preserving omnipotence proved relevant in relation to the Vietnam War. In a 1975 article called 'Home to

Roost', Arendt showed how the disaster in Vietnam was coming home to America as a historically rooted sense of omnipotence came severely under threat. Living in New York, Arendt warned against fleeing defeat in Vietnam into an escalating violence against Cambodia, and she highlighted 'the boomerang effect, the unexpected ruinous backfiring of evil deeds on the doer'.[11] More specifically, she said that the violence, lying and magical thinking nurtured in Vietnam had come 'home to roost' in the form of Nixon's Watergate scandal.[12] Arendt argued that the US executive's determination to wage war as it saw fit had fed a systematic secrecy and a growing contempt for the legislative arm of the US government as well as for the press: then, as now, if you were defending a fake story, you ended up pointing your finger at a 'fake media'. Arendt also highlighted the deployment *within America* of an extensive intelligence apparatus that had grown in the context of the Cold War in general and the Vietnam War in particular. Prefiguring the rise in domestic surveillance in the context of the 'war on terror', America's security apparatus was turned by Nixon on some of his 'internal enemies', while the 'big lies' of Vietnam logically morphed into repression at home. After noting the strong influence of 'public relations' and 'Madison Avenue' on the American government during the Vietnam War, Arendt observed:

> when all signs pointed to defeat, this whole official outfit strained its remarkable intellectual resources on finding ways and means to avoid admitting defeat and to keep the image of the 'mightiest power on earth' intact. It was at this moment, of course, that the administration was bound to clash head-on with the press and find out that free and uncorrupt correspondents are a greater threat to image-making than foreign conspiracies or actual enemies of the United States.[13]

That reference to an officialdom that 'strained its remarkable intellectual resources' to maintain a certain idea and image points back to the dangers of what I have called 'elite magical thinking'. Much more recently, Dan Kahan at Yale University has found that conservatives with high scientific literacy are more prone to dismiss global warming than conservatives with low scientific literacy: the former have tended to use their skills to dismiss information they didn't like. In the context of the Vietnam War, and not for the first time or the last, a war on the enemy had turned into a war on truth, and Arendt noted that:

> the policy of lying was hardly ever aimed at the enemy ... but chiefly if not exclusively destined for domestic consumption, for propaganda at home and especially for the purpose of deceiving Congress ...[14]

Whether in the McCarthyite witch-hunts after the Korean War or later during the Vietnam War, we can see how anti-Communist sentiments and the sense that the country was threatened by fiendish enemies at home and abroad were used to re-label dissent as disloyalty or even treason.

While American democracy survived Nixon's more authoritarian instincts, the war in Vietnam was still a salutary example of a disaster 'coming home'. If part of this was a crisis of democracy, another part was the contribution that defeat in Vietnam made to the US government's emerging 'war on drugs' and 'war on crime'. These were projects that in turn created the foundation of another disaster, the mass incarceration that today sees some two million Americans in jail or prison alongside the mass disenfranchisement of some one in seven Black Americans under felony legislation.[15] As the Vietnam War receded, both the language and logistics of war were imported into the domestic sphere in the form of an escalating 'war on drugs/crime'. In the process, the racialized enemies of the Vietnam War morphed into the racialized enemies of the 'war on drugs/crime'.

Moreover, the emerging 'war on drugs/crime' appears to have served an important function in accommodating domestic backlash from the Vietnam War itself. Firstly, it was a distraction from defeat. Secondly, it served as a response to those who blamed soldiers' consumption of drugs for military defeat. Thirdly, it helped to reframe the enemy as the kind of permissive 'drug-fuelled' and 'radical' culture that Nixon in particular was linking rhetorically with protests against Vietnam.[16]

On top of all this, the Vietnam War also played a significant role in stoking extreme right-wing movements in the US, with significant involvement from Vietnam veterans and a strong narrative that centred on the 'betrayal' of American soldiers by a fickle government in Washington.[17] Right-wing extremism was subsequently fed, too, by the 1990–1 Gulf War, as was highlighted by the 1995 Oklahoma City bombing for which Gulf War veteran Timothy McVeigh was subsequently executed. McVeigh's antipathy to the US federal government had been encouraged, in part, by witnessing the mass killing of Iraqi soldiers retreating from Kuwait. Today, as noted, right-wing terrorism is responsible for the majority of deaths from terrorism within the US,[18] and the narrative that Washington cannot be trusted remains extremely influential.

In our discussion of disasters in the Global South, we noted that when wars mutate into some new form with a new (or modified) enemy, many of war's underlying and hidden *functions* – for example, maintaining social control, distracting from grievances, and facilitating exploitation – remain in place. It's important to keep this possibility in mind when wars in the Global North mutate, often at dizzying pace – for example, from the 'war on Communism' to the 'war on drugs', the 'war on crime', the 'war on terrorism' and the 'fight against illegal migration'. The causes of the relevant shifts are complicated, and certainly no individual 'war' is simply the product of another. But the underlying and undeclared functions of a war, in whichever part of the world, tend to encourage a constant reinvention of 'wars' with a constant redefinition or modification of 'the enemy'.

Today, as in the Vietnam War era, one relevant mutation has been a *turning inwards*. Even as Trump turned his back on some parts of a failing 'war on terror', he followed Nixon in importing the language of war into the domestic sphere. Again, a racialized enemy was carried over from the foreign to the domestic sphere (with Muslims now featuring in *both* definitions of the enemy). The 'enemy' category was subsequently expanded to include not only Muslims but migrants/refugees arriving from the south and at least some elements of the Black Lives Matter protests. Trump tweeted in November 2015 'Eight Syrians were just caught on the southern border trying to get into the US. ISIS maybe? I told you so. *We need a big & beautiful wall!*'.[19] Throughout his 2016 campaign, as Stephen Wertheim put it in the *New Yorker*, Trump 'jumbled "radical Islamic terrorism" and Central American migrants into a single specter of nonwhite threat'.[20] In the context of the caravan, he tweeted about 'criminals and unknown Middle Easterners' who had allegedly infiltrated the exodus. Like Nixon, Trump played up the threat of crime.

Magic and Intimidation in the 'War on Terror'

Vital elements in the process of disasters 'coming home' have been a *truth crisis* and a closely related *law crisis*. These have been intimately linked not only to each other but also to the 'war on terror' from 2001. The story illustrates once more how a 'big lie' can lead towards many kinds of violence and disaster.

Of course, the terror attacks of September 2001 were themselves an example of disaster 'coming home': firstly, terrorism 'came home' in the simple and uncontroversial sense that it took place in the United States; secondly, a case can be made that violence was 'coming home to roost' – in other words, that the terror attacks were linked to resentment at American interference in the Middle East.[21]

On top of this, the violent US-led response to these attacks was *disaster-producing* in at least four crucial respects. First, violent counter-terrorism predictably fed into terrorism itself. For one thing, Iraq *became* a major locus for terrorism (and eventually a key originator of ISIS) *as a result of* the US-led invasion. Moreover, the number of fighters in Islamist-inspired terrorist organizations around the world rose by more than three times between 2000 and 2013 – from 32,200 to over 110,000.[22] Meanwhile, the total number of recorded terrorist attacks rose from 3,329 in 2000 to 29,376 in 2015.[23] These attacks included the July 2007 bombings of the London bus and underground railway network (with attackers specifically citing the invasion of Iraq as a key grievance) as well as the attacks in Madrid in 2004 and Paris in 2015.

A second way in which the 'war on terror' has been disaster-producing is that it has served as cover in numerous countries around the world for human rights abuses in the name of 'counterterrorism'. We have discussed two striking examples of this in Syria and Sri Lanka. Insofar as racism and long-running conflicts create conditions for organizations like ISIS, this mechanism can also rebound in acts of terrorism against Western democracies. It also feeds into the movement of refugees and hence into the various humanitarian disasters that have grown up around this migration.

Third, the 'war on terror' set a dangerous precedent, whether domestically or internationally, in terms of pushing law to one side. The move beyond the law was exemplified when the criminal acts of 9/11 were met with the invasion, without specific UN authorization, of entire countries. Since Iraq had no connection to the 9/11 attacks and since the alleged 'weapons of mass destruction' in Iraq did not actually exist, the concept of being punished for something you have done was radically set aside. Some influential supporters of the 'war on terror' were very clear that they envisaged a domestic sphere in which law was to be obeyed alongside an international sphere that demanded a much 'tougher' and more pre-emptive approach.[24] For example, Robert Cooper, a prominent adviser to Tony Blair, explicitly supported the idea of pre-emptive attack and noted, 'Among ourselves, we keep the law but when we are operating in the jungle, we must also use the laws of the jungle.'[25] The focus on Saddam Hussein's bad *intentions* when it came to international terrorism was a key shift, underlining the move away from the normal legal emphasis on *punishment for what you have done* and towards a more Orwellian emphasis on *thought crimes*. This brings us back to Arendt's comment that once the link between crime and punishment has been broken, no one is safe.

A fourth way in which the 'war on terror' was disaster-producing centred on the violent defence of magical thinking and a corresponding expansion in the 'enemy' category. From the outset, the 'war on terror' was itself deeply informed by magical thinking, and, as we've seen, such fantasies tend to demand an escalating intimidation to 'make them true'.[26]

While Trump's admiration for his own intuition has been noted, it did not arise in a vacuum. US President George W. Bush explicitly and shamelessly revered his own instincts, both in relation to the 'war on terror', and more generally. In fact, Bob Woodward said of Bush, 'His instincts are almost his second religion.'[27] Treasury Secretary Paul O'Neill reported that the Bush administration was dominated by two major ideological beliefs – a belief in pre-emption and a belief in the inherent value of tax cuts. O'Neill commented, 'Ideology is a lot easier, because you don't have to know anything or search for anything. You know the answer to everything. It's not penetrable by facts. It's absolutism.'[28] Once Bush made a decision, he also expected complete faith from others.[29]

Notwithstanding the commonly expressed reverence for 'evidence-based policy' at the time, the attack on Iraq in particular was a clear example of setting aside science and evidence, with a strong accompanying dose of intimidation. UN chief weapons inspector Hans Blix said the Bush administration had leant on his inspectors to produce more damning language in their reports,[30] while MI6 Chief Sir Richard Dearlove famously told a Downing Street meeting in July 2002 that in the US 'the intelligence and facts were being fixed around the policy'.[31] When irrationality was enthusiastically embraced, the trappings of 'science' – from satellite pictures, 'secret intelligence', 'precision' weapons, and expertise in 'winning hearts and minds' – offered a great deal of phony reassurance. Meanwhile, the insistence by Bush and his team that the Iraq War would not cost anything represented another significant element of magical thinking. In the event, by mid-2005 the Iraq War had already cost about $300 billion (over and above the annual $400 billion Pentagon budget), plus tens of billions for the botched reconstruction. Hugely profitable for companies close to the Bush administration,[32] the war still had to be paid for.

Significantly, the 'war on terror' was not just a precedent for aggressive magical thinking in the US domestic arena but also part of what Trump was pushing *against*. He was critical of the Iraq War in his 2016 campaign, linking the money it had absorbed to the neglect of Americans back home.

As for the attack on Iraq itself, the flight from evidence was underlined by the many similarities between the invasion and a *witch-hunt*: the demand that Saddam confess to possession of weapons of mass destruction he did not have; the focus on Saddam's presumed evil intentions; the targeting of Iraq based on its weakness and inability to strike back; and the magical belief that removing one individual would fix the problem. When interventions manifestly did not solve the problem of terrorism but actually *increased* the number of global terrorist attacks as well as the violence within Iraq, US policy hawks suggested that *more targets should be found*. Attacking Afghanistan morphed into attacking Iraq and deposing Saddam morphed into a never-ending hunt for individual terrorists and diverse terrorist groups within Iraq and the Middle East more generally, and the growing problems in occupied Iraq in turn fed into renewed determination to make a 'success' of Afghanistan. Since the witch-hunt was not working, more witches had to be found.

Especially neglected in Iraq and Afghanistan was the lesson that it is extremely difficult to remake societies by force. Edward Said observed in 2003: 'It is quite common to hear high officials in Washington and elsewhere speak of changing the map of the Middle East, as if ancient societies and myriad peoples can be shaken up like so many peanuts in a jar.'[33]

This was magical thinking that went deep into the heart of the American and the British establishment, a kind of imperialist mindset that spared neither major political party within these well-established democracies. When 9/11 saw UK Prime Minister Blair declaring, 'Let us re-order this world around us', new life was being breathed into an old imperial dream. The Iraq invasion also involved an assumption that *enemies and obstacles would magically melt away* as history took its predictable course. A lot of hopes were pinned on getting rid of Saddam Hussein himself, but it turned out that there was more to the Ba'athist state than Saddam and that key players stubbornly refused to disappear from history. In particular, when Saddam's army was disbanded *en masse* in Iraq, many of its members resolutely declined to melt away and went on to form the basis for Al Qaeda in Iraq and, to a significant extent, ISIS.[34]

Blair's own manipulations of the 'enemy' category were evident when he lumped opponents of 'modernity' into the same category as Islamist terrorists, invoking for example 'the age-old battle between progress and reaction, between those who embrace the modern world and those who reject its existence'.[35] While it's true that Blair's domestic policies made a positive difference to the UK (for example, in a substantial reduction of child poverty), his ideology also displayed a kind of *fetishizing* of modernity that magicked away opposition and stigmatized those who disagreed.

When we think about disasters coming home, it is instructive to put these assumptions alongside the assumption that *domestic* opposition will also melt away. Blair was a particularly self-conscious 'moderate' – and this stance had done a great deal to revive the Labour Party's electoral fortunes. But a major downside of this stance was that those whose views differed sharply were implicitly (and sometimes explicitly) positioned as 'extremists' – notably as reactionary forces who stood in the way of modernization and globalization. The ultimate representative of these forces (for Blair as he looked outwards) was the terrorist. But Blair was also looking inwards and sending an intimidating message to opponents – including critics of his wars – at home.

A wider overconfidence also seems to have contributed to the anger of those overlooked. For almost two decades following the end of the Cold War, the triumph of liberalism, capitalism, peace and democracy was widely held to be *inevitable*. In Blair's formulation (and he was far from alone in this), this relentless process implied the irrelevance, invisibility and eventual disappearance of those who thought otherwise.[36] But there were crucial problems here. As noted, if all decent and reasonable people agreed on a particular path, it followed logically that anyone who did not agree was *neither decent nor reasonable*. Further, the idea that those who 'rejected the modern world' were *disappearing from history* was itself a kind of provocation.[37] With the rise of the UK's far right and the rise of the UK Independence Party (and with the rise of Trump too), it became increasingly clear that many of the 'disappearing' (including those deemed superfluous by globalization) were rather keen to put themselves on the map once more. We have noted the allure of what Arendt called 'access to history', and this allure – perhaps the simple desire to say 'we are still here!' – will surely always be greater among those who have been written out of the script and written out of history. Consensus politics, as Belgian political theorist Chantal Mouffe predicted in 2005, could easily shade into a dangerous *abolition of politics* that sowed the seeds for more virulent, and even violent, disagreements. Mouffe suggested that this emerging politics would be built in large part around the reassertion of ethnic identity and the loud expression of suppressed passions – and to a large extent she was right.

Crucially, once a magical path had been chosen, a floundering 'war on terror' seemed to 'require' a progressive deepening of self-delusion if it was to be sustained – along with a definition of the enemy that conveniently expanded so as to include the many critics of this failing endeavour.[38] Much of the logic here was spelled out in the aftermath of September 11 in President George W. Bush's notorious and threatening observation: 'Either you are with us, or you are with the terrorists.'[39] In the UK, BBC news director Richard Sambrook said, 'It is our firm view that No. 10 [the Prime Minister's office in Downing Street] tried to intimidate the BBC with its reporting of events leading up to the [Iraq] war and during the course of the war itself.'[40]

We have stressed that when magical thinking runs up against reality, the denigration of experts tends to deepen and the retreat into delusion may easily intensify. In his May 2018 *New Yorker* piece on governance under Trump, Evan Osnos compared the growing sense of unreality in government circles under Trump with Osnos's personal experience of a growing sense of unreality in Iraq from 2003. More specifically, the writer recalled that Baghdad's Green Zone (from which the US-led occupation was directed) became a place where US officials could insulate themselves not only from the chaos and violence of Iraq but also from the gathering chorus of information about how badly the occupation was going. Inside the Green Zone, Osnos recalled:

> The philosophy of governance – defined by loyalty, hostile to expertise, and comfortable with lies – created a disaster, even as its adherents extolled American values. Those who recognized the self-delusion and incompetence began referring to the Green Zone as the Emerald City.[41]

Coming back to the Trump administration at the end of his article, Osnos noted:

> Midway through its second year, Trump's White House is at war within and without, racing to banish the 'disloyals' and to beat back threatening information. Bit by bit, the White House is becoming Trump's Emerald City; isolated, fortified against nonbelievers, entranced by its mythmaker, and constantly vulnerable to the risks of revelation.[42]

Following profound military setbacks in Afghanistan, Iraq and Libya and a growing sense that the 'external enemy' could not be realistically taken on and beaten, there was also a growing focus on the *internal* enemy. As the reality of a floundering 'war on terror' began to dawn, an emphasis on physically shutting out immigrants gained traction. Particularly as Trump came to prominence, there was a shift of emphasis from the 'problem' of Muslims abroad to the 'problem' of Muslims coming to – or already inside – the United States, with those coming across the US's southern border frequently amalgamated (as we've seen) into this flexible threat.

Importantly, in its intensifying intimidation of certain kinds of dissidents and 'internal enemies', the US government was able to draw on a surveillance apparatus that had been significantly strengthened in the context of the evolving 'war on terror', so that this apparatus too could be said to be 'coming home'. Again, this mirrored in certain respects the tendency at the end of the Vietnam War to redirect the intelligence apparatus towards *internal* enemies.

In the UK, the government's 'Prevent' initiative was ostensibly aimed at preventing terrorism but often ended up stirring tensions via ethnic/religious profiling, while eroding free speech through positioning 'extreme' views as a threat.[43] In their important 2011 report, Choudhury and Fenwick found that Prevent had alienated many Muslims in the UK through stop-and-search and through stigmatizing them as potential terrorists. They also found that criticism of UK foreign policy or of the mistreatment of Palestinians was often seen by British Muslims as attracting unwelcome attention from the British police.[44] When it came to the 'war on terror', a key truth was that this overambitious and violent project was fuelling grievances and anger in targeted countries and well beyond. Yet this truth became *unsayable* by British Muslims (many of whom had relatives in these targeted countries and were in a good position to know). Meanwhile, beliefs classified as extremist came to include the belief that Muslims 'cannot legitimately and/or effectively participate in our democratic society'.[45] So, logically, the view that democratic freedoms and opportunities were being weakened by counterterrorism policies could *itself* classify you as an extremist. Adding to the dangers here was an official focus on ideas and intentions rather than on *what people had actually done*, a move that mirrored the drift from law to 'thought crimes' that had already been manifest in the outwardly directed 'war on terror'.

Meanwhile, UK citizens were routinely encouraged to inform on each other – a practice one might associate with the Stasi in East Germany or the KGB in the former Soviet Union rather than with a Western democracy. Children as young as four were being referred to Prevent by teachers, and everyday life was said to demand constant vigilance, so that while waiting (say) for a flu vaccination in the chemist's, a notice would advise 'It's probably nothing, but ... If you have any concerns or wish to speak to someone, contact the Celesio UK Prevent Team safeguarding against radicalism.' We should note here that this is not 'safeguarding against terrorism' but 'safeguarding against radicalism.' Emphasizing internal and as well as external intimidation, Deepa Kumar introduced the concept of 'terrorcraft', noting in 2020:

> Terrorcraft as ideology is reinforced through rituals such as the 'see something, say something' campaign in its ubiquitous staging in public spaces and through 24/7 news media coverage of every attack carried out on western targets ... [Yet] the number of deaths in the US due to Jihadi terrorism after 9/11 is 107, a figure that is dwarfed by gun deaths during that same period or the hundreds of thousands killed in the US's war on terror.[46]

Importantly, the evolution of the 'internal enemy' did not stop there. Partly to avoid explicit focus only on Muslims (but also convenient when it comes to suppressing dissent more widely), there was a growing concern with *extremism in general*. In the context of the 'war on terror' and the July 2005 terror attacks in London, the UK government's claim to be targeting extremists *of all kinds* had grave implications for freedom of speech. Faced with the obvious difficulty of saying who *were* the extremists, the government's definition turned on those who did not subscribe to 'fundamental British values'.[47] But this immediately threw up the problem of who got to define these values, as well as pushing the policy framework and the defence of freedom into a mode that was explicitly nationalist as well as profoundly intrusive.

Again, we see the dangers in expanding the category of the 'enemy'. Significantly, those placed into the category of 'extremist', and therefore on the margins of the law's protection, came to include those protesting against inequality (Occupy London)[48] and those protesting climate change (Extinction Rebellion).[49] Extinction Rebellion was sometimes tarred with the brush of 'terrorism' in UK government documents,[50] and was subject to a judicial crackdown that forms just one part of a more general tendency to criminalize climate protest in countries as diverse as India, the Philippines, Mexico and the United States.[51] In the US, Pennsylvania's Office of Homeland Security hired a private contractor to gather intelligence on anti-fracking groups.[52]

In the UK, the Truss government was accusing environmental groups of being part of an 'anti-growth coalition'. The reckless expansions in the 'enemy' that have been associated with counterterrorism and anti-environmentalism should be set alongside those that accompanied the 'Brexit' process, where even judges weighing the relevant law were labelled in the press as 'enemies of the people'. Under the provisions of the Police, Crime, Sentencing and Courts Act, we are now seeing major restrictions on peaceful protest that causes 'disruption' or 'public nuisance' (with extensive powers for the Home Office to define these concepts in practice).[53] And as we have seen many times in the Global South, nothing polices a particular definition of an emergency or enemy quite so effectively as the possibility of expanding the 'enemy' category so as to include those who question these definitions.

Conclusion

The 'war on terror' helped to lay down conditions in which law and truth could be rather systematically set aside. Both the 'war on terror' *and* Trump reflected a wider tendency, even and perhaps *especially* among elites, to lurch into a world of magical thinking and then defend it with violence. This goes back to Vietnam and beyond, as Arendt and Hofstadter have shown in their different ways. Certainly, the 'war on terror' was a particularly extreme flight into a fantasy world, a journey from which it has proven difficult to return. A particular construction of the enemy – and the associated 'alternative realities' – encouraged a shift in the focus of violence towards targets *at home*; at the same time, preserving omnipotence in the face of defeat encouraged narratives of betrayal and a turning inwards of aggression. Under Trump, the assumption of omnipotence was manifest in the idea that he personally would always win – not least in presidential elections. When Trump lost in 2020 and quickly invoked the narrative of betrayal by various parties including the media and even fellow Republicans, it was an exceptionally dangerous moment in American history. But Trump was also following a long tradition of attempting to preserve omnipotence in the face of defeat – and we suggested in Chapter 7 that modern-day Democrats have hardly been immune. Trump's version of conspiracy theory, like many others before, was not just an outbreak of madness; it also followed logically from *the assumption of always winning*, an assumption that inevitably crashes at some point into the rocks of reality. Meanwhile, millions of Americans have been promised a 'win' in wealth and life that has not, in the end, arrived.[54] In this context, Trump perhaps understood better than anyone how widespread has been the need to escape from shame to blame, a reflex that has always been his personal habit and inclination. He constructed a story that was magical in crucial respects but which felt true and felt exhilarating to millions of people, and he set about defending this story with a widening array of accusations. Whether under Trump or in numerous wars that preceded him, this is how the flight into fantasy does much of its damage.

9

Action as Propaganda

We have suggested that magical thinking infuses the current disaster-producing system. Part of the problem is that magical thinking is inherently bad at solving real-life problems. Significant additional problems arise, as we've seen, from the *defence* of magical thinking – sometimes the *violent* defence. At the same time, the intimidation of critics may prove to be an unreliable way of sustaining lies and delusions. Bullying may begin to look like desperation; and in a democracy, if you expand the 'enemy' category *too far*, you will lose your majority.[1]

Why is it, then, that magical and disaster-creating policies are often so persistent, whether these are pushed by democratic or authoritarian leaders? Part of the answer is the enduring allure of certainty and responsibility avoidance, as we saw in Chapter 7. People will not readily let go of delusions, particularly if some valued aspect of their identity is attached to the relevant delusion. Whether in politics or consumer capitalism, the impulse to fix on some kind of magical solution is one that can attach itself to a range of policies or objects, many of them repackaged from earlier versions – the 'new and improved' version of the 'war on terror' under President Obama, for example, now with added drones. Since hope springs eternal (and hope, for Arendt, was often a dangerous emotion), there is generally some new 'fix' that can be packaged and sold.

Another part of the explanation for the persistence of policies that are not working, as we've seen many times in the Global South, lies in the practical benefits that these polices are conferring or promising to confer, benefits that tend to accrue disproportionately to those who are shaping these policies while the costs fall on others.

We also need to understand how disaster-producing policies are *legitimized*, and here it's helpful to look more closely at Arendt's concept of 'action as propaganda'. We've noted Arendt's view that action, especially violent action, often serves as a more effective form of propaganda than mere words or images. More specifically, violence could help to generate a significant degree of plausibility for big lies and alternative realities. Arendt noted that 'action as propaganda' was 'foolproof against arguments based on a reality which the [totalitarian] movements promised to change'.[2] So, while conventional propaganda simply presented a distorted impression of reality, 'action as propaganda' worked through shaping the world in such a way that reality began to conform to the relevant delusions. Arendt observed that 'Once the [totalitarian] movements have come to power, they proceed to change reality in accordance with their ideological claims.'[3] In this way, outrageous lies could be made to seem more plausible as time went by. Arendt also suggested that central fictions or big lies could be used to build up 'even under nontotalitarian circumstances a society whose members act and react according to the rules of a fictitious world'.[4]

A supplementary part of Arendt's explanation of the power of 'action as propaganda' was her observation that Nazism's ability to attract believers collapsed almost overnight when military defeat in 1945 and ejection from power meant that Nazism could no longer back up its lies with 'impressive' actions that made the Nazis seem to be in command of history.[5]

Although Arendt developed the concept of 'action as propaganda' as part of her analysis of totalitarian regimes in Germany and the Soviet Union in particular, it's a concept that turns out to be disturbingly relevant in the context of today's Western democracies and more specifically in the context of the various crises, whether real or hyped-up or both, that these democracies are confronting, manipulating and sometimes creating. Of course, democracies do not generally have the power to shape reality in quite the 'total' way that a totalitarian regime does. But democratic politicians can still push reality more into line with their claims, ideas and predictions. The concept of 'action as propaganda' can be particularly helpful in understanding why blowback, instead of leading to policy change, often reinforces the dangerous and disaster-producing policies that led to blowback in the first place. Such processes help to explain why even democratic systems do not necessarily prevent or correct disasters, but may tolerate or actively feed on them.

Arendt deployed the concept of 'action as propaganda' to help explain how the big lie of the-Jews-as-existential-threat, along with many other lies, could become sufficiently plausible to allow something on the scale of the Holocaust to take place. As part of her analysis, she stressed that the fictional world constructed by the Nazis became a 'reality' that most people in Germany were ready to accept. An important factor here was the way the Nazis acted *as if* the alleged 'laws of history' were true.

The expansion of the 'enemy' category that we discussed in Chapter 7 could perhaps be seen as a form of 'action as propaganda'. After all, targeting an ever-wider group of people sends a powerful practical message that no one is safe and that official truths or untruths cannot sensibly be challenged. But this process of intimidation is in many ways a relatively old technique of authoritarian government, and Arendt wanted to highlight something newer and even more terrifying: the use of violent action *to bring reality into line with outrageous propaganda*.

Five Types

Though Arendt herself doesn't set things out in this way, five types of 'action as propaganda' can be distilled from her writing and each turns out to have played a significant role in legitimizing the *current* disaster-producing system.

Reproducing the enemy

The first type of 'action as propaganda' centres on *reproducing the enemy*. Since emergency politics tends to thrive on enemies, reproducing them may sometimes, paradoxically, be more of a solution than a problem. Arendt observed that 'Practically speaking, the totalitarian ruler proceeds like a man who persistently insults another man until everybody knows that the latter is his enemy, so that he can, with some plausibility, go and kill him in self-defence.'[6] Eliminating the Jews was sometimes defended by the Nazis on the grounds that the Jews 'were bent on wiping us out' as Himmler put it.[7] Fear of revenge was part of this, so that violence was in a sense constructing its own bogus 'legitimacy' by creating the presumption of impending revenge and hence the 'necessity' of preventing the revenge through mass killing.[8] (This perverse logic is certainly not confined to the Holocaust, and fear of revenge also fed into extreme brutality in Rwanda and Cambodia, for example.)[9] Arendt suggested that, by generating hostility, violence could also generate dubious 'legitimacy' for military expansion: '... by forcing the Jews into uncompromising hostility against them, the Nazis had created the pretext for taking a passionate interest in all nations' domestic policies'.[10]

Today, action appears to be serving as a powerful form of propaganda when it reproduces enemies such as 'the terrorist' or 'the human smuggler' in ways that legitimize complex (and profitable) systems of repression.

The most startling contemporary manifestation of reproducing the enemy is probably the 'war on terror'. In the wake of 9/11, Iraq was said by President Bush to be a source of terrorism. It became a major centre of terrorist activity *as a result of* the US-led invasion. More generally, the terrorist has been reproduced in a highly predictable manner, and this has had the effect of escalating the sense of threat. In turn, this legitimizes expensive counter-terror operations and huge military spending (most notably in the US but also in many other Western democracies) as well as shoring up a range of repressive governments that claim to be waging a 'war on terror'. A variety of 'cooperating' governments have *themselves* engaged in violence that reproduces grievances and, at the extreme, terrorism, while advertising their cooperation in ways that bring international aid and local impunity. We may say, then, that the figure of 'the terrorist' has for some time served as a focal point for an elaborate and evolving system of profit and repression based around the ostensible attempt to eliminate the terrorist – a useful enemy.

Today, 'enemies' are also being routinely reproduced in the so-called 'fight against illegal migration', and notable here is the much reviled 'human smuggler'. Part of the mechanism is that tighter borders have tended to make smugglers more 'essential' for people trying to move. Another mechanism is that tighter borders boost incentives for smugglers by raising prices. Yet, at the same time, the role of smugglers has also been cited as justification for the further tightening of borders. Meanwhile, sealed borders also systematically produce the 'illegal immigrants' who themselves are frequently demonized by populist politicians who point to such 'illegality' as necessitating tougher restrictions,[11] a self-reinforcing system that is brilliantly analysed by Ruben Andersson in his book *Illegality Inc.* Yet very often, as noted, there is no other way to claim asylum than to enter a country in a way that is deemed to be 'illegal'.

To legitimize the systems of suffering that are emerging around migration (including the widespread denial of asylum, the forcible returns, the inhuman conditions and the practice of allowing people to die), it becomes convenient to focus on the allegedly 'humanitarian' task of *preventing dangerous journeys*. Alongside this there has frequently been a righteous condemnation of those who are seen as facilitating these journeys. In these circumstances, the 'human smuggler' actually plays a key role in legitimizing an elaborate system of profit and repression. Indeed, this demon figure has stepped conveniently into the paradigm of 'useful enemy' already inhabited by 'the terrorist'.

And just as the 'terrorist sympathizer' becomes a category rather central to controlling the behaviour, speech and thought of potential critics of a 'war on terror', so too the accusation that people are 'complicit with human smugglers' has become a pivotal accusation on the part of those who are seeking to control the behaviour, speech and thought of potential critics of a heavily securitized and exclusionary approach to the movements of migrants/refugees. Aid agencies have found themselves in the 'front line' of such criticisms in both contexts – and since migrants are sometimes accused of 'bringing in terrorism', these contexts may also overlap considerably.

Creating inhuman conditions

A second main form of action as propaganda highlighted by Arendt (and again of relevance in today's 'migration crisis') centres on the *creation of inhumane conditions* and then the implementation of drastic 'solutions' for these conditions, 'solutions' that typically lead to even more inhumane conditions. Such a process may contribute powerfully to the impression that the victims are less than human.

The key historical example that Arendt gave here was the Nazis' action in confining Jews to insanitary ghettos and eventually to the concentration camps. These confinements helped to produce the diseases, and even sometimes an appearance of 'inhumanity', that Nazi propaganda had long sought to link to being Jewish. Moreover, the public-health crisis centring on the ghettos served both as a reason and an excuse for shifting from the policy of ghettoization to the policy of mass murder in concentration camps.[12] Measures like dressing people alike and assigning them numbers in concentration camps further dehumanized them, while according to the SS newspaper *Schwarze Korps* one of the advantages of an enforced mass Jewish emigration was that it would convince recipient nations that the Jews were 'scum' and 'unidentifiable beggars' (in line with the vicious denunciations in Nazi propaganda).[13]

Of course, there are always dangers in comparing present-day abuses with the extreme horrors of the Holocaust, as noted. But again it seems much more dangerous to *ignore* the past. When I was in Calais in 2016, I was struck by the relevance of Arendt's 'action as propaganda' and part of it was the practice of *making people resemble what you (erroneously) say they are*. Right-wing populism's instrumentalization of suffering in Calais depended on a number of stereotypes about the migrants – a highly contentious, contradictory and politicized script in which migrants were some combination of *violent*, *terrorists*, *disease-ridden*, *desperate*, *crazy*, *lazy*, *'desperate for our jobs'* and *driven by the lure of 'benefits'*. A key thing that went missing in most accounts was that most of the problems presented as emanating from the migrants could actually be traced to the way they were treated and mis-treated. For example, tight UK border controls in France had created the informal and insanitary migrant settlements around Calais and these settlements were then used to underline the necessity of strong controls. Later, when French police destroyed part of the camp in February–March 2016, this exacerbated the overcrowding and fuelled tensions, disease and desperation in the camp. In general, poor conditions associated with mistreatment helped to stoke a sense of threat that played well to audiences that were being whipped up into fear and indignation. As often happens, even critics of the abuses found themselves using words that risked dehumanizing people. Examples included the 'jungle' label (which was also widely used by camp residents) and references to the 'herding' or 'hounding' of migrants/refugees by the police.

In the camp itself, migrant/refugee and volunteer initiatives created plenty of positive things – mosques and churches, art and language lessons, restaurants and shops. These were elements, in fact, of an improvised city, and British jazz singer Ian Shaw became well known in the camp not just for his singing but for helping a number of businesses. The ramshackle restaurants played an important role in the social life of the camp as well as helping to plug the shortfalls in free food distributions as migrant numbers rose. But, while enterprise and resilience are qualities that are routinely lauded in the aid world, these traits were frequently *punished* in Calais. There were repeated police attacks on the elements of *civilization* or *city* that the migrants/refugees were seeking to build, with the inhabitants repeatedly reduced by the police to conditions that were closer to what Agamben called 'bare life' – essentially a condition of pure need and pure desperation where people lack the ability to shape their own lives. In July 2016 we witnessed a series of large-scale police raids on shops and restaurants, with police citing violations of 'health and safety'.

In October 2016, inhuman conditions were used as justification for the total destruction of the camp, with the UK and French governments and even UNHCR now citing health and safety. Revealingly, some of the destruction was also framed as 'concern for the environment' and French officials went so far as to announce that the 'jungle' camp site was to become part of an area of 'ornithological and ecological excellence'.[14] In other words, it would be good for the birds. In the event, the destruction of the whole camp in 2016 led to *worse* conditions for migrants who were now harder to help. Often they were woken not by birdsong but by the police, whose Sisyphean task of endlessly harassing the migrants extended through the night.

More widely, we may notice that so-called 'blighted' neighbourhoods from Detroit to hurricane-hit New Orleans to the 'jungle' camp in Calais have been earmarked for destruction in the name of eradicating the 'scandal' of poor conditions. In this sense, poverty creates the conditions that are said to justify the ejection of the poor, a manoeuvre that is familiar from the destruction of slums in many parts of the world. But, while areas may sometimes be 'improved' or made to look better or 'gentrified', the fate of those living in those areas is a different matter.

All this is not to say that there was an evil plan in relation to Calais or other struggling areas, a plan on the lines of 'Let's make some inhuman conditions and then we can portray the inhabitants as inhuman!' But these *systems of suffering*, as they evolve, do acquire a complicated set of functions. Neglect becomes functional, while violence is legitimized by the conditions that violence helps to generate.

Blaming the victim

A third aspect of 'action as propaganda' (quite closely related to the second) is *using violence to imply that the victims are guilty*, on the basis that punishment implies a crime. In a key statement, Arendt observed that in the context of the Nazi Holocaust 'Common sense reacted to the horrors of Buchenwald and Auschwitz with the plausible argument: "What crime must these people have committed that such things were done to them!"'[15] On somewhat similar lines, Arendt noted that the existence of a secret police could easily mislead observers 'into thinking there is some secret resistance'.[16] Here, one might also think of the popular saying that 'there is no smoke without fire'. In the Global South, tarring innocent civilians with the brush of 'rebel sympathizer' has been a common way of justifying abuse, and one way of asserting that such sympathy-with-rebels exists has been precisely by physically attacking people. More generally, victim-blaming has often been rather central to legitimizing many human-made disasters, as we have seen in the case of Sudan's Darfur region, for example.

In the diverse 'migration crises' affecting and preoccupying Western democracies, heavily securitized responses have served to underline the seriousness of the alleged threat. In Calais, actions to combat the 'migrant threat' tended only to underline fears around the migrants/refugees. At one point when we were there in 2016, fully twenty police-vans were lined up on the west side of the camp, along with eight police cars. Police with shields and helmets came at the camp from both sides, as if in a military operation. Even small details told their own story: plastic covers on police boots announced that the police did not wish to be contaminated by the squalor. In general, police 'overkill' served to dramatize the alleged 'threat' from the migrants, and this was an important element in the theatrical repertoire of 'action as propaganda'.

Significantly, many of the migrants/refugees in Calais expressed the feeling that they were being punished without having committed a crime. Therapists Charlotte Burck and Gillian Hughes noted the prevalence of 'We are human too' slogans in the jungle camp, and observed, 'It was a continual challenge to counter the internalization of negative identities ... In the current migration crisis, seeking asylum has become framed as a crime, not a right.'[17]

The assumption that there is no smoke without fire and no punishment without crime inevitably hovers over other situations of confinement and has frequently been manifest in other locations – as with Lampedusa in Italy, islands in Greece, and innumerable detention centres for asylum-seekers around the world. *If these people have not committed a crime and are not a threat, then why are they being confined in such a manner?* Depending largely on one's attitude to authority, that sentence can be read either as a well-meaning plea for the release of those confined or as endorsement of their confinement on the grounds that they must indeed have done something wrong. Across the Atlantic, and just days before the 2018 Congressional mid-term elections, Trump ordered the dispatch of 5,200 troops to confront the exhausted caravan of refugees heading towards the US from Mexico (and later said he'd send as many as 15,000).[18] Again, from one point of view, there was no better 'demonstration' of the severity of the threat than the size and nature of the forces that were sent to confront it.

Often fuelling perverse distributions of blame is something called 'just world thinking'. This, broadly, is the view that there must be a good reason for violence, often linked to deference to authority and the fear that violence might be indiscriminate.[19] The subtext of such 'just world thinking' is often that 'since they *deserved* to suffer, I will be safe'. In one 2018 BBC documentary, a woman of Mexican origin was asked if she did not feel disturbed by Trump's talk of Mexican rapists and criminals, and she replied that she did not have to worry because Trump was only going after the 'bad hombres'.[20] Meanwhile, for those who are sufficiently scared or suggestible or who simply have a sufficient degree of deference towards the relevant government authorities, aggressive measures like Trump's banning of immigrants from seven Muslim-majority countries or various kinds of 'walling off' may serve as their own propaganda, so that the best argument for the existence of criminal intent among Muslims or Mexicans or others who are portrayed as 'threats' and 'outsiders' may be the ban or the wall itself. Given such measures and given the frequency with which asylum-seekers are called 'illegal immigrants', it will not be very difficult to convince at least some of your audience that they are indeed criminals.

More generally, the far right can (as noted) point to problems profoundly shaped by neoliberal policies (mass incarceration, the alleged non-assimilation of minority groups and so on) and claim that this is a cultural problem or something intrinsic to the nature of certain ethnic or racial groups.[21]

Even when it came to the disaster of the 2007–8 financial crisis, victim-blaming proved to be an important part of how suffering was legitimized, with 'action as propaganda' once more playing a destructive role. We know that many of those responsible for the 2007–8 financial crisis were protected and even rewarded, notably via government bailouts for the banks and, meanwhile, long-lasting programmes of austerity hit several poorer countries hard (including Greece) as well as inflicting suffering on poorer people within a wide range of countries. Austerity programmes in Greece and elsewhere also served greatly to erode the sovereignty of national governments themselves, including not just how much governments could spend but also what they could spend their money *on*.[22] Again, such sanctions are not only a humiliation and a route to impoverishment; they may easily be seen as implying the existence of some fundamental 'crime' or 'sin' among those who are being 'punished' in such drastic ways. In the case of Greece in particular, the implied guilt of imposed austerity was compounded by a great deal of rhetoric about Greek irresponsibility, laziness, and so on. Even the xenophobia and nationalism that were boosted by mass hardship and the rough international treatment of Greece could then be used to stigmatize the Greeks as backward and in need of rescuing or reforming by more enlightened Europeans.

Undermining the idea of human rights

In today's overlapping disasters, a fourth important element of 'action as propaganda' has been the process of *trampling on human rights and thereby 'demonstrating' that they do not exist*. Arendt argued that bold and abusive action could be used by totalitarian rulers to 'reveal' the irrelevance of humanitarian ideals. She emphasized that human rights may not appear to be real if they are not in practice respected. She also stressed that without a political authority to enforce human rights (usually a national government), the human rights that are assumed and proclaimed to exist may count for little or nothing. Hence, in part, her notion of 'the right to have rights'.

The faltering international commitment to asylum in the 1920s, 1930s and 1940s was a major concern of Arendt's, as noted, and she observed in *The Origins of Totalitarianism*:

> The first great damage done to nation-states as a result of the arrival of hundreds of thousands of stateless people was that the right of asylum, the only right that had ever figured as a symbol of the Rights of Man in the sphere of international relations, was being abolished.[23]

Many governments throughout Europe and in the US were punishing would-be refugees not for any crime that they had committed but simply for being stateless, and Arendt saw this as a massive blow to the clear link between crime and punishment that national and international law demands or should demand. For those (like the Nazis) who wished to insist that there was no such thing as human rights, there was perhaps no better propaganda than ruthlessly to remove or ignore them. This also brought the 'bonus', from the point of view of Nazi propagandists, of exposing what they said (in many ways, accurately) was the hypocrisy of Western democratic countries who claimed to care about the Jews. In a key passage, Arendt referred to the exodus of people from Nazi rule and noted:

> the incredible plight of an ever-growing group of innocent people was like a practical demonstration of the totalitarian movements' cynical claims that no such thing as inalienable human rights existed and that the affirmations of democracies to the contrary were mere prejudice, hypocrisy, and cowardice in the face of the cruel majesty of a new world. The very phrase 'human rights' became for all concerned – victims, persecutors, and onlookers alike – the evidence of hopeless idealism or fumbling feeble-minded hypocrisy.[24]

Hitler himself suggested that the project of expelling the Jews had revealed democratic nations' lack of belief in their own ideas about human rights, notably the right to asylum. He mocked Western democracies for turning their backs on the very same Jewish people that they claimed to be so 'precious'.[25]

The current assault on asylum, like the pre-emptive attack on Iraq without evidence of a connection to 9/11, represents a major blow to the idea of human rights. Where rights are allowed to wither on the vine, what reason is there to imagine that these rights actually exist?

Totalitarianism took the de-linking of crime and punishment to a catastrophic extreme. It moved away from a long-established authoritarian determination to punish political opponents and towards a more 'radical' stance in which certain people were to be punished simply *for being* – or *for being who they were*. Naturally, the category of those-who-could-be-punished-without-a-crime could expand with extreme rapidity since clearly no crimes were necessary to 'allow' or 'justify' this expansion. Eventually, the targeted group expanded even to the German people as a whole, whose only crime (from the Nazis' point of view) was to have lost the war. When the Allies advanced towards Berlin in 1945, some Nazi leaders began to say it was necessary to 'prepare an easy death' for the defeated German people.

Today it seems strikingly clear that bold and abusive actions can build 'charismatic' authority while also sometimes underlining a sense of emergency. Arendt helps us to see that such actions may also erode the impression that human rights *actually exist*. Indeed, the infringement of democratic safeguards may imply that what we thought were rights were actually a mirage or something that was in effect granted conditionally by those who have now (perhaps because of an emergency) changed their minds.[26] Safeguards like the independence of the press or the ability of judges and courts to block emergency legislation may be portrayed as 'elite' attempts to block 'public opinion' or 'the will of the people', a pretty standard part of the armoury of right-wing populism. At the extreme, the relevance of these safeguards may be 'proven', through confident action, to be a thing of the past. On top of this, a key 'power play' today and a key means of selling officially endorsed interpretations of today's overlapping crises has been the use of the 'rightless' as an example of what might happen to *others*. This manoeuvre is perhaps clearest and most dangerous when condemnation is turned towards those who speak for, or assist, the rightless. Meanwhile, big lies not only confuse people but may even disrupt the idea of a truth that exists independently of those who believe in different values or positions. Without a belief in such a shared 'truth', enforcing rights is going to be difficult; believing that these rights exist may also be difficult.

Sometimes the threat to the concept of rights comes in a very 'moderate' guise. In the UK, Tony Blair suggested in 1996 that 'For every right we enjoy, we owe responsibilities',[27] while his Home Office Minister Mike O'Brien stated: 'Rights flow from duties, not the other way.'[28] This kind of language was part of New Labour's 'middle way' and its self-conscious 'moderation'. But the implications were potentially very extreme. In the US at around this time, Bill Clinton had his own versions of making rights conditional, as when welfare was cut and explicitly linked to 'character'.[29] But if rights are going to be linked to responsibilities, who gives themselves the power to specify these responsibilities? What if the responsibilities (for whatever reason) are not being met? Rights that are made conditional in this way are not actually rights at all. And why should rights be assumed to be in the power of the government when the main point of rights, historically, was to limit arbitrary government?[30] Significantly, it has often been undemocratic governments (like the old Soviet regime) who have most explicitly linked rights to duties[31] and it's noticeable that the current Orbán government, with its distinctly anti-democratic tendencies, has emphasized this link. Today in the UK a growing emphasis on removing people's citizenship underlines the impression that rights are *conditional*; again this pushes towards a situation in which rights are not actually rights.

Making predictions come true

Arendt highlighted a fifth important element of 'action as propaganda'. This was using violent action *to make your predictions come true* and to show that you have somehow been 'vindicated' by history and by your own 'success'. Arendt argued that totalitarianism was often less concerned with causal processes than with prophesy and its fulfilment, and she showed that totalitarian demagogues rely heavily not only on projecting certainty but also on displaying their powers of prophesy. Arendt put this quite strongly, observing that 'Mass leaders in power have one concern which overrules all utilitarian considerations: to make their predictions come true.'[32] Meanwhile, the demagogue's 'principal quality is that he "was always right and will always be right."'[33] Crucially, demagogues could often *make* their predictions come true through violent actions and through inflammatory statements (including predictions about the 'inevitability' of certain kinds of violence).

In more recent times, the 'war on terror' has illustrated how bold and abusive action can 'confirm' the prediction that old institutions and laws will no longer provide protection. One 'confirmation' was provided by the conspicuous de-linking of crime and punishment that came with attacking Iraq in response to 9/11. Related to this was the immediate discrediting of international law and international institutions, which were sometimes openly disparaged. In the run-up to the 2003 US-led invasion of Iraq, for example, prominent American neo-conservative Richard Perle argued that the US should reject international law if this law was not changed to permit the actions Washington wanted to take. This was certainly an interesting conception of law and, just after the invasion began, Perle elaborated his position: 'As we sift through the debris of the war to liberate Iraq, it will be important to preserve, the better to understand, the intellectual wreckage of the liberal conceit of safety through international law administered by international institutions.'[34] The idea was that the US would quite literally drive a tank through the notion that the UN and international law were relevant and could keep people safe. That takes us back to Arendt's observation in the face of large-scale violence Nazi violence and mass exodus: 'The very phrase "human rights" became for all concerned – victims, persecutors, and onlookers alike – the evidence of hopeless idealism or fumbling feeble-minded hypocrisy.'[35]

For Arendt, action could serve effectively as propaganda when violent actions accelerated what was portrayed as the 'inevitable' triumph of historical 'laws', while massive force could 'demonstrate' that history was on your side. More specifically, alleged historical laws about the triumph of a particular group or idea could be 'revealed' as accurate by mass persecutions. In the case of the Nazis, the most relevant long-term historical law was a kind of racial Darwinism; for Stalin, it was the inevitable and scientifically predicted triumph of the proletarian class. Arendt pointed out that the Nazis spoke of soon-to-be-extinct races and the

Soviet regime of dying classes, and that the murderous actions of these totalitarian regimes helped to underline their power and omniscience by making such predictions come true.[36] In one sense, it was a version of the old saying that 'might is right'. Encapsulating a kind of collective flight from reality and a belief that bold actions could somehow *prove themselves right*, a senior adviser to President George W. Bush notoriously accused the journalist Ron Suskind of being 'in what we call the reality-based community ... [those who] believe that solutions emerge from your judicious study of discernible reality', adding, 'We're an empire now, and when we act, we create our own reality.'[37]

Sometimes Nazi 'predictions' were very precise and very directly linked to the act of *blaming*. Notably, Hitler 'predicted' that the Jews, said by him to have caused the First World War, would create 'another' war. On 30 January 1939 (the day he became Chancellor of Germany), Hitler said the Jews had ridiculed his prophesies that he would become head of state and 'settle the Jewish problem' but now were 'laughing on the other side of their face'. He added:

> Today I will once more be a prophet: if the international Jewish financiers in and outside Europe should succeed in plunging the nations once more into a world war, then the result will not be the Bolshevization of the earth, and thus the victory of Jewry, but the annihilation of the Jewish race in Europe!

Again, the point here is not to assert any kind of equivalence between twentieth-century totalitarianism and the more recent past – far from it. But if we turn again to the 'war on terror', there is evidence of a conscious attempt to use massive violence to *legitimize itself*. Under President George W. Bush, 'winning' was revered as a way of convincing those who might otherwise feel that going to war would fly in the face of truth and evidence. Thus George W. Bush's close adviser Karl Rove said of the war on terrorism: 'Everything will be measured by results. The victor is always right. History ascribes to the victor qualities that may not actually have been there. And similarly to the defeated.'[38] (One is reminded of a comment by Arendt on colonial officials in her discussion of the British empire: 'It is obvious that these secret and anonymous agents of the force of expansion felt no obligation to man-made laws. The only "law" they obeyed was the "law" of expansion, and the only proof of their "lawfulness" was success.')[39] Bush and Blair projected a strong sense that they understood the general direction of history, that democratization and liberalization were inevitable, and that those who stood in the way of these processes could be pushed aside, violently if necessary.

We've seen how both Bush and Trump revered their own instincts. Although Trump has often and plausibly been accused of coming up with crazy 'solutions', Trump has consistently portrayed himself as exceptionally *in touch* with a reality to which most commentators are said to be blind. As part of this, he has repeatedly lauded his own intuition and his powers of prediction. Indeed, Trump has been in the habit of claiming that what might at first appear to be a lie or a mistake is actually a far-sighted statement or prediction that will one day be revealed to others as true. When Trump was asked about his accusation that Obama had conducted wiretapping against him, Trump told *Time* magazine, 'I predicted a lot of things, Michael. Some things that came to you a bit later.' He also mentioned his 'Sweden! Who would believe it?!', statement, saying it was immediately followed by riots: 'I predicted a lot of things that took a little bit of time ...'.[40] In this connection, he also mentioned Brexit.

One is strongly reminded of Arendt's insight that a totalitarian leader's statements 'cannot be disproved by facts, but only by future success or failure',[41] and that '... demagogically speaking, there is hardly a better way to avoid discussion than by saying that only the future can reveal its merits'.[42] Arendt also noted in the context of totalitarianism:

> ... ideological thinking becomes emancipated from the reality that we perceive with our five senses, and insists on a 'truer' reality concealed behind all perceptible things, dominating them from this place of concealment and requiring a sixth sense that enables us to become aware of it ...[43]

Trump personalized and in some ways secularized the dangerous trope of Bush and Blair. Uninterested in ideas, he seemed to have little sense of any 'wider' laws of history – the inevitable triumph of certain ideas. This may have been a blessing, particularly when it came to waging wars abroad. But Trump too expressed the belief that history was following a particular path. Indeed, while Bush and Blair focused on their part in history, Trump concentrated on history's part in Trump. And all three were obsessed with *winning*. Whether Trump was President or a presidential candidate, the 'law' that he liked to follow was not so much the inevitable triumph of liberalism, democracy and globalization, but rather the unwritten law that says Trump will always win, Trump is always right, and Trump's prophesies and predictions will always come true. Such a world-view would seem to culminate, quite logically, in the attempt to overturn the 2020 election results (including the Capitol invasion of 6 January 2021). Significantly, Trump had already covered himself against losing – for example by claiming in advance that the election would be 'the most corrupt in history'.[44]

Arendt suggested:

> The totalitarian dictator, in sharp distinction from the tyrant, does not believe that he is a free agent with the power to execute his arbitrary will, but, instead, the executioner of laws higher than himself. The Hegelian definition of Freedom as insight into and conforming to 'necessity' has here found a new and terrifying realization.[45]

Looked at from this standpoint, Trump's more authoritarian tendencies have made him look more like a tyrant than a totalitarian ruler. The freedom that Trump showed himself to value was the freedom to execute his own will. As Fintan O'Toole observes, Trump took a blowtorch to regulation, especially environmental regulation, and supplemented this abroad with 'the trashing of international agreements, the withdrawal from the Paris climate accord, sucking up to the leaders of mafia states, and open contempt for female leaders like Angela Merkel and Theresa May'. Was this about pushing through a right-wing political agenda? No doubt in part it was. But O'Toole comments perceptively, 'Trump's aim, in the presidency as in his previous life, was always simple: to be able to do whatever the hell he wanted. That required the transformation of elective office into the relationship of a capricious ruler to his sycophantic courtiers.'[46]

At the same time, Trump's determination to be proved right implied a huge project of intimidating dissenters and a determination to refashion the world so that it conformed more closely to the world as he said it was or predicted it would be. This is where Trump's insistence on infallibility became especially dangerous. For the claim to predict and control events in a sense 'demands' a push to control those who might otherwise be disturbingly unpredictable in their behaviour. Arendt saw the lie as feeding the will to power, if only because some approximation to absolute power would be necessary to make outrageous lies appear true. That brings us back, once again, to the attempts to overturn the 2020 presidential elections. Arendt noted that 'Terror is needed in order to make the world consistent and keep it that way; to dominate human beings to the point where they lose, with their spontaneity, the specifically human unpredictability of thought and action.'[47] In elections people make a choice, and predictions can be proven wrong. Arendt helps us to see why Trump could not accept that.

Conclusion

We can see then that what Arendt calls 'action as propaganda' – the use of violent action to make false claims appear more and more true as time goes by – has been an important technique through which our disaster-producing politics has been sustained and legitimized. While not all the elements of 'action as propaganda' have been intended or planned from the outset, there are many kinds of violence that have conveniently and often predictably created legitimacy for themselves, giving little reason to change course.

In the context of our current home-grown disasters, action is serving as dangerous propaganda not only in the age-old targeting of critics but also through a number of mechanisms that reflect Arendt's more specific understanding of 'action as propaganda': they are bringing reality into line with outrageous statements. Key mechanisms here include: reproducing the enemy; creating an impression of inhumanity (and the perceived need for dramatic solutions) through fostering inhuman conditions; victim-blaming; implying that human rights do not exist by abusing or neglecting them; and using success to 'demonstrate' righteousness while suggesting that violent actions are simply following or accelerating the inevitable triumph of certain historical laws, predictions or prophesies.

A key element of 'action as propaganda' has been the use of bold and abusive actions to construct a kind of 'charismatic' authority: such actions not only imply the gravity of the highlighted 'threat' but also dramatize the 'disloyal' or even 'treasonous' nature of criticism. At the extreme (as with Extinction Rebellion in the UK), dissent can be relabelled as threats to public order or even as terrorism. More generally, bold and transgressive actions erode the impression that human rights *actually exist*. For example, while the 'right to asylum' is often mentioned, the widespread failure to *provide* asylum sends a powerful message to Western electorates and to would-be migrants that these rights do not in practice exist. If, in the face of the inability to claim asylum, a young person fleeing conflict in the DRC or Sudan still wishes to adhere to the view that human rights exist, then he or she may be propelled towards the conclusion that those to whom rights are not in practice extended are not considered human – a message that is as demoralizing as it is provocative.

10

Choosing Disaster

If action is one of the most effective forms of propaganda, another is what Arendt called 'the argument of the lesser evil'.[1] According to this argument, which has at least some degree of logic and validity, 'If you are confronted with two evils ..., it is your duty to opt for the lesser one.'[2] Today, a complex set of disaster-producing policies has been encouraged and legitimized by framing the relevant decisions as choices between a 'lesser evil' and some ostensibly more disastrous alternative. While this is by no means new, it's clear that today a 'lesser evil' politics is damagingly influencing policy across a wide range of issues from climate change to migration, crime, terrorism, and disease.

The Politics of the 'Lesser Evil'

Again, Arendt can help us to understand this process, and she went to considerable lengths to explain her deep reservations around the 'lesser evil' argument. 'The extermination of the Jews was preceded by a very gradual sequence of anti-Jewish measures', she wrote, 'each of which was accepted with the argument that a refusal to cooperate would make things worse – until a stage was reached where nothing worse could possibly have happened.'[3] Arendt pointed out that even at this final stage, the 'lesser evil' argument in favour of quietude and cooperation was not abandoned – for example in the Vatican's apparent concern that protesting mass persecution could make things worse. Arendt's antipathy to the 'lesser evil' also stemmed from a critique of Nazism and Soviet Communism themselves and indeed of US officials making policy in Vietnam, all of whom advanced some version of the old adage that 'You can't make an omelette without breaking eggs.'[4] Pushing back against this ruthless reflex in her essay 'The eggs speak up', Arendt noted, 'Each good action, even for a "bad cause", adds some real goodness to the world; each bad action even for the most beautiful of all ideals makes our common world a little worse.'[5] A key concern for Arendt was the dangerous idea that a certain amount of pain would be worth it *in the long run*.

In our contemporary politics, the success of the 'lesser evil' argument or manoeuvre typically depends on evoking a sense of crisis – usually a crisis that is said to be about to get much worse – while playing down the damage (often some kind of abuse of human rights) that is involved in 'averting' this disaster. By invoking the spectre of a greater and impending catastrophe such as 'terrorism with weapons of mass destruction' or 'the triumph of the deep state' or 'mass migration' or indeed 'the rise of fascism', it has often been possible to sell and justify a range of policies that themselves play a considerable role in undermining democracy and human rights. Pushing a heavily securitized response to some high-profile 'greater evil' not only leaves the roots of disasters un-tackled but also tends itself to be *disaster-producing*. Such a procedure tends to depend, in turn, on invoking an underlying 'science', theory or prediction that is rarely set out with sufficient clarity or scepticism.

Of course, the idea that one should choose the path of 'the lesser evil' need not necessarily be unethical or unhelpful. Surely, we *should* do something harmful when we know it will prevent something worse? Why, in weighing two alternatives, would anyone actually choose the *greater* evil? Every time the dentist drills our teeth, we see the principle of choosing 'the lesser evil' in action and, on the whole, this particular procedure seems helpful (if not at the time).

Problems with the 'lesser evil' argument

When we look more closely at the logic of the 'lesser evil' argument, however, several problems arise. Many of these centre on the way the argument *is applied*. Whether knowingly or not, advocates of 'lesser evil' arguments have frequently ignored at least six major difficulties.

The first is the way that alternatives are being *framed*. An invitation to choose between a lesser and greater evil tends to ignore the possibility that there are other alternatives available.[6] Some of these alternatives, moreover, may not actually involve inflicting harm.[7]

A second problem with invoking the 'lesser evil' argument is that the predictions being made about impending 'greater evils' may be based on *limited or non-existent evidence* or may even go against the available evidence. This is where the problem of hype – and playing on people's fears – tends to loom large.

A third problem is that the evidence that a 'lesser evil' will actually *prevent* a greater one may itself be thin or non-existent. The causal processes that are invoked (but often not discussed) tend to be very complex, while the emotional response to a vividly invoked 'greater evil' – notably, fear – tends to close down the possibility of calmly and carefully exploring these causal connections.

A fourth objection to the 'lesser evil' argument (closely related to the third) is that 'lesser evils' may themselves actually *feed into* the occurrence of 'greater' ones. Arendt warned that 'those who choose the lesser evil forget very quickly that they chose evil',[8] and she noted:

> The natural conclusion from true insight into a century so fraught with danger of the greatest evil should be a radical negation of the whole concept of the lesser evil in politics, because far from protecting us against the greater ones, the lesser evils have invariably led us to them.[9]

Arendt elaborated, 'The greatest danger of recognizing totalitarianism as the curse of the century would be an obsession with it to the extent of becoming blind to the numerous small and not so small evils with which the road to hell is paved.'[10]

Famously critical of the Jewish Councils in the Nazi-created ghettos, Arendt said that their cooperation with the Nazis – largely in the hope of saving some people from annihilation – had actually contributed to the unfolding disaster. This argument was extremely controversial for a number of reasons: its empirical basis was debatable (and of course it was essentially a hypothetical argument); it was stated too boldly (a not uncommon problem in Arendt's writing); and it was often interpreted as a kind of *victim-blaming*. Nevertheless, Arendt's controversial criticisms here were very much in line with, and helped to inform, her more general wariness around the possibility of preventing a greater evil by accepting or embracing some lesser version.

A fifth difficulty with the 'lesser evil' argument is that in practice the weighing of alternatives cannot usually be divorced either from some element of *ideology* or from some element of *self-interest*. Indeed, both these elements may take the 'lesser evil' argument in dangerous directions.

Here we can go back to Arendt once more, who showed in her book *Eichmann in Jerusalem* just how destructive it can be when alternatives are framed in line with particular ideologies. Arendt pointed out that senior Nazi officials sometimes presented the Holocaust itself as, in effect, 'a lesser evil' – an astonishing manoeuvre. More specifically, some senior Nazis advocated what they chose to call 'mercy killings' (in gas chambers), and this path was painted as preferable to (and even sometimes as more 'humane' than) available 'alternatives', including mass starvation or large-scale face-to-face killing.[11] (The latter method, incidentally, was seen as particularly distressing *for the perpetrators.*)

While this type of framing was about as murderous and indeed ludicrous as one could imagine, it does illustrate something of relevance to politics more generally: a great deal turns on what is presented as 'inevitable', on how the relevant alternatives are framed, and on what the audience is invited to believe is the 'the least bad' way of carrying out a process that has been presented as both beneficial and unavoidable. Again, both the conception of what is inevitable and the listing and weighing of 'alternatives' are likely to be strongly shaped by ideology and by self-interest. Anyone thinking about how decision-making is framed in the workplace may recognize variations of such framings.

When it comes to the possible influence of *self-interest*, we should note that there may be substantial *benefits accruing to decision-makers* from choosing what they present as a 'lesser evil'. Across a wide range of policy issues, there are likely to be significant pay-offs from the shaping of agendas, including from the common practice of narrowing down a wide range of alternatives to two or three that are said to be 'practical' or 'realistic'.[12] Meanwhile, the costs of this path frequently do not fall – surprise! – on the decision-makers themselves, so that the 'short-term pain' that is being sold as a way of warding off disaster turns out very frequently to be *the pain of others*. We have seen this process play out strongly with migrants/refugees and also in the case of the 'austerity' that was said, after the 2007–8 financial crisis, to be necessary in order to ward off economic collapse.

Across a range of policy spheres, the gravity of the crisis that is supposedly being averted may be exaggerated for self-interested reasons. And the parties claiming to prevent the 'greater evil' may have an entirely different set of objectives in mind, so that combating the 'greater evil' becomes in effect a *cover* for other more self-interested agendas. This is something I have found to apply rather consistently in my investigations of civil wars in many parts of the world and also in relation to the 'war on terror'. The demon enemy serves in effect as cover for a wide range of violent actions that are carried out by a diverse coalition of actors who claim to be confronting this 'greater evil'. Meanwhile, the 'lesser evils' that these diverse actors perpetrate, ostensibly with a view to tackling this 'greater evil' but actually for a wide range of political and economic purposes, turn out rather frequently to be more damaging than the 'greater evil' that is purportedly being averted or diminished. (Of course, averting the 'greater evil' may still be one of the relevant and actually existing aims.)

The five problems set out above relate broadly to the possibility of *misrepresentation*: key actors may inaccurately represent either the underlying problems or the alternatives available or the relevant causal mechanisms or some combination of these; and this misrepresentation may be strongly contaminated by ideology, self-interest or both. But there is also an important sixth problem with the 'lesser evil' argument, one that centres not on misrepresentation but on *the temptation actively to stoke* the 'greater evil' that is ostensibly being averted.

In general, it is not easy to prove that someone is actively and covertly stoking a problem they claim to be addressing. That party is certainly not going to admit this subterfuge. Nevertheless, one can sometimes get a good sense of collusions on these lines. I was able to investigate some of these mechanisms in some detail during Sierra Leone's civil war, and I wrote a book about it called *Conflict and Collusion in Sierra Leone*.[13] Here, the proclaimed intention of confronting rebels tended to serve as cover for a wide range of violent and exploitative acts, not least by government soldiers. Government soldiers' behaviour included attacking and looting civilians, coordinating movements with rebels, and even selling arms to rebels, all of which predicably *stoked* the threat that was ostensibly being confronted.[14] Of course, the intentions here were complex, and it would be foolish to interpret everything as *a plot to strengthen the enemy*. A key problem was that priorities *other than confronting the rebels* took precedence.

Even when a detailed on-the-ground investigation is not feasible and even where intentions cannot be very precisely proven, it may be possible to detect behaviour that is (a) predictably stoking a problem and (b) continuing long after it has become known that the behaviour is having this effect.[15] A commonly occurring example is an indiscriminate counterinsurgency (involving attacks on unarmed civilians over a long period) or a largely indiscriminate counterterrorism project that proves similarly enduring. We have already seen that actions that predictably reproduce the enemy can be part of what Arendt called 'action as propaganda', having the effect of legitimizing further aggression. If we think about the possibility of *stoking* in the context of Western democracies, a notable historical event was the 1933 Reichstag fire in Berlin, which was used by the Nazis as a reason to introduce emergency legislation in order, they said, to ward off an impending Communist uprising. This helped to kill off democracy under the Weimar Republic. While responsibility for the fire has never been fully established, some historians believe that it was started by the Nazis themselves – and the Nazis certainly had the motive. Another example is the terror bombings in Russia, under suspicious circumstances, that helped to precipitate war in Chechnya. We might also think of the urban unrest in the US in 2020, to the extent that this was actively stoked by Trump for political purposes.

The Road to Hell

If we reflect a little more on the 'war on terror' and the contemporary 'migration crisis' alongside these various objections to 'lesser evil' arguments, we can see, firstly, that these arguments were frequently used to justify the 'war on terror' and, secondly, that a wide range of objections to this manoeuvre are well grounded.

Notoriously, the 'greater evil' of terrorism-with-weapons-of-mass-destruction was poorly based in evidence since these weapons did not actually exist. Nor was a 'war on terror' an effective means of preventing terrorism. A criminal justice framework offered a better alternative. Yet the latter was hardly considered, partly because of the *vested interests* that lined up behind the preferred policy of war. The fact that many people were radicalized by the 'war on terror' is a key point here. It shows how the 'lesser evil' was not an effective route to reducing the 'greater evil' of terrorism, and it shows too how the underlying problem was being actively *stoked*.

After 9/11, even some liberal commentators began to argue that some forms of torture (sometimes rendered as 'coercive interrogation') should be considered to be a 'lesser evil' if they extracted information that could prevent the 'greater evil' of a terrorist attack.[16] But we know from what is now a long experience of the 'war on terror' that such reasoning invites abuse on a massive scale (as in the Abu Ghraib prison). We know, too, that torture can easily *nurture* terrorism (as it did in many prisons in Iraq),[17] and that information extracted via torture is in any case unreliable (not least because a tortured person will often say anything to make it stop). Many of the critiques of torture also apply more widely – for example to the practice of indefinite detention at Guantanamo Bay and elsewhere.

In general, the overriding rhetorical priority given to defeating terrorism has helped to cement and legitimize increased repression, surveillance and disrespect for human rights and this applies both inside and outside Western democracies. A key danger is that such 'emergency' measures come to serve major functions in suppressing dissent more widely and that they depend on a continuing state of emergency for their legitimacy and longevity.[18] We have seen many times how a doctrine of 'the lesser evil' allows damaging government impunity (as in Sri Lanka, Syria and Yemen for example), reinforcing grievances that may in turn fuel rebellion. After 9/11, politicians often stressed the need to 'strike a balance' between security and liberty; yet, when liberal values were trampled in the 'war on terror', this only tended to fuel grievances and to *undermine* security.[19]

The realm of 'migration control' also illustrates grave dangers with the 'lesser evil' argument. In Europe, as noted, 'getting tough' has involved the EU pushing migrants back to Libya, where it was known that many of them would be tortured. The various 'get tough' policies of which this practice is a part have been defended on the grounds that they will tackle the evil practice of human smuggling, that they will pre-empt the 'disaster' of mass immigration, and even that they will prevent a 'racist' backlash from the far right.

More generally (and again ostensibly to ward off 'greater evils'), Western policy-makers have repeatedly engaged in actions that shift migration flows to more dangerous routes, that encourage inhumane conditions, and that stoke important longer-term *causes* of migration – for example by bolstering authoritarian regimes that promise to rein in migration.[20]

The very extremity of these particular 'solutions' illustrates a key point emphasized by Arendt: that 'lesser evils', so far from averting disaster, tend to lead us rather directly towards it. Since the Libyan torture camps to which people have been returned have been credibly described by UN officials as 'hell-holes', Arendt's description of a 'lesser evil' being a 'road to hell' is directly applicable in this case. Moreover, in ostensibly warding off 'racism', many policies deeply *infused by* racism have been widely and persistently embraced. Far from protecting democracy against fascism, neglecting asylum *itself* has a powerfully corrosive effect on democratic values and practices, not least when those speaking against this neglect or helping with practical assistance (as we saw in Chapter 5) are silenced and vilified.

In her discussion of totalitarian movements, Arendt referred to 'the sympathizers' who 'can hardly be called single-minded fanatics', noting that it is through these people that totalitarian movements 'can spread their propaganda in milder, more respectable forms, until the whole atmosphere is poisoned with totalitarian elements which are hardly recognizable as such but appear to be normal political reactions or opinions'.[21]

That is a timely warning when it comes to the common invitation today to embrace 'lesser' versions of racism so as to ward off the 'greater' versions. If racism is to be the 'game', then the exponents who speak most clearly and who benefit most substantially are likely to be the extremists rather than the self-styled 'moderates' who (in ostensibly warding off the 'greater evils' of one kind or another) are often busy abandoning the concept of 'rights' to which in theory they subscribe.[22] Even some well-established Oxford academics now say they are trying to prevent political crisis in the West by arguing that assistance to refugees should be concentrated in countries near to their country-of-origin;[23] according to this argument, large-scale asylum-in-the-West is politically destabilizing while a policy of helping-in-the-region represents a pragmatic alternative (and your money goes further). But not only does this ignore the enormous political pressures that come from 'containing' migrants in countries like Greece, Turkey, Lebanon, Mexico and so on; it also ignores the more general erosion of human rights and democratic values that takes place when the principle of asylum is further neglected.[24]

The redefinition of 'normal' is a key danger today. In France's 2007 presidential elections, Nicolas Sarkozy's focus on immigration contributed to a temporary fall in support for the National Front. So it was easy to conclude that Sakozy's 'lesser evil' had prevented a greater one. But Aristotle Kallis refers to Sarkozy's 'legitimization of some ideas and policies previously considered extremist',[25] adding that measures like banning Muslim female dress (and the face-covering veil) 'break taboos and produce a kind of license to think the previously unthinkable'.[26] In the event, the National Front/National Rally rebounded strongly and is today a serious challenger to President Macron. As its leader, Marine Le Pen was sometimes presented as more moderate than her father, and she also presented herself in 2022 as more palatable than 'Great Replacement' theorist Eric Zemmour. So several 'lesser evil' manoeuvres were operating simultaneously.

More generally, while those taking a 'tough' line on immigration and refugees have sometimes claimed that they are pre-empting extremists, there is little sign that extreme racist individuals are in a state of mourning that their thunder has been stolen by mainstream politicians or academics. More often, the 'extreme' racists have been celebrating and spurred on by the new 'respectability' that their hatreds, fears and predictions have been accorded. In fact, both far-right and violent jihadist groups stand to benefit from policy initiatives, such as banning public veiling, that are put forward in an ostensible attempt to 'pre-empt' the far right.[27] One research team who looked at twelve western European countries going back to the 1970s found that

> fighting far-right parties by adopting their migration policies is at best fruitless and at worst counterproductive. By legitimizing a framing that is associated with the radical right, mainstream politicians can end up contributing to its success.[28]

The normalization of extremism was starkly illustrated in a 2017 documentary called *White Right: Meeting the Enemy*. Jeff Schoep, commander of the National Socialist Movement (which reveres Hitler and until recently had the swastika as its symbol), said a lot of statistics showed that whites were going to be a minority in America, and noted that in these circumstances his National Socialist Movement was demanding a homeland for white people.[29] He also noted that his movement was growing and it was partly because of Trump:

> A lot of the things that he [Trump] was saying – build a wall, stop illegal immigration, bring back American jobs – so he was saying a lot of the things that are right out of our playbook that we've been saying for years. We've been kind on the fringes for a long time and it ends with our talking points finally appearing in the White House. Nationalism has become more mainstream.[30]

We should also consider the possibility that extremists (even as they are stirred up and encouraged on a regular basis) have themselves become an important means of pushing through and justifying policies that many 'moderates' (who may not be found wanting when it comes to ruthlessness and racism) are themselves more than willing to advance.

In the UK, a referendum on the EU was put forward as a way of dealing with hardliners, notably within the Conservative Party. The far right had also been making headway and benefiting from anti-Brussels sentiment. But stirring up fears around Brussels opened the door for numerous abuses. Subordination to Brussels (and later going against 'the will of the people') was positioned as a 'greater evil' than all the measures – the untruths, intimidation and erosion of democratic procedures – that were deemed necessary to 'get Brexit done'. In relation to the 'war on terror', the 'fight against illegal migration' and indeed the Brexit process, we should ask: at what point does the ostensible 'defence' of tolerance, democratic values and sovereignty actually morph into an abandonment of these values?

The UK's Conservative Party has long been split on Europe, which would seem to be a major thorn in the party's side. Yet we should also notice that this 'damaging split' has actually proved compatible with long years of Conservative dominance (whether one considers the last fifty years since the UK joined the EU or the unbroken period of office since Cameron became Prime Minister in 2010). This latter period of dominance is perhaps *especially* remarkable given the economic downturn and austerity from 2007–8. Perhaps one clue here is that politics, like war, is not only a contest but also a system. In particular, between right-wing 'moderates' and 'extremists', there seems to have been a kind of symbiosis as well as a tension. Relatively 'mainstream' right-wing politicians have given encouragement to extremism by turning nationalist and racist policies like the 'hostile environment' into everyday politics, by stirring up xenophobia, by offering the encouragement of a referendum on the EU, and by exhibiting (Johnson-style) both a significant degree of contempt for democratic procedures and a contempt for sticking to the Covid rules of his own government. Despite an element of splitting the 'right-wing vote', the BNP and UKIP absorbed some of the growing discontent that might easily have helped the Labour Party, channelling it more towards nationalism than radicalism. And, meanwhile, relatively 'moderate' elements in the Conservative Party have also made a show of offering 'protection' against extremism, sometimes claiming to take the wind out of its sails through 'pragmatic' and 'hard-headed' measures. Yet many of these ostensibly pragmatic policies have themselves been extremely damaging: the fostering of 'hostile environments' in the UK and abroad; the erosion of democratic norms; and the potentially UK-splitting project of Brexit itself (which could easily reignite outright conflict in Ireland while reinforcing the dominance of right-wing politics in England itself and pushing Wales into deeper subordination to England or perhaps a financially precarious independence). Interpretations along these lines are no doubt contestable. But the key underlying point is that a 'moderate' version of something bad is probably not something good.

A final example of dangers in the 'lesser evil' argument takes us back to Covid. Particularly in the early months of Covid-19, lax controls were embraced by UK government officials on the grounds that they would ward off grave economic damage, prevent a collapsing health service the following winter, and promote 'herd immunity'. Yet this was a deadly disease in the 'here and now' with no vaccine available, and evidence for these various projections was generally weak; at any rate, the government made little effort to set the evidence out. The general message was that this was a crisis in which one had to defer to 'science', while the science itself remained rather opaque. To the extent that infection was encouraged to *spread*, this itself fed into the economic damage that was ostensibly being prevented.

Referring to the fears of a 'second wave' of infections, Harvard epidemiologist William Hanage eloquently summarized a key problem with this position in March 2020: 'Let me be clear. Second waves are real things, and we have seen them in flu pandemics. This is not a flu pandemic. Flu rules do not apply. There might be a second wave, I honestly don't know. But vulnerable people should not be exposed to a virus right now in the service of a hypothetical future.'[31] A key problem centred on allowing and even welcoming a massive health crisis in the here and now in order to avoid a possible health crisis – and an NHS that could not cope – in the future.[32]

As the virus took hold, Trump insisted in May 2020, 'We can't keep our country closed down for years.'[33] Yet, as Nicholas Kristof and Stuart Thompson noted pithily in the *New York Times*, '... the best way to protect the economy is to rein in the pandemic',[34] while Adam Serwer pointed out, 'Economists are in near-unanimous agreement that the safest path requires building the capacity to contain the virus before reopening the economy – precisely because new waves of deaths will drive Americans back into self-imposed isolation ...'.[35] Meanwhile, Nafeez Ahmed observed of the UK, 'the government's fatalistic refusal to consider a pathway of trying to "squash" the virus appears to have locked itself into an avoidable trajectory bound to kill both the economy and many vulnerable people'.[36]

Again, with a largely vaccinated population a different balance becomes appropriate. Indeed, there is a danger (as China reminds us) that the 'greater evil' of Covid infection is allowed over a long period to justify a very wide range of 'lesser evils' in terms of restrictions on people's lives that, taken together, turn out to be not so 'lesser' after all. The difficulty of making judgements here only underlines the importance of facilitating dissent, querying 'the science' and the alternatives that are being presented or squashed, and avoiding the temptation to channel one's own fear and indignation into shutting down the debate.

Conclusion

This chapter has stressed that counterproductive policies have been encouraged by particular framings. Crucial here is what is framed is *inevitable*. Also pivotal is the presentation of limited, often binary, alternatives, so that even a course of action in which few people seriously *believe* can nevertheless be presented as preferable (and a 'lesser evil') in comparison to some 'disastrous' alternative. This manoeuvre depends on successfully evoking a sense of threat and a sense of emergency.

Once a convincing vision of hell has been conjured into people's minds, it then becomes surprisingly feasible to sell a given 'solution', even if this is a solution (as Arendt argued in relation to mass bombing in Vietnam) that almost no relevant policy-maker actually believes will work. Again, one of the confusing things about Brexit was that key leaders backed a policy of leaving the EU, which they had either voted against in the past (Theresa May), or written against in the past (for Boris Johnson notoriously argued the case for both Leaving *and* Remaining in two drafts of the same article).

As the securitization of global warming gathers force, boosting the military and an escalating attempt at *walling off* are already being presented as 'lesser evils' in comparison to the 'greater evils' of mass migration and drought-driven conflicts. Yet such measures will surely only feed into the 'greater evil' of a heating planet, fuelling 'growth', complacency and war. Again, the framing of alternatives is crucial, as is the construction of what is 'inevitable' and what is not. A key danger with climate change (as with a range of other disasters) is that responses will be geared towards walling off the consequences. A second danger lies in the propensity for instrumentalizing the consequences rather than engaging in fundamental reforms that tackle the underlying problem. Even responses that are predictably counterproductive, like attempts to seal richer countries from the effects of their own behaviour, are likely to be embraced as sensible measures in the face of the 'inevitability' of climate change. (Of course, some future climate change *is* now inevitable; but there is still a difference between adaptations and dealing with the root of a problem.) Meanwhile, a sophisticated system of profit-making, both around the causes of global warming and, increasingly, around responses to it, is already supporting very particular framings.

Today, the embrace of violent methods even by more moderate players (such as EU officials) and the active manipulation of home-grown disasters (whether by right-wing populists or 'moderates') should be a resounding wake-up call. A proper awakening would include recognizing the degree to which hard-headed 'means' are not warding off catastrophe but bringing it quickly and concretely into the present.

11

Home to Roost

An extraordinary number of crises and emergencies are today impacting and threatening the world, and Western democracies are very far from being immune. Relatively sudden disasters afflicting these democracies have included: terrorism, weather-related disasters, financial crisis, migration crises, Covid-19 and war in Ukraine, with more extended disasters including longer-term economic crisis, climate crisis and a complex political crisis that involves the erosion of democratic norms. These overlapping disasters are not just proliferating; they are feeding off each other.

Part of the approach in this book has been to look at a range of disasters in the Global South and to see what light they might throw on crises affecting the Global North. In Chapter 2, we noted that disasters in the Global South have routinely yielded beneficiaries, and that these benefits can help to explain why these disasters occurred and why they have frequently persisted. Today, as a great many disasters have in effect 'come home' to the Global North, so too have some of the *benefits* of disaster as well as the closely related *instrumentalization* of disaster. Suffering is increasingly being welcomed and put to use in Western democracies, mirroring a disturbing phenomenon that has been documented in Africa, Asia and Latin America over several decades. In the West as elsewhere in the world, a disaster-producing system can be said to be feeding on the very crises it is helping to produce.

Today a condition of *permanent emergency* seems to have enveloped Western democracies along with much of the rest of the world. Why is this? While the answer is clearly complex, part of it is that emergencies have their uses. Although we are often told that special measures are needed to deal with an emergency, the emergency may itself be 'needed' in order to allow the special measures. If civil wars around the world exemplify this, Nazism too had elements of this reversal. Hitler is reported to have told his subordinates, 'the war had made possible for us the solution of a whole series of problems that could never have been solved in normal times', adding that, no matter how the war turned out, 'the Jews will certainly be the losers'.[1]

Many of the current disasters in Western democracies are 'coming home' not just in the sense of encroaching on this historically privileged geographical zone but also in the sense that disasters represent a kind of 'blowback' from earlier abuses and misadventures. Both jihadist and white supremacist terrorism have been fed by the 'war on terror'. Weather-related disasters have been encouraged by growth-induced climate change. And large-scale migration has been fuelled by a combination of colonialism, neoliberalism, the 'war on drugs', and (again) the 'war on terror'. Unfortunately, many of the fantasies that helped to create contemporary *disaster-producing policies* are today being reinforced precisely by the blowback that they have induced, so that the perennially proposed remedy is, in effect, 'the hair of the dog' – or 'more of the same'. In short, we are seeing the emergence of a *disaster-producing politics* that is in many ways *self-reinforcing*. An increasingly toxic politics is encouraging and exacerbating emergencies and disasters of various kinds while feeding off the disruption, fear, collective delusions and migration that these disasters bring in their wake.

Part of what is entrenching disasters is a phenomenon to which Arendt and Agamben were both eager to draw attention: namely that the exception, including the rightlessness of 'the camp', is always threatening to become the rule. A key problem is that once human rights are set aside and once the link between punishment and crime is broken, then the category of victims may expand extremely quickly; indeed, it may come right to your door.

Once it has been accepted that it is permissible and desirable to create a 'hostile environment' within a Western democracy, policy-makers and even the public may be led to ask, in effect, *how* hostile it should be and *to whom* this hostility can usefully be extended. In practice, this has come to include many of those trying to draw attention to, and ameliorate, the suffering of migrants and refugees.

Once it has been accepted that the problem of terrorism demands a direct, unilateral and (to a significant extent) extra-legal response, then policy-makers and even the public may be led to ask to whom the label 'terrorist' can usefully be extended. Hence, in part, Trump's invocation of the need 'to clean out this beehive of terrorists' in relation to Black Lives Matter protests in Portland, Oregon. Soon many Democrats in particular were keen to label the mob invading the Capitol as 'terrorists';[2] perhaps there is a better case to be made here than with Trump's denunciations. But the import of 'war on terror' language into the domestic arena tends only to exacerbate the current polarization of politics.

Truth is another problem. Once a basic respect for truth-telling is set aside in the context of foreign wars, that habit too can rebound with a vengeance. When winning becomes *too* important, you start bending the truth, and today the cavalier approach to both law and evidence in the 'war on terror' shows every sign of 'coming home' into the domestic politics of the US in particular. To use the term that Arendt employed in relation to Vietnam, some of the habits nurtured in relation to Iraq and Afghanistan have 'come home to roost' within the US itself.

Part of the problem is that fantasies of omnipotence and the recurrent fantasy of *always winning*, which seems to have been nurtured at the ever-expanding American frontier and later pursued in an expansive 'war on terror', can easily dovetail into narratives of 'betrayal'.[3] As we've seen, the idea of betrayal maintains a sense of omnipotence since history can still be seen as dictated by 'us'. From a religious point of view, too, it is not God who has deserted us but nefarious humans. Conspicuous setbacks (in Korea, in Vietnam and later in the 'war on terror') have repeatedly fed into narratives of betrayal and, along with this, into a search for internal enemies. After the US's defeat in the Vietnam War, Arendt observed from her home in New York: 'When the facts come home to roost, let us try at least to make them welcome. Let us try not to escape into some utopias – images, theories, or sheer follies.'[4] In warning against a flight from reality (including in this case an escalation of bombing in Cambodia), Arendt stressed two themes of considerable relevance in our present era. One is the habit of fleeing from one misadventure to another, the habit of *not learning lessons*. The second is the way one disaster tends to facilitate other disasters – not least in the *flight from truth*.

We may also notice that, to a degree, the physical means of violence have also 'come home' to the US. Photographs of police protests against killings by the police in Ferguson and Baltimore reveal heavily armed police with assault rifles and lines of armoured vehicles. This suggests an element of what Derek Denman calls 'a collapse of war zone and home front', with the international 'war on terror' in particular blurring into a military-style mobilization against anti-racism protesters.[5] Armoured vehicles have been recycled from military deployments to the police via the Defense Department's Defense Logistics Agency.[6] More generally, foreign wars may serve as testing grounds for the burgeoning internal security market.[7]

Since democracy is indeed under threat, it is perhaps natural that those who see themselves as defending democracy are today pumped up and primed for 'battle'. But, on the domestic front in the US, the idea of defending democracy has led to some pretty intemperate language that again seems to offer very little when it comes to softening the deep political rifts that are themselves such a significant threat to democracy. In a January 2022 speech in Atlanta, President Biden addressed the topic of Republican voter suppression measures, referring to the domestic 'enemies' of democracy, noting the need to 'hate evil, love good', and asking 'Will you stand for democracy? Yes or no?'[8] US House speaker Nancy Pelosi went further and said Republicans in Congress who were pushing voter suppression measures were 'enemies of the state'.[9]

Meanwhile, the fierce defence of democracy and a domestically generated sense of indignation seem to be expanding *outwards*. In fact, in both the foreign and domestic spheres, leading Democrats seem to be elevating the idea of a 'threat to democracy' to the status of an *absolute evil* – a position that may justify all manner of 'lesser evils' that turn out to be not so small after all; here we might briefly mention a world war, perhaps involving Russia, China or both.

We've noted the elevation of Russia to the status of a mortal threat to American democracy, a move that served important domestic political functions but that was hardly constructive in terms of international diplomacy. The war in Ukraine, certainly cruel and vicious and an alarming manifestation of Russian aggression, was quickly elevated to the status of an existential crisis for Western democracy itself (and apparently the only humanitarian crisis in the world) with some *40 billion* US dollars quickly mobilized (and mostly channelled to US defence companies) for weaponry and other assistance. In April 2022, US Defense Secretary Lloyd Austin expanded the war aims from defending Ukraine and declared that the West's goal was to 'weaken Russia' to the point where it could no longer invade or threaten its neighbours.[10] Yet such a stance can only have played into Putin's rhetoric that this was an existential war for national survival. On 25 April 2022, Russian Foreign Minister Sergei Lavrov warned of the risks of a nuclear conflict and said NATO was 'in essence ... engaged in a war with Russia through a proxy and is arming that proxy'.

British politicians jumped in with their own dangerous rhetoric. A day after Austin's comments, UK Junior Defence Minister James Heappey said it would be 'completely legitimate' for Ukraine to use Western weapons for striking *inside Russia* if need be.[11] (Imagine if Moscow had armed Iraq and said it would be 'completely legitimate' if such weapons were used to strike against the UK or the US.) When UK Health Secretary Sajid Javid was asked about a Russian attack on a Ukrainian military base about ten miles from the Polish border, he said 'Let's be very clear ... if a single Russian toecap steps into NATO territory, there will be war with NATO.'[12] Two days after Russian Foreign Minister Lavrov's suggestion that NATO was engaged in a proxy war with Russia, the then UK Foreign Secretary Liz Truss declared, 'We are doubling down. We will keep going further and faster to push Russia out of the whole of Ukraine.'[13] Yet even if it were possible to eject Russia from the Donbas and its predominantly ethnic Russian population, it would surely involve a dangerous degree of humiliation for Russia. Rhetoric like Truss's tends to have significant domestic functions; but what goes down well with the right-wing Tory party members who elected Truss as Prime Minister is not necessarily the best approach for avoiding a global conflagration or even for helping the people of Ukraine.

In August 2022, as the focus shifted briefly from Ukraine, we were suddenly being told that the future of democracy rested on Taiwan. Nancy Pelosi, whose visit to Taiwan prompted China to cut ties with the US on a number of issues, declared that 'We cannot stand by as the CCP [Chinese Communist Party] proceeds to threaten Taiwan – and democracy itself.' But a significant element of grandstanding – or what Robert Daly at the Woodrow Wilson has called 'escalation games' – had again crept into the picture, and Todd Hall, director of Oxford University's China Centre, commented 'My major worry is that Beijing will take measures that Washington, in turn, will see itself forced to respond to in order to avoid appearing irresolute or passive, thus potentially triggering a spiral of escalation.'[14] The rhetoric was all about defending freedom. But self-righteousness is always a danger when politicians think they know exactly where the 'greater evil' lies. If we take Bernie Sanders' definition of freedom seriously and recognize that freedom involves *economic security*, we may rather quickly lose the Pelosi- or Truss-style sense that everything in foreign affairs can be simplistically reduced to a confrontation between 'the free' and the 'unfree'. In other words, a little modesty is called for.

More generally, we may say that some of our most trumpeted emergencies (notably the 'migration crisis') have been greatly exaggerated, while several deeper underlying crises are being allowed to proceed largely unchecked. In the midst of these overlapping disasters, we are tending to focus on symptoms rather than causes. Yet we need to understand how simultaneous habits of hype and neglect interact. We also need to recognize how addressing *the wrong disaster* (which is often 'trumped-up' in the sense of being manufactured and/or hyped) is stirring up dangerous fantasies while severely inhibiting our responses to the graver underlying disasters. A key part of the problem is that many disasters are being harnessed to a form of right-wing populism that offers big emotional and political payoffs and largely magical solutions for real-world problems while simultaneously turning against (or perhaps we should say turning *further* against) the world of evidence. There is also a problem of 'crying wolf'. Particularly since many contemporary emergencies have been trumped up or trumpeted or both (from 'oppression by Brussels'[15] to 'the caravan is coming!'[16] to the more mundane and often profit-driven insistence in the workplace that 'our organization is in crisis!'), Western publics now face a major challenge in sorting out the real emergencies from the fake ones.

Sometimes it seems that we all have very short attention spans and very short memories and that we collectively decide, in a rush of fear and indignation, to focus on one problem which has been so far elevated in our media-fuelled imagination that we cannot even imagine the other problems or remember to enquire about how all of these various problems came about.

Many current responses centre on building various kinds of 'walls' around the most obvious consequences of deep-lying crises. To a large extent, current responses to emergency centre on securitization, on the theatrics of getting tough, and on selling the fiction that you are protecting people while simultaneously neglecting what would *really* protect them. We need to take much better account of the *actually existing* disasters within people's own lives (such as ill health, bad housing, unemployment, being rendered economically superfluous) as well as a range of neglected and related 'macro' disasters such civil war, global precarity, and global warming. This demands a very fundamental re-think about how social and economic life is fashioned, but it is hard to think clearly when trumped-up disasters are constantly being placed before our eyes and mixed in with the real ones. That impediment to thinking may indeed be a key *function* of various high-profile disasters. Our more fake or fabricated emergencies and associated scapegoating tend to shore up a (gainful) world of delusions, while distracting people from a range of all-too-real disasters and from a proper understanding of their causes.

We've noted Sen and Drèze's argument that democracy and a free press protect against famines, a protection that would seem to extend (on the same logic) to other disasters. But democratic governments may also cover up disasters. And democracies, more broadly, may have important *disaster-producing qualities*. Whether in relation to famines or other disasters, we need to interrogate the nature of actually existing democracies and the nature of the media operating therein and how these relate to the protection that is or is not being provided. This applies in any part of the world. A key factor here is the extent to which particular groups are exposed to disasters through lack of political muscle or influence. Another is the extent to which disaster is actually welcomed. A third is the degree to which the media is interested in preventing or promoting disasters. A fourth is the extent of intimidation that accompanies democratic rule. And a fifth is the extent to which the essence of democracy is actually being eroded or surrendered, whether in the suppression of dissent or in various versions of 'emergency rule' and 'emergency management'. The protection that democratic institutions are often presumed to provide turns out to depend on how disaster is conceptualized and whether the will and energy exist to inject these institutions with the vitality they require. Democracy is still a kind of lifebelt in an increasingly stormy sea; but if we forget to breathe air into this lifebelt, it will not save us.

In this book, we've seen how emergency politics in the Global South is partly about sealing yourself off from the costs of disasters. At the extreme, elites creating a crisis obtain many benefits and incur very few costs, a situation that feeds into disasters themselves and even into 'permanent emergency'. In Chapter 2, we noted that the *trajectory* of disasters in the Global South has been closely related to *changes in the distribution of costs and benefits*. So relatively powerful groups will tend to relieve disasters when they are incurring costs and they will tend not to relieve disasters (and indeed to make them worse) when they are reaping benefits.

When we think about the disaster-producing system in the Global North within this kind of framework, we can better understand possible trajectories, which are also likely to reflect the changing distribution of costs and benefits. Mapping this changing distribution offers a promising framework for analysing how these various disasters (from financial crisis to global warming) are panning out and how they may evolve in the future. We can also see clearly the dangers that arise when potential costs (like defeat at the ballot box) are neatly and dangerously turned into benefits through a politics that instrumentalizes disaster and disorder.

Naturally, the idea that countries or individuals can be physically sealed off from 'blowback' greatly erodes the incentive to prevent or tackle disasters. It encourages reckless behaviour. We saw this when the idea that banks were 'too big to fail' encouraged lending far in excess of one's assets. We've seen it in the 'war on terror' and with global warming.[17] A key 'sealing off' has been reinforcing borders as conflicts and humanitarian crises proliferate under the strain of conflict and global heating. Indeed, we may expect that this walling off will be a central strategy for those who wish to focus on consequences not causes and to pursue 'business as usual'. In *No Go World*, Ruben Andersson shows that in marking out large parts of the world as 'no go zones', in trying to push risk away,[18] and in outsourcing 'migration control' to abusive regimes and militias, Western policy-makers are fuelling discontent and stoking the very abuses that bring these risks closer.[19] 'Escape strategies' in relation to global warming include such small-scale 'adaptations' as pumping Florida beaches and building luxury homes on higher ground from Miami to New Zealand. We are also seeing a proliferation of 'gated communities', often in response to crime, while in the financial markets hedging against future disasters is now a huge industry. In a small but telling incident from the UK, leading 'Brexiteer' Jacob Rees-Mogg's company Somerset Capital Management set up offshoots in Dublin to guard against the economic effects of Brexit.

Within and on the fringes of Western democracies, the *micro-disaster zones* created by global 'wars' (on terror, on 'illegal migration') – from burgeoning US prisons to Guantanamo Bay to the sites of migrant suffering like Calais, Lesbos, the Arizona desert and the Mediterranean Sea – have become a kind of seedbed for a politically regressive and increasingly anti-democratic project. Meanwhile, disaster zones themselves may serve as a testing ground and an intimidating 'showpiece' for a brand of politics that has grown increasingly confident and brazen in setting human rights to one side. In this way, 'emergencies' have increasingly been used to justify a resort to special powers and to legitimize a wider project of strong government and the policing of dissent. The 'climate change' emergency appears to be headed in the same direction, with intimidation of environmental NGOs in the Global South already widespread, Extinction Rebellion recently being told that it could not engage even in peaceful protest within central London, and such 'radical' organizations as the Royal Society for the Protection of Birds now informed they are part of the 'anti-growth coalition'.

We looked in Chapter 2 at how disasters in the Global South have been routinely legitimized through the way they are framed, and later in the book we examined some ways in which disasters impacting the Global North (as well as ineffective responses) have been legitimized. In this discussion, we explored the important roles played by magical thinking, by 'action as propaganda', and by 'the argument of the lesser evil'.

Magical thinking has involved the embrace of bogus solutions for (real or bogus) crises. It is intimately linked with *not learning lessons*. Closely associated with magical thinking (and more specifically to the *defence* of magical thinking) has been a strategic expansion of the 'enemy' category so as to include critics of the disaster-producing system. In wars in the Global South, we have many times seen how critics have been quickly and conveniently incorporated into a shifting category of enemy, particularly in the context of some wider national or international war. This has been a key part of the *function* of often-enduring civil and global wars that have continuously legitimized repression and bolstered extreme inequality. Today, a closely related process is unfolding around disasters in the Global North. A growing vilification and even prosecution of humanitarian actors and activists mirrors the vilification of, and violence against, humanitarian workers and activists that has long been a feature of functional disasters within the Global South.

When it comes to Arendt's 'action as propaganda', a key aspect has been the active fuelling of disasters, which are then used to terrify the public and to channel politics in very particular (disaster-producing) directions. 'Lesser evil' politics has been no less insidious. Allegedly pre-empting terror, a 'war on terror' has helped to nurture it. And in the name of warding off future disaster (including extreme right-wing politics and even fascism), politicians in Western democracies have pushed through a set of migration/immigration policies *that are themselves extreme* and that lead rather *directly* to disaster; left unchecked, this will only reinforce our more fundamental underlying disasters in the future.

If Trump, Johnson, Brexit and right-wing populism more generally are actually symptoms rather than causes, then focusing only on these prominent phenomena will not get us very far. In fact, it may sometimes represent *another kind* of magical thinking.[20] Our current focus on abusive or irresponsible individuals tends to obscure *what made them possible*. The growing prominence of right-wing populism in many countries around the world represents an invitation to learn from experience and to re-think the practices that have helped to generate these movements. In highlighting the 'crisis' of Trump or Brexit, we often sideline awareness of the complex causes and functions of right-wing populism. Today, even opponents of the status quo risk being mesmerized by particular phenomena that are perhaps better seen as variations on a global theme and as *epiphenomena* produced by deeper processes, of which widening inequality would seem to be the most important.[21] Such a reflex represents, in effect, another version of focusing on symptoms rather than underlying problems, on consequences rather than causes.

Arendt emphasized that it was dangerous to be so mesmerized by totalitarianism that one forgot to investigate and address the conditions that had made it possible (and that were always threatening to recreate it). She noted, for example, that 'If homelessness, rootlessness, and the disintegration of political bodies and social classes do not directly produce totalitarianism, they at least produce almost all of the elements that eventually go into its formation'.[22]

Many observers have expressed amazement that Trump could win the presidency despite his casual cruelty, his cavalier attitude to the truth, and his general shamelessness. But cruelty can be strangely appealing, as we have seen. It can sometimes even feel more 'honest' than the politically correct statements of those who have been subject to a growing suspicion over many years that they do not really mean what they say. People do not always want the 'truth' that they have been sold many times before. And shamelessness has its own allure, particularly for those who have been routinely and systematically shamed. In many ways, Trump won not despite his many faults but because of them, and Arendt can help us to understand this shocking phenomenon.[23]

Tempting as it may be to position disasters as something 'over there' or 'far away', those living in Western democracies have now been sharply reminded that they are, in the words of Shylock in Shakespeare's *The Merchant of Venice*, 'subject to the same diseases, healed by the same means'. Today, powerful Western governments continue to fuel wars, to stoke inequality, to bolster repressive regimes, and to heat the planet, while at the same time looking to build a variety of walls around the most obvious consequences.[24] In this context, Shylock's famous speech may also help us to remember that we are 'warmed and cooled by the same winter and summer'. Our shared vulnerability to climate, disease and violence and the shared propensity for revenge that Shylock also highlighted underline the fact that our most pressing social problems urgently require collective and collaborative solutions.

Such joint solutions are needed internationally, too. A long-established reflex to condense all problems (and all 'evil') into one person (a Castro, a Saddam Hussein or a bin Laden) is as unhelpful internationally as it has been domestically with Trump. The case of Russia and the Ukraine is complicated of course, and such a catastrophe always brings the danger (as 9/11 did) that explaining will be seen as excusing. But Putin's extreme aggression in Ukraine is not wisely separated from the complex conditions that nurtured it. Important here was the failure to disband NATO at the end of the Cold War and the failure to push through a radical downsizing of US military spending in particular. Instead, NATO was significantly and repeatedly expanded despite the warnings of many experts. As for US military spending, it might be useful to pause and ask how much the US commits to the military compared to Russia. Maybe a bit more? Maybe twice as much? In reality, today the United States is spending 801 billion dollars a year on the military, some *twelve times* the military spending of Russia (66 billion). The US total is also greater than the *next nine countries* put together.[25] That is a scandal, a provocation and a waste of resources on a truly epic scale. It can only be justified with resort to the idea that America has a special gift for freedom and a special responsibility for spreading it, ideas that have already got us into a lot of trouble. Even domestically, that 'special gift' idea tends to obscure all the ways in which people in America are not actually free and to reduce the perceived need to do something radical about it.

As for NATO, veteran US diplomat George Kennan had observed back in 1997 that 'Expanding NATO would be the most fateful error of American policy in the post-cold-war era'; it would 'inflame the nationalistic, anti-Western and militaristic tendency in Russian opinion'. Yeltsin told President Clinton that NATO expansion towards Russia would be 'a new form of *encirclement*', and we know that the fear of encirclement is a major theme in Russian history. Putin himself was visibly furious that Western governments had gone back on assurances that NATO would not expand eastwards at the end of the Cold War. Of course, it's not hard to see why eastern European countries would want to be inside NATO, and some of the push for expansion has certainly come from them. But building this particular 'wall' offered little to Western democracies and, insofar as it provoked Russia, perhaps rather little to 'eastern democracies' either. Andrei Tsygankov at San Francisco State University noted in 2018 that

> In the early 1990s, Russia perceived NATO as an alliance of Western democracies that it was looking forward to joining ... [By 2014] the Kremlin was no longer eager to become a part of the Western civilization and instead sought to shield itself against the West's potential harmful influences ... Russian military planners and policy makers now assume that the only way to stop NATO's encroachment on Russia's perceived spheres of influence is to clearly signal red lines and act firmly to defend Russia's interests as it was done with respect to Georgia [in 2008] and Ukraine [in 2014].[26]

Of course, Russia has gone far beyond acting 'firmly'. But the switch is still notable. Apart from Moscow's security concerns, NATO enlargement damaged Russia's idea of its own status.[27] In many ways, US foreign policy after the Cold War was not simply about exporting and defending freedom; it was about *exhibiting* freedom. Serbia was bombed by NATO in 1999 without UN Security Council approval, leading to the overthrow of Milošević and prompting anger in Russia. The US unilaterally withdrew from the Anti-Ballistic Missile Treaty with Russia in 2001–2. In 2003, the United States and its allies invaded Iraq without UN Security Council approval, another blow to Russia's view of its great power status, particularly given its veto in the Security Council. And, in 2011, a UN Security Council-approved NATO mission against Gaddafi in Libya morphed into a regime change operation, something that Russia opposed.[28] What felt like freedom in Washington was often interpreted as disrespect, even humiliation, in Moscow, where many still clung to Russia's status as a 'great power'.[29] Perhaps the thrill of 'winning' the Cold War had been too intoxicating for the victors.

At any rate, the story of NATO's retention and expansion would seem to be a strong illustration of Nafeez Ahmed's more general comment on disaster-producing security structures that was quoted earlier: 'It is often assumed that ... contemporary structures are largely what need to be "secured" and protected from the dangerous impacts of global crises, rather than transformed precisely to ameliorate these crises in the first place.'[30]

A second background cause of Russian aggression has been the extent of corruption in the country and the past consolidation of all the vested interests that are today threatened by genuine democratization (including the 'threat of a good example' in Ukraine itself). This corruption and these vested interests did not arise in a vacuum. When economic liberalization was rapidly pushed out to Russia at the end of the Cold War, this process fuelled both poverty and corruption as welfare provisions were severely eroded and a small number of well-connected Russians gained control of oligopolistic businesses at knock-down prices, with criminal networks playing a major role.[31] There was no equivalent of the post-Second World War Marshall Plan to help to build a fair democratic society out of the ruins of totalitarianism. And since the oligarchs' ill-gotten gains were welcomed with open arms from Geneva to London to New York, these influential individuals had relatively little incentive to push for the kind of rule-of-law-based democracy that could have offered a better path for Russia and a more secure environment to protect their wealth.[32]

The extreme wealth of the oligarchs and the entrenchment of corruption in Russia also had a significant 'boomerang effect' abroad as the Kremlin pushed its tentacles of corruption into Western democracies, funding right-wing groups (as with France's National Front party) and sometimes using corruption (as it had domestically) to gain influence and win loyalty through compromising information.[33] These tactics in turn fuelled anti-Russian feeling and helped to revive Cold War antipathies, notably after Russian meddling in America's 2016 elections.

We should acknowledge that 'West-splaining' (or attributing all events in the world to the West) remains a danger here; at the extreme, such explanations may represent *their own* fantasy of omnipotence. It's clear, too, that primary responsibility for Russian aggression remains with Putin.

Nevertheless, it is hard to avoid the conclusion that Russia's growing belligerence means that several chickens have once again been coming home to roost. Again, the extreme violence we have recently been witnessing from Russia in Ukraine cannot sensibly be de-linked, as Arendt always argued in relation to totalitarianism, from all that has gone before. When the Berlin Wall fell, the rapid spread of capitalism and of NATO looked very much like an endless winning as the frontiers of 'the American way' were pushed relentlessly outwards alongside the violent export of democracy in the form of the 'war on terror'. While blowback is usually a force to be reckoned with, there is always the possibility of *incorporating blowback into the system that produced it*, not least in the demand for 'more security' and 'more military spending'.

Such a perverse system demands quite a high degree of forgetting and even intimidation when it comes to the actual causes of things or the complex historical processes that led us to where we are. But such things are often possible in what Gore Vidal once called the United States of Amnesia.

Once – on one of Oxford's less drizzly days – I went with an old friend to see a film in the *Phoenix* cinema, an appropriate name as it turned out. During the movie (a thriller), I noticed that the curtains at the side of the screen seemed to be displaying a kind of 'flame'. At first, I wondered if it might be part of a curtain design, or even a special effect to enhance the tension of the movie. Soon I observed that the flames were getting more and more pronounced and that some kind of smoke effect was being added to the mix. Belatedly, I realized that the cinema was actually on fire, an adverse turn of events that was not made more palatable by the movie's title, *No Exit*. When I went to the lobby, I tried to project a great deal of calm (and perhaps overdid it since the usher was under the impression that I wanted a bag of sweets).

Fairly soon the audience was out on the street and we were watching the fire-brigade battle raging flames that were threatening an old people's home to the back of the cinema. When the fire was finally extinguished, I got into conversation with a fireman and I asked him if he knew how the fire had started. He looked at me suspiciously: 'Well, *you* seem to know an awful lot about it!'

Many of us have been slow to react to major crises, finding ways to discount or 'explain away' unwelcome information, most notably in relation to global heating. Some of our crises have had a hyped-up and theatrical quality: we may be mesmerized by the drama even as the cinema itself is burning down. Meanwhile, raising the alarm in relation to climate change or suffering around migration can easily bring recriminations: enquiring too closely or even asking about the causes of things may precipitate the accusation, as we've seen, that we are part of the problem.

The thinking needed for such enquiries is not helped by economic crisis itself or the prospect of being surplus to requirements. Automation and artificial intelligence mean that human minds as well as bodies can be replaced. The only things that cannot be replaced, perhaps, are creativity, kindness and the willingness to think for oneself. But these can certainly be discouraged or even made illegal, as with the criminalization of humanitarian aid. If we think or feel or question too much, moreover, the machines are ready to step in and provide their own more acceptable version of working and thinking.[34] The rise of artificial intelligence is putting even professional jobs at risk as the prospect, and reality, of being 'superfluous' extends outwards from manual workers to others. Whether at work or in national politics, the idea that we are in a financial 'emergency' never quite recedes. And if we still have a job, a sense of crisis (along, perhaps, with an escalating debt) will keep us hoping that the crisis will pass if we can somehow work harder and longer and do not ask too many awkward questions. Of course, there is a world of difference between a modern workplace and a Nazi-constructed ghetto, but Howard Stein has insightfully compared the fearful worker with the desperate occupant of these ghettos in at least one key respect: both may have the hope (and Arendt wrote about this too in relation to the ghettos) that if they can only work hard enough and continue to make themselves useful and not show any sign of rebellion, then the system will eventually be merciful and will choose not to dispense with them altogether.[35]

However, disasters are a chance to wake up, to protest, and to change – and multiple overlapping disasters even more so. We know from past experience that disasters can radicalize people, but this does not always work out well. We might think here of the role of the First World War in giving birth to both Communism and Nazism. Radical solutions may bring their own versions of magical thinking and their own forms of intimidation, as we saw many times with Communism. And Nazism should remind us that radical politics may also trigger a political backlash that ends up bolstering important existing interests while embracing its own disastrous kinds of magic. To my mind, the point is not to 'rebel' in any violent sense. As Gandhi stressed, such violence tends to legitimize security structures while also reinforcing the sense of self-righteousness within and around these structures.[36] In both the Global South and the Global North, violent protest has sometimes been quickly and effectively instrumentalized to strengthen state repression. This can easily become part of a toxic politics of distraction-and-fear that sells people the 'lesser evil' of state repression on the grounds that it prevents a greater one that is rather quickly labelled as 'terrorism'.[37] A better path, to my mind, is to think for oneself, to question one's own assumptions, to talk with others, to speak very plainly about what is happening, to organize protest, and to refuse to cooperate. In that sense, we are back to Gandhi and 'non-violent non-cooperation', a path that helped to bring about Indian independence, which strongly informed the Arab Spring, and which remains much more threatening to power than we often imagine.[38]

Meanwhile, rights can be affirmed in small ways as well as large, and that means the rights of everyone and not simply the rights of privileged groups or the rights of those who have comfortably progressive views. Faith in the existence of rights rests on their observance, as Arendt showed. In the middle of a devastating civil war, it is hardly surprising that people are often sceptical about the relevance and even the existence of human rights. At one workshop in Sierra Leone, some local people said human rights were irrelevant because everybody ignored them. In 1995, during one of the peaks of Sierra Leone's civil war, a local doctor told me 'This country needs to be saved. People don't believe they have rights as human beings. People here are so innocent.' A priest commented: 'There's little concept of justice and rights, more of an overwhelming anger.'

When I was doing research in Serbia in 1999, I learned that many people did not actually believe in the concept or existence of human rights – essentially, because *their own* human rights had not been upheld. Given that domestic political support for national law, for international law and for international humanitarianism seems to be perched on a knife-edge in the US and the UK and elsewhere, it would seem helpful to ask what kinds of support and inclusion can help to regenerate a sense of generosity and a sense that rights, in a real and practical sense, actually do *exist* and can benefit everyone. In the UK, organizations like Oxfam are beginning to wonder whether a neglect of the interests of ordinary people *in Britain* has helped to generate a political climate in which it becomes difficult to address the rights of people *anywhere*. In July 2014, just north of San Diego in California, residents of Murrieta protested the arrival of Central American children. One protester said, 'We can't take care of others if we can't take care of our own.'[39] For a sceptical individual, the best advertisement for the importance and existence of human rights may well be some kind of practical demonstration that *your own* rights as a human being are being taken seriously. That also means including you in the working definition of the community rather than labelling you as irrational or 'beyond the pale'.

From Arendt's perspective the hope lies partly in good actions, however small, which push in the opposite direction to those 'lesser evils' that generally turn out to be not so small after all. If every infringement of human rights is a kind of denial of legal and moral frameworks, it is also the case that every action upholding human rights – on whatever scale – is correspondingly a crucial affirmation that these rights do in fact exist: in fact, it is 'action as propaganda' in reverse. In the face of the current migration crisis, there has been a huge wave of volunteer humanitarianism, with people from all walks of life offering their time and services to help the refugee populations.[40] This is not so much an old-style ideological movement with a prescription for a new world order as it is an amazing accumulation of the 'small and not so small' acts of kindness that Arendt sees as making a better world. Each act of helping carries the message, which may or may not be widely heard, that human rights do exist and that they exist because there are people who are still willing – rather against the odds and in many ways against the *Zeitgeist* – to make them real. Even if not widely noticed, this kind of affirmation will almost always be noticed by those whose rights are being affirmed. This opens at least the possibility of a virtuous circle, a circle that is already playing out every day in countless ways alongside all the bad things that are happening and being encouraged to happen.

Notes

1 Disasters Coming Home

1 Keen, 1994.
2 See e.g. Africa Watch, 1991; Duffield, 1994a; de Waal, 1997; Kaldor, 1998.
3 E.g. Keen, 1994; Keen, 2008.
4 *Oxford Dictionary of English*, 2010, 498.
5 Wikipedia (drawing on aid agency sources). The definition goes on to refer to a situation that exceeds a community's ability to cope.
6 Other sites of significant terrorist attacks included Germany, Belgium, Norway, Sweden and Canada.
7 Stevenson, 2019.
8 Miller-Idriss, 2021, 56.
9 Stevenson, 2019.
10 E.g. Watts, 2021.
11 Gutiérrez et al., 2021.
12 E.g. Blaikie et al., 2003.
13 E.g. White, 2015a.
14 E.g. Loewenstein, 2017.
15 E.g. McQuarrie, 2017 on the effects on labour; Wade, 2009 on largely unregulated capital movements.
16 Wade, 2009, 1169.
17 On manufacturing output, see for example Lincicome, 2021.
18 Duffield, 2019.
19 McQuarrie, 2017, S135.
20 Saez and Zucman, 2016.
21 E.g. Coronese et al., 2019.
22 Ibid.
23 Varoufakis, 2021.
24 Mishra, 2017, 341.
25 For example, in Spain and the UK.

26 Cf. Duffield, 2019.
27 Alexander, 2019.
28 E.g. Keen and Andersson, 2018.
29 See, notably, Andersson, 2014 and Andersson, 2019.
30 E.g. Said, 1991.
31 Keen, 2005; Keen, 2012.
32 E.g. Evans-Pritchard, 2002.
33 Freud, 1960, 3.
34 Ibid., 86.
35 Ibid., 87.
36 Ibid., 87.
37 Ogden, 2010, 319.
38 Freud, 1960, especially ch. 3 'Animism, magic and the omnipotence of thoughts'.
39 See discussion in Favila, 2001.
40 Freud, 1960, 88.
41 Ibid., 88.
42 Ibid.
43 Arendt, 1968, 437.
44 Ibid., 437.
45 *Oxford Dictionary of English*, 184.
46 Césaire, 2000, 36.
47 E.g. Graham, 2013.
48 Arendt, 1986, 222–3 (Arendt is quoting from Ernst Hasse's *Deutsche Politik*); see also Gerwarth and Malinowski, 2009.
49 Comaroff and Comaroff, 2013, 114.
50 E.g. Lazar, 2020.
51 Comaroff and Comaroff, 2013, 12.
52 Haug, 2021.
53 Comaroff and Comaroff, 2013.
54 Lazar, 2020, 6.
55 Woodward, 1995.
56 Todorova, 2009, 13.
57 Said, 1991.
58 Todorova, 2009.
59 Applebaum, 2020, argues convincingly against such a separation.
60 Ibid., 2020.

2 Lessons from 'Far Away'

1 E.g. Comaroff and Comaroff, 2013.
2 Foucault, 1977.
3 Foucault, 1980.
4 E.g. Keen, 2008.
5 Sen, 1984.
6 Rangasami, 1985.
7 Keen 1994; Verhoeven, 2011.
8 Chabal and Daloz, 1999, xviii.
9 Browning 1992; Wyman, 1984.

10 See also Browning, 1992 on the Nazi Holocaust
11 See e.g. Wisner, 2001.
12 Klein, 2007.
13 Andersson and Keen, *Wreckonomics* (forthcoming).
14 Hoyos, 2012.
15 Klein, 2017, has interesting material on this.
16 See e.g. Norberg, 2008. War boosted early rises in state power (Tilly, 1985; Cramer, 2006).
17 Hoyos, 2012; Foucault, 1980.
18 E.g. de Waal, 2015; cf. Keen and Andersson, 2018.
19 Chabal and Daloz, 1999.
20 Sen and Drèze, 1989.
21 E.g. Rubin, 2009.
22 Cf. Rangasami, 1985.
23 de Waal, 2000.
24 de Waal, 1997; de Waal, 2000.
25 Keen, 1994.
26 Venugopal, 2018; ICG, 2007; Spencer, 2008.
27 Weiss, 2012.
28 Levitsky and Ziblatt, 2019, 5. See also Rigi (2012) on 'the corrupt state of exception' in Russia.
29 Levitsky and Ziblatt, 2019, 204.
30 E.g. Keen, 2008.
31 Cf. Rangasami, 1985.
32 E.g. Keen, 2008; Keen, 2014.
33 E.g. Weiss, 2012.
34 E.g. Keen, 2014; Allié, 2011; see also Weissman, 2011, on MSF's decision-making.
35 Stoakes, 2017.
36 UN Panel of Experts, 2011.
37 Jaspars, 2018.
38 E.g. Stockton, 1998; Bradbury, 2010.
39 Stockton, 1988; see also Marriage, 2006.
40 E.g. Menkhaus, 2012; Gordon, 2020.
41 Keen, 2013.
42 Cf. Keen, 1994; Kalyvas, 2004.
43 Arendt, 1968, 363.
44 E.g. Keen, 2017.
45 Keen, 2012; Attree, 2016.
46 Weissman refers to MSF choosing 'the lesser evil' in choosing not to denounce the government of Sri Lanka but help survivors (Weissman, 2011, 33).
47 E.g. Bartov, 2000.
48 Cohn, 2007.
49 Mamdani, 2001, 207
50 Muana, 1997, 84.
51 Ibid., 88.
52 Allen, 1997.
53 Hickel, 2015.

54 Jaspars, 2018.
55 Duffield, 2019, viii.
56 Ibid.; cf. Zuboff, 2019; Andersson, 2019.
57 Keen, 2003.
58 See notably Venugopal, 2009.
59 E.g. Cutler, 1989; Keen, 1994.
60 Duffield, 2019; Andersson, 2019.
61 Robinson et al., 2021.
62 E.g. Keen, 1994, 2014; Weissman (ed.), 2004.
63 E.g. Armstrong, 2009.

3 A Self-Reinforcing System?

1 We see this in nature when the product of a reaction leads to an increase in that reaction.
2 Bigo suggests securitization comes from actions as well as speech (e.g. Bigo, 2014).
3 Duffield, 1994b. On global systems, see e.g. Duffield, 2019.
4 Ahmed, 2011; see also Keen, 2017 on Syria.
5 Ahmed, 2011, 351.
6 Ibid., 345.
7 Ibid., 348.
8 Ibid., 351.
9 Ibid., 336.
10 Klein, 2015; Klein, 2017.
11 E.g. Klein, 2017.
12 Klein, 2017, 156; Sylves, 2006.
13 Keegan, 2021.
14 Gotham and Greenberg, 2008; see also Gotham, 2012.
15 Brand and Baxter, 2020; see also Tierney, 2015.
16 Gotham, 2012, 642.
17 Klein, 2017, 153; cf. Nuba complaints on land-stealing in Sudan: we 'began to know that the Sudan Government is not our government.' (African Rights, 1995, 49).
18 See e.g. Keen, 2017, on drought/war in Syria.
19 Sylves, 2006.
20 Kellner, 2007.
21 CNN, 2009.
22 Sylves, 2006, 54.
23 Thomas and Warner, 2019.
24 Klein, 2017, 154.
25 Ibid., 201.
26 Ambrose, 2021.
27 See also Keen and Andersson, 2018.
28 Davidson and Saull, 2017.
29 Fletcher, 2012.
30 Ibid.
31 Duffield, 2001.
32 See also Duffield, 2007.

33 Agamben, 2014.
34 Cunningham and Warwick, 2013, 445.
35 Alexander, 2019.
36 E.g. Mkandawire, 2010.
37 Harvey, 2004; cf. Wade, 2009.
38 Rector, 2017, 314.
39 Ibid.; see also Stern, 2022.
40 Rector, 2017; 335; Wilde-Anderson, 2016.
41 Rector, 2017.
42 Kirkpatrick, 2016.
43 Schmitt, 2005, 5.
44 Ibid., 14.
45 Rector, 2017, 304.
46 Ibid.
47 Stern, 2022.
48 Fasenfest, 2019.
49 Klein, 2018.
50 Johnson and Barnes, 2015.
51 Stubbs and Lendvai-Bainton, 2019
52 Kornai, 2015, 38.
53 Ibid.
54 Ibid., 39.
55 Stubbs and Lendvai-Bainton, 2019, 549.
56 See for example Frank, 2012.
57 Agamben, 2014.
58 Ibid.
59 Freud, 1997.
60 Berlant, 2011, 28.
61 See also Keen, *The Politics of Shame* (forthcoming).
62 Mouffe, 2005.
63 Sommerlad, 2022.
64 Cf. Snyder, 2021.
65 Cf. Arendt, 1968.
66 Masco, 2017, 573.
67 Ibid.

4 *Emergency Politics*

1 Lerer and Corasaniti, 2020.
2 Danner, 2016.
3 Ibid. Fear of terrorism predicted support for Trump among Republican primary voters, along with an inclination towards authoritarianism (MacWilliams, 2016).
4 Volokh, 2017.
5 Chan, 2017.
6 Trump's aides said he'd been referring to a documentary the night before.
7 This was not quite true, but Obama did slow the visa process.
8 Coscarelli, 2017.
9 Topping, 2017.
10 Ibid.

11 Mencken, 2009, 54.
12 Lerer and Corasaniti, 2020.
13 Ibid.
14 After me, the deluge (or flood).
15 Udall and McGovern, 2020.
16 *Guardian*, 2020.
17 McGreal, 2020.
18 Ackerman, 2021, 325.
19 Ibid., 318.
20 Ibid., 318.
21 Wertheim, 2020.
22 Ibid.
23 Savage, 2021.
24 Ibid.
25 Blake, 2021.
26 Ibid.
27 Levine, 2021.
28 Bartov, 2000.
29 E.g. Hochschild, 2016; Haslett, 2016; Keen, *The Politics of Shame* (forthcoming).
30 Smith, 2017.
31 Bush, 2022.
32 Elias, 2000.
33 Mennell, 1990, 205.
34 Ibid.
35 Arendt, 1968, 190.
36 Arendt, 1973b.
37 Arendt, 1968, 330–1.
38 Ibid., 351. Or in ads, 'the solution *they* don't want you to know about.'
39 Cf. Arendt, 1968.
40 Hochschild, 2016.
41 *Guardian News*, 2018.
42 E.g. *Guardian* staff and agencies, 2021.
43 https://medium.com/@ericdmunoz/rationalizing-normalization-he-tells-it-like-it-is-8774eecb3f24 (Paul Noth).
44 Cf. Gerges, 2005.
45 Saez and Zucman, 2016.
46 Kuttner, 2022.
47 E.g. Shaxhon, 2018; Bullough, 2019.
48 Frank, 2004.
49 Akerlof and Shiller, 2015.
50 Hochschild, 2016, 52.
51 Keller and Kelly, 2015a, 439.
52 Keller and Kelly, 2015b, 3.
53 Ibid.
54 Hacker and Pierson, 2010.
55 Kuttner, 2022.
56 Hacker and Pierson, 2010, ebook version.
57 Jessop, 2014.

58 Ray, 2017.
59 Gilens and Page, 2014, 576.
60 Reich, 2016.
61 Abdul-Razzak et al., 2020.
62 Vogel and Kelly, 2021.
63 On the latter, see Freedland, 2021.
64 Piketty, 2014; also Akerlof and Shiller, 2015, and Bartels, 2016.
65 Hacker and Pierson, 2010.
66 McQuarrie, 2017, S127.
67 Ibid., S133.
68 Ibid.
69 Ibid.
70 Reich, 2016.
71 McQuarrie, 2017, S146.
72 Snyder, 2021; cf. Frank, 2004; cf. also Mayer, 2020.
73 E.g. Chang, 2012.
74 This was actually dwarfed by the Fed bailout to European banks. Both sets of loans seem to have been repaid though the political damage was done (e.g. Frank, 2012; Cassidy, 2018).
75 See notably Putzel, 2020.
76 Danner, 2016.
77 Jackson, 2016.
78 Frank, 2012.
79 Putzel, 2020.
80 Harvey, 2020.
81 Ibid., 49.
82 Wodak, 2019.
83 Jones, 2012, 223.
84 E.g. Ford and Goodwin, 2014; O'Toole, 2018.
85 Arendt, 1968, 332.
86 E.g. Anderson, 2021.
87 White, 2019.
88 The UK Supreme Court held that Parliament had been unlawfully prorogued (House of Commons Library, 2020).
89 Freedland, 2019.
90 White, 2019.
91 Applebaum, 2020, 86 and 92.
92 Ibid., 94.
93 Ibid., 93.
94 E.g. Müller, 2016.
95 Bielik, 2019.
96 E.g. White, 2019.
97 Applebaum, 2020, 70.
98 O'Toole, 2020b.
99 Alston, 2018, 3.
100 Case and Deaton, 2015.
101 E.g. Giroux, 2006.
102 On pollution, see Harvey, 2016.

103 Gotham and Greenberg, 2008; see also Gotham, 2013.
104 See also Loewenstein, 2017.
105 Gotham, 2012.
106 *Harvard Law Review*, 2015; Ponder and Omstedt, 2022.
107 Factbase, 2016.

5 Hostile Environments

1 Jones, 2015.
2 CNCDH, 2015.
3 Jones, 2015; Channel 4, 2015.
4 E.g. Human Rights Watch, 2017; Refugee Rights Data Project, 2016.
5 Amnesty International, 2019; Keen, 2021.
6 Cf. Mbembé, 2003.
7 Arendt, 1968, 299.
8 Ibid., 291–2.
9 Carr, 2012, 128.
10 *Défenseur des Droits*, 2015, 13.
11 Within the UK itself, centres for those waiting to claim asylum have been part of a deterrence structure, with some state-run and some privatized (e.g. Loewenstein, 2017).
12 Cf. Andersson, 2014.
13 Khomami, 2016.
14 Cf. Brown, 2010.
15 E.g. O'Toole, 2018.
16 Newton and Boyle, 2016.
17 Helm, 2021.
18 Nazi propaganda portrayed Jewish people as *less than human* but also *super-intelligent and scheming*.
19 *Sun*, 16 January 2015, in Berry et al., 2015, 41.
20 *Daily Mail*, 2015.
21 Sommer et al., 2018.
22 Ackerman, 2021, 261.
23 Grandin, 2019.
24 Amnesty International, 2017a, 15.
25 Ibid.
26 De León, 2015, 34.
27 Cornelius, 2001, 675.
28 Ibid., 678.
29 Grandin, 2019.
30 Ibid., 251.
31 Ibid.
32 Ibid., 266.
33 Amnesty International, 2017a, 7.
34 Ibid., 8.
35 E.g. Taylor, 2015.
36 Ibid.
37 IOM, 2019.
38 Amnesty International, 2017b.

39 E.g. Andersson, 2014; Andersson and Keen, 2019.
40 See also Andersson, 2014.
41 Ibid.; Keen and Andersson, 2018.
42 E.g. Baldo, 2017a; Baldo, 2017b.
43 E.g. Duffield, 2019; Jaspars, 2018; Baldo, 2017a; Baldo, 2017b; Jaspars and Buchanan-Smith, 2018.
44 E.g. Baldo, 2017a, 2017b; Jaspars and Buchanan-Smith, 2018.
45 E.g. Keen, 2012; Keen and Andersson, 2018; Andersson and Keen, 2019.
46 HRW, 2017.
47 Amnesty International, 2019.
48 See e.g. Sandri, 2018.
49 E.g. Cuttitta, 2017.
50 Cf. Pallister-Wilkins (2020); Harrell-Bond (1986).
51 Cuttitta, 2017.
52 Townsend, 2017.
53 Cf. Bartov, 2000.
54 Serwer, 2018.
55 Lind, 2018.
56 Serwer, 2018.
57 Anapol, 2018.
58 HIAS, 2018.
59 Smith, 2019.
60 E.g. Mollat, 1986.
61 Arendt, 1968, 281
62 Ibid., 281–2.
63 The League of Nations noted in 1933 that states had an obligation to accept refugees from a neighbouring country and not to expel them 'unless the said measures are dictated by reasons of national security or public order' (League of Nations, 1933, Article 3).
64 Arendt, 1968, 288.
65 Ibid.
66 Ibid.
67 Ibid., 289.
68 Keen and Andersson, 2019.
69 Bescherer, 2017.
70 Larking, 2012, 70
71 Ibid.
72 Arendt, 1968, 285.
73 Ibid.
74 Ibid.
75 Ibid. 290.
76 E.g. Grandin, 2019.
77 Laughland, 2018.
78 E.g. Siddique, 2019.
79 O'Loughlin and Gillespie, 2012, 120; see also Saddique, 2021.
80 Arendt, 1968, 276.
81 Ibid., 296.
82 Ibid., 296.

83 Wyman, 1984, 105.
84 See particularly Benhabib, 2017.

6 Welcoming Infection

1 Worldometers, 2020.
2 Costello, 2021.
3 E.g. Schreiber, 2022.
4 E.g. Rangel et al., 2020; Colombo, 2021.
5 Cf. Schaffer, 1984.
6 Stewart and Busby, 2020.
7 Parker et al., 2020.
8 Ibid.
9 Suppression involves trying to get the 'R' (reproduction) number below 1 while mitigation does not.
10 Islam, 2020.
11 Horton, 2020a.
12 *Newsnight*, BBC, 2020.
13 Ahmed, 2020a.
14 SAGE secretariat, 2020.
15 WHO was saying globally around 3.4 per cent of reported Covid-19 cases had died (Coronavirus [Covid-19] Mortality Rate, 5 March 2020, www.worldometers).
16 See e.g. discussion in Fox, 2021.
17 E.g. Fox, ibid.
18 House of Commons Science and Technology Committee (UK), 2021.
19 SPI-M-O, 2020c.
20 SAGE also noted on 17 February that 'Current estimates for the fatality rate for people hospitalized in China, who primarily have pneumonia and/or other severe symptoms, are around 15%' (SPI-M-O, 2020b, 1).
21 Mitigation would still bring down mortality (e.g. Ferguson et al., 2020) but postponements put it up.
22 Sample, 2020a.
23 Hanage, 2020.
24 Henley and Jones, 2020.
25 McCoy, 2020a.
26 Henley and Jones, 2020.
27 E.g. Kim, 2020; Shorrock, 2020.
28 Tapsfield, 2020.
29 Hellewell et al., 2020.
30 Tapper, 2020; Costello, 2020b.
31 Topping, 2020.
32 *Telegraph* reporters, 2020
33 ITV News, 2020.
34 SPI-M-O, 2020a, 1.
35 Ibid.
36 Ibid.
37 Morris, 2020.
38 Tapper, 2020.
39 Mahase, 2020.

40 Shipman and Wheeler, 2020; see also Jukes, 2020.
41 Walker, P., 2020.
42 Hancock, 2021.
43 Ibid.
44 Shipman and Wheeler, 2020.
45 Roberts, 2020.
46 Bump, 2020.
47 Ibid.
48 Facebook, 2020.
49 Ahmed, 2020b
50 On Britons' 'inalienable right' to go to the pub, see O'Toole, 2020a; cf. O'Toole, 2018.
51 Mueller, 2020b.
52 Swinford, 2021
53 Yong, 2020b.
54 Horton, 2020b.
55 Ibid.
56 Serwer, 2020.
57 Ibid.
58 Butcher and Massey, 2020.
59 Mohdin, 2020.
60 Serwer, 2020.
61 Van Dorn et al., 2020, 1243.
62 Almagro and Orane-Hutchinson, 2020.
63 Yong, 2020b.
64 Ibid.
65 Luce, 2020.
66 Wise, 2020.
67 Blake, 2020.
68 Wehner, 2020.
69 Ibid.
70 Fournier, 2001.
71 In the Cold War, a common slogan was 'Better dead than red.'
72 Yong, 2020a.
73 Maxeiner, 2020, 214.
74 Van Dorn et al., 2020, 1244.
75 Luce, 2020.
76 Yong, 2020a.
77 Ibid.; Packer, 2020.
78 Freedland, 2020a.
79 Packer, 2020.
80 Calvert et al., 2020.
81 Lawrence et al., 2020.
82 Mueller, 2020a.
83 E.g. Press Association, 2020.
84 Hattenstone, 2020; in the US, there was a shortage of ventilators, with doctors and nurses also frequently lacking basic protective gear (Menon and Kucik, 2020).

85 Stewart and Busby, 2020.
86 Johnston, 2020.
87 Ryan, 2021.
88 Booth, 2020b.
89 Pegg et al., 2020.
90 Booth, 2020b.
91 Booth, 2020a.
92 Sinclair and Read, 2020, citing Hurst, 2020.
93 Singh, 2020.
94 Cadwalladr, 2020.
95 Hattenstone, 2020.
96 White House task force briefing, 2020.
97 E.g. Channel 4, 2018.
98 Monbiot, 2020.
99 E.g. Costello, 2021
100 Maxeiner, 2020, 221.
101 Klein, 2020.
102 Foa et al., 2022.
103 Adebajo, 2020.
104 *Telegraph*, foreign staff, 2020.
105 'The UK dragged its feet for an interminable eight weeks and the US ignored clear warning signs for 70 days' (Liu, 2020).
106 Dalglish, 2020, 1189.
107 Johns Hopkins Bloomberg School of Public Health/Nuclear Threat Initiative, 2021, 6.
108 Doward, 2020; United Nations, 2020.
109 Waterson, 2020.
110 Werleman, 2020.
111 E.g. American Progress, 2022.
112 Frum, 2020.
113 Smith, 2020.
114 Applebaum, 2020.
115 Weigel, 2020.
116 Foa et al., 2022, 1.
117 See e.g. United Nations, 2020. Such developments, of course, may make it harder to disabuse the likes of QAnon.
118 Ibid., 16.
119 Freedland, 2020b.
120 Applebaum, 2020.
121 Doward, 2020.
122 See also Honig, 2014.
123 House of Commons Science and Technology Committee (UK), 2021, para. 44.
124 Campbell, 2020; see also Horton, 2020b, 1178.
125 Horton, 2020b, 1178.
126 McCoy, 2020b.
127 Costello, 2020a.
128 Hunter et al., 2022.

129 Ward, 2020; Jones, 2020.
130 Van Dorn et al., 2020.
131 Maxeiner, 2020, 218.
132 Packer, 2020.
133 Ferguson, 2020.
134 Sample, 2020b.
135 E.g. Rangel et al., 2020; McKie, 2022.
136 Chakrabortty, 2020.
137 Packer, 2020.

7 *Magical Thinking*

1 Chait, 2017.
2 Scherer, 2017.
3 Osnos, 2018.
4 Ibid.
5 O'Toole, 2020b.
6 Nelson, 2017. Conway's comments came after Trump mocked the disability of a reporter.
7 Netflix, 1977.
8 E.g. Hochschild, 2016, 227.
9 Hochschild, 2016.
10 Arendt, 1968.
11 Ibid., 356, 477.
12 Ibid.
13 Ibid., 474.
14 Arendt, 1994b, 349–50.
15 Arendt, 1968, 356.
16 Ibid., 437.
17 Ibid.
18 Ibid., 439, citing especially Bettelheim.
19 Ibid.
20 See, notably, Bartov, 2000.
21 Girard, 1977.
22 Arendt, 1994c, 292–3.
23 Ibid., 292.
24 Ibid.
25 Ibid.
26 Manjoo, 2008.
27 *Guardian*/Associated Press, 2018.
28 Christensen and Santiago, 2018.
29 Lind, 2018; Collins, 2018.
30 Arendt, 1973a. Even the South Vietnamese government had many important priorities other than winning the war (e.g. Corson, 1968).
31 Arendt, 1973a, 31.
32 Ibid., quoting Ralph Stavins et al.'s *Washington Plans an Aggressive War*.
33 Ibid., 15.
34 Ibid., 15; Cohn, 1987.
35 Arendt, 2006, 253–4.

36 Ibid., 256.
37 E.g. Frank, 2004; Hochschild, 2016.
38 Hofstadter, 2008, 106.
39 See e.g. Parten, 2021.
40 Hofstadter, 2008, 133.
41 Grandin, 2019, 223.
42 Ibid.
43 Ibid; see also Belew, 2018.
44 Grandin, 2019.
45 Ibid., 229.
46 Ibid.
47 Ibid., 255.
48 Ibid.
49 Ibid.
50 Ibid., 266.
51 Ibid.
52 Ibid., 273.
53 Ibid.,
54 Ibid., 273–4.
55 Belew, 2018, 7–8.
56 CNN.com, 2001.
57 Woodward, 2002, 38–9.
58 E.g. Jones, 2016.
59 See notably Applebaum, 2020.
60 Belton, 2020; Applebaum, 2020.
61 Gawthorpe, 2022; Garamvolgyi and Borger, 2022.
62 Gawthorpe, 2022.
63 Applebaum, 2020, 20.
64 Buchanan, 2013.
65 Bartov's excellent *Mirrors of Destruction* (2000) discusses some material issues involved.
66 E.g. Bartov, 2000. This mechanism also informed the 1994 Rwandan genocide.
67 Applebaum, 2020.
68 E.g. Kornai, 2015.
69 Applebaum, 2020.
70 Ibid., 45; see also Krastev, 2016.
71 E.g. Davies, 2016.
72 Cooper, 2021. In Poland and Hungary, mass privatizations in 1990s did help lots of former Communists translate their political connections into economic power (e.g. Applebaum, 2020).
73 E.g. Frank, 2016; McQuarrie, 2017.
74 Sanders is an obvious one.
75 E.g. Fogleson, 2020.
76 Siddiqui, 2019
77 E.g. Gessen, 2017.
78 NPR, 2018.
79 Lukyanov, 2020.

80 Siddiqui, 2019. Of course, this not the same as concluding that the Trump campaign *did not* conspire with Russia.
81 E.g. Gessen, 2017.
82 Ibid.
83 Sakwa, 2021, 276–7.
84 Ibid., 265.
85 Ibid., 268.
86 Gessen, 2017; remarks by Naomi Klein in *Intercepted*, 2019.
87 Fraser, 2017a.
88 See e.g. Brenner's (2017) critique.
89 Isaac, 2019.
90 McQuarrie, 2017, S127.
91 Michaels, 2008, 34.
92 Fraser, 2017b.
93 Ibid.
94 Fraser, 2017a.
95 E.g. McQuarrie, 2017; Harrington, 2022.
96 FirstPost, 2022.
97 Harrington, 2022.
98 Robinson et al., 2021.
99 Andersson and Keen, *Wreckonomics* (forthcoming); Keen and Andersson, 2018.
100 Wade, 2009, 1167.
101 Comaroff and Comaroff, 2013, 124.
102 Wade, 2009, 1177.
103 Cf. Beck, 1992.
104 O'Toole, 2018.
105 Pilkington, 2022.
106 Hochschild, 2022.
107 Krastev, 2016, 10.
108 Ibid., 11.

8 Policing Delusions

1 Arendt, 1968, 392.
2 See e.g. Armstrong, 2009 on the Soviet Union and Becker, 1996 on China.
3 Arendt, 2006, 240.
4 Ibid., 241.
5 Snyder, 2021.
6 Ibid.
7 Stanley, 2018, 64
8 Smith, 2018.
9 Müller, 2016.
10 Hofstadter, 2008.
11 Arendt, 2003b, 271.
12 Cf. Belew (2018) on the Vietnam War fuelling domestic right-wing extremism.
13 Arendt, 2003b, 263–4.
14 Arendt, 1973a.
15 Alexander, 2019; Kuzmarov, 2008.
16 Ibid.

17 See notably Belew, 2018.
18 Stevenson, 2019.
19 Khan et al., 2021, 7.
20 Wertheim, 2020.
21 There was an element of provoking America too (e.g. Gerges, 2005).
22 Goepner, 2016, 113.
23 Global Terrorism Index, 2015 and 2016.
24 Cooper, 2002; Ignatieff, 2004a; Ignatieff, 2004b.
25 Cooper, 2002.
26 E.g. Keen, 2006.
27 Woodward, 2002, 342.
28 Suskind, 2004a, 292.
29 Ibid.
30 Smith, 2003.
31 Smith, 2005, citing civil service paper for 23 July 2002 Downing Street meeting.
32 E.g. Klein, 2007.
33 Said, 2003.
34 E.g. Gerges, 2005; Dodge and Wasser, 2014.
35 Blair, 2007.
36 Mouffe, 2005.
37 Cf. Fanon, 2008.
38 Cf. Armstrong, 2009.
39 The White House, 2001.
40 Extracts from letter to Alastair Campbell, *Guardian*, 28 June 2003.
41 Osnos, 2018, 65.
42 Ibid.
43 Kundnani, 2014.
44 Choudhury and Fenwick, 2011.
45 Kundnani, 2014, 168.
46 Kumar, 2020, 38.
47 Allen, 2021; Kundnani, 2014; Chaudhury and Fenwick, 2011.
48 Kundnani, 2014.
49 Dodd and Grierson, 2020.
50 Grierson and Scott, 2020.
51 E.g. Taylor, 2021.
52 Klein, 2015, 362.
53 E.g. Malik, 2021.
54 We can see this in the work of Hochschild, 2016; Bageant 2007; and Frank, 2004, for example.

9 Action as Propaganda

1 One example was the 2015 electoral defeat of Sri Lankan President Mahinda Rajapaksa.
2 Arendt, 1968, 363.
3 Ibid., 470–1.
4 Ibid., 364.
5 Ibid.

6 Ibid., 424.
7 Arendt, 1968, 429
8 E.g. Bartov, 2000.
9 E.g. Hinton, 1998.
10 Arendt, 1968, 415.
11 See notably Andersson, 2014.
12 E.g. Browning, 1992.
13 Arendt, 1968, 269.
14 Hagan, 2018; Hagan, 2019.
15 Arendt, 1968, 446.
16 Ibid., 422.
17 Burck and Hughes, 2018, 227; see also Davies et al., 2017.
18 Smith and Agren, 2018; Gonzales, 2018.
19 E.g. Lerner and Simmons, 1966.
20 Balls, 2018.
21 E.g. Davidson and Saull, 2017.
22 White, 2015a; White, 2015b.
23 Arendt, 1968, 280.
24 Ibid., 269.
25 Hitler, 1939.
26 Cf. Schmitt, 2005.
27 Petley, 2009, 79.
28 Ibid.
29 E.g. McQuarrie, 2017.
30 Petley, 2009.
31 Ibid.
32 Arendt, 1968, 348–9.
33 Ibid., 383.
34 Perle, 2003.
35 Arendt, 1968, 269.
36 Ibid., 333.
37 Suskind, 2004b.
38 Woodward, 2002, 338.
39 Arendt, 1968, 215.
40 Scherer, 2017.
41 Arendt, 1968, 383.
42 Ibid.
43 Ibid., 4701.
44 Vazquez and Judd, 2020.
45 Arendt, 1994b, 346.
46 O'Toole, 2020b.
47 Arendt, 1994b, 349–50.

10 Choosing Disaster

1 Arendt, 2003a, 35.
2 Ibid., 35–6.
3 Ibid., 37; cf. Arendt, 1994a.
4 Arendt, 1994b, 276.

5 Ibid., 281.
6 See Spielthenner, 2010.
7 Ibid.
8 Arendt, 2003a, 36.
9 Arendt, 1994b, 271.
10 Ibid., 271–2.
11 Ibid., 1994a.
12 E.g. Schaffer, 1984.
13 Keen, 2005.
14 Ibid.
15 E.g. Keen and Andersson, 2018.
16 Dershowitz, 2003; cf. Ignatieff, 2004a.
17 E.g. Gerges, 2005.
18 E.g. Keen, 2012.
19 E.g. Keen with Attree, 2015.
20 E.g. Andersson, 2014.
21 Arendt, 1968, 367.
22 E.g. Kallis, 2013.
23 Betts and Collier, 2017.
24 Betts and Collier fall into this double standard.
25 Kallis, 2013, 237.
26 Ibid., 238; Wodak, 2019.
27 E.g. Kallis, 2013; Ebner, 2017.
28 Krause et al., 2022.
29 Netflix, 2017.
30 Ibid.
31 Hanage, 2020.
32 As Jana Bacevic, 2020 notes, 'following the science' ignores the political nature of decisions, including trade-offs.
33 Serwer, 2020.
34 Kristof and Thompson, 2020.
35 Serwer, 2020.
36 Ahmed, 2020b; Walker, A., 2020.

11 Home to Roost

1 The *Goebbels Diaries*, 1948, 314 in Arendt, 1968.
2 The *Oxford Dictionary of English* (2010, 1837) defines terrorism as 'the unofficial or unauthorized use of violence and intimidation in the pursuit of political aims'. But such a definition risks positioning rebellion as terrorism.
3 Hofstadter, 2008.
4 Arendt, 2003b, 275.
5 Denman, 2020, 1139.
6 Ibid.
7 Graham, 2013.
8 White House, 2022.
9 Connolly, 2020.
10 Sabbagh, 2022.
11 Ibid.

12 Harris, 2022.
13 Truss, 2022.
14 Ni, 2022.
15 O'Toole, 2018.
16 Andersson, 2014.
17 E.g. Klein, 2017.
18 Andersson, 2019.
19 Ibid.
20 Ousting Saddam did not solve the problems of Iraq.
21 Cf. Putzel, 2020.
22 Arendt, 1994b, 271.
23 See also Keen, *The Politics of Shame*, forthcoming.
24 E.g. Andersson, 2014; Klein, 2017; Ahmed, 2011.
25 Figures from SIPRI, 2021, 2.
26 Tsygankov, 2018, 109.
27 Marten, 2020, emphasizes status concerns.
28 Ibid.
29 E.g. Forsberg and Pursiainen, 2017; Tsygankov, 2018.
30 Ahmed, 2011, 336.
31 E.g. Klein, 2007; Castells, 1998.
32 Markus, 2017; cf. Giustozzi, 2004.
33 Belton, 2020.
34 Cf. Arendt, 1998; Duffield, 2019.
35 Arendt, 1968; cf. Stein, 2009.
36 Stephan and Chenoweth, 2008.
37 E.g. Keen, 2017.
38 Stephan and Chenoweth, 2008.
39 Grandin, 2019, 265.
40 E.g. Sandri, 2018.

References

Abdul-Razzak, N. et al. 2020. 'After citizens united', *Electoral Studies*, 67.

Ackerman, S. 2021. *Reign of Terror*. Viking.

Adebajo, A. 2020. 'Trump vs The WHO', *Business Day*, 20 April.

African Rights. 1995. *Facing Genocide.*

Agamben, G. 2014. 'For a theory of destituent power', *Critical Legal Thinking*, 5 February.

Ahmed, N. 2011. 'The international relations of crisis and the crisis of international relations', *Global Change, Peace and Security*, 23(3), 335–55.

— 2020a. 'This is how America and Britain are maximizing coronavirus deaths', *Insurge-Intelligence*, 12 March.

— 2020b. 'Leaked Home Office call reveals government wants economy to "continue running" as "we will all get" COVID-19 anyway', *Byline Times*, 9 April.

Akerlof, G. and R. Shiller. 2015. *Phishing for Phools*. Princeton University Press.

Alexander, M. 2019. *The New Jim Crow*. Penguin (first published 2010).

Allen, T. 1997. 'The violence of healing', *Sociologus*, 47(2), 101–28.

Allié, M-P. 2011. 'Acting at any price?' in C. Magone et al. (eds), *Humanitarian Negotiations Revealed*. Hurst & Co.

Almagro, M. and A. Orane-Hutchinson. 2020. 'Disparities in exposure to Covid-19 across New York City neighbourhoods', *Covid Economics*, 13, 31–50.

Alston, P. 2018. 'Report of the Special Rapporteur on extreme poverty and human rights on his mission to the United States of America', UN General Assembly. 4 May.

Ambrose, T. 2021. 'World's militaries avoiding scrutiny over emissions', *Guardian*, 11 November.

American Progress. 2022. 'The Title 42 Expulsion Policy does nothing to prevent the spread of Covid-19', 10 May.

Amnesty International. 2017a. *Facing Walls*.

— 2017b. *Libya's Dark Web of Collusion*. 11 December.

— 2019. *Targeting Solidarity*. June.

Anapol, A. 2018. 'Fox Business drops guest who blamed migrant caravan on "Soros-occupied state department"', *The Hill*, 28 October.
Anderson, P. 2021. 'The Breakaway', *London Review of Books*, 21 January.
Andersson, R. 2014. *Illegality Inc.* University of California Press.
— 2019. *No Go World.* University of California Press.
Andersson, R. and D. Keen. 2019. *Partners in Crime?* Saferworld, July.
Andersson, R. and D. Keen (forthcoming). *Wreckonomics*, Oxford University Press.
Applebaum, A. 2020. *Twilight of Democracy*. Allen Lane/Penguin.
Arendt, H. 1968. *The Origins of Totalitarianism.* Harvest/Harcourt (first published 1951).
— 1973a. 'Lying in politics', in Arendt, *Crises of the Republic*. Penguin.
— 1973b. 'On violence', in Arendt, *Crises of the Republic*. Penguin.
— 1994. 'On the nature of totalitarianism', in Arendt, *Essays in Understanding, 1930–1954* (ed. J. Kohn). Schocken.
— 1994a. *Eichmann in Jerusalem.* Penguin.
— 1994b. 'The eggs speak up', in Arendt, *Essays in Understanding, 1930–1954* (ed. J. Kohn). Schocken (paper written circa 1950).
— 1994c. 'At table with Hitler', in Arendt, *Essays in Understanding, 1930–1954* (ed. J. Kohn). Schocken (first published 1951–2).
— 1998. *The Human Condition*. University of Chicago Press (first published 1958).
— 2003a. 'Personal responsibility under dictatorship', in J. Kern, *Responsibility and Judgement*. Schocken, 17–48 (first published 1964).
— 2003b. 'Home to roost', in Jerome Kern, *Responsibility and Judgement* (ed. J. Kern) Schocken, 257–75 (first published 1975).
— 2006. 'Truth and politics', in H. Arendt, *Between Past and Future*. Penguin, 223–59 (first published 1967).
Armstrong, S. 2009. 'Stalin's witch-hunt', *Totalitarian Movements and Political Religions*, 10(3–4), 221–40.
Attree, L. 2016. *Blown Back*. Saferworld, February.
Bacevic, Jana. 2020. 'There's no such thing as just "following the science" – coronavirus advice is political', *Guardian*, 28 April.
Bageant, J. 2007. *Deer Hunting with Jesus*. Crown Publishers.
Baldo, S. 2017a. 'Border control from hell', The Enough Project, April.
— 2017b. 'Ominous threats descending on Darfur', The Enough Project, November.
Balls, E. 2018. 'Travels in Trumpland with Ed Balls', BBC2, 29 July.
Bartels, L. 2016. *Unequal Democracy*. Princeton University Press.
Bartov, O. 2000. *Mirrors of Destruction*. Oxford University Press.
Beck, U. 1992. *Risk Society*. Sage.
Becker, J. 1996. *Hungry Ghosts*. John Murray.
Belew, K. 2018. *Bring the War Home*. Harvard University Press.
Belton, C. 2020. *Putin's People*. William Collins.
Benhabib, S. 2017. 'Nothing is more dangerous for human beings than to be forgotten', blog, 10 March.
Berlant, L. 2011. *Cruel Optimism*. Duke University Press.
Berry, M. et al. 2015. 'Press coverage of the refugee and migrant crisis in the EU', UNHCR/Cardiff School of Journalism, December.
Bescherer, K. 2017. 'Borders, industry, logistics', Humboldt University, Masters.
Betts, A. and P. Collier. 2017. *Refuge*. Allen Lane/Penguin.

Bielik, S. 2019. 'With its lurch to the right, Britain is no longer special in Europe', *Guardian*, 24 December.

Bigo, D. 2014. 'The (in)securitization practices of the three universes of EU border control', *Security Dialogue* 45(3), 209–25.

Blaikie, P. et al. 2003. *At Risk*. Routledge (first published 1994).

Blair, T. 2007. 'A battle for global values', *Foreign Affairs*, January/February.

Blake, A. 2020. 'Trump's continually strange comments on possibly "overrated" coronavirus testing', *Washington Post*, 15 May.

—2021. 'The role of violent threats in Trump's GOP reign, according to Republicans', *Washington Post*, 14 October.

Booth, R. 2020a. 'Ministers were warned two years ago of care homes' exposure to pandemics', *Guardian*, 13 May.

— 2020b. 'Why did so many people die of Covid-19 in the UK's care homes?' *Guardian*, 28 May.

Bradbury, M. 2010. 'State-building, counterterrorism, and licensing humanitarianism in Somalia', Feinstein International Center, September.

Brand, A. and V. Baxter. 2020. 'Post-disaster development dilemmas', in S. Laska (ed.) *Louisiana's Response to Extreme Weather.* Extreme Weather and Society/ SpringerLink, 217–40.

Brenner, J. 2017. 'There was no such thing as "progressive neoliberalism"', *Dissent Online*, 14 January.

Brown, W. 2010. *Walled States, Waning Sovereignty*. Zone Books.

Browning, C. 1992. *The Path to Genocide*. Cambridge University Press.

Buchanan, P. 2013. 'Putin's paleoconservative moment', *American Conservative*, 17 December.

Bullough, O. 2019. *Moneyland*, Profile.

Bump, P. 2020. 'The problem with Trump's "herd mentality" line isn't the verbal flub. It's the mass death', *Washington Post*, 16 September.

Burck, C. and G. Hughes. 2018. 'Challenges and impossibilities of "standing alongside" in an intolerable context', *Clinical Child Psychology*, 23(2), 223–37.

Bush, S. 2022. 'How "vice-signalling" swallowed electoral politics', *Financial Times*, 23 June.

Butcher, B. and J. Massey. 2020. 'Why are more people from BAME backgrounds dying from coronavirus?' *BBC News*, 7 May.

Cadwalladr, C. 2020. 'They can't get away with this', *Guardian*, 20 April.

Calvert, J. et al. 2020. 'Coronavirus: 38 days when Britain sleepwalked into disaster', *Sunday Times*, 29 April.

Campbell, D. 2020. 'NHS staff "gagged" over coronavirus shortages', *Guardian*, 31 March.

Carr, M. 2012. *Fortress Europe*. Hurst & Co.

Case, A. and A. Deaton. 2015. 'Rising morbidity and mortality in midlife among white non-Hispanic Americans in the 21st century', *Proceedings of the National Academy of Sciences in the United States of America*, 112(49), 15078–83.

Cassidy, J. 2018. 'The real cost of the 2008 financial crisis', *New Yorker*, 17 September.

Castells, M. 1998. *End of Millennium*. Blackwell.

Césaire, A. 2000. *Discourse on Colonialism*. Monthly Press Review, ProQuest Ebook Central (first published 1950).

Chabal, P. and J.-P. Daloz. 1999. *Africa Works*. James Currey.

Chait, J. 2017. '"I alone can fix it" becomes "It's not my fault,"' *New York Magazine*, 25 August.

Chakrabortty, A. 2020. 'Right now, the only thing staving off a collapse in the social order is the state', *Guardian*, 13 May.

Chan, S. 2017. 'Last night in Sweden?' *New York Times*, 19 February.

Chang, H.-J. 2012. 'We must stop protecting the rich from market forces', *Guardian*, 24 October.

Channel 4. 2015. 'Calais Jungle Camp littered with asbestos', November.

— 2018. 'How generous have the Conservatives been with the NHS?' 20 June.

Chaudhury, T. and H. Fenwick. 2011. *The Impact of Counter-Terrorism Measures on Muslim Communities*. Equality and Human Rights Commission.

Christensen, J. and L. Santiago. 2018. 'Despite rhetoric, illness threat from migrants is minimal, experts say', *CNN*, 2 November.

CNCDH (Commission Nationale Consultative des Droits de l'Homme). 2015. 'Opinion on the situation of migrants in Calais and in the Pale of Calais', July.

CNN. 2001. 'Falwell apologizes to gays, feminists, lesbians', 14 September.

— 2009. 'Court: Army Corps of Engineers liable for Katrina flooding', 19 November.

Cohn, C. 1987. 'Sex and death in the rational world of defense intellectuals'. *Signs*, 12(4), 687–718.

Cohn, S. 2007. 'The Black Death and the burning of Jews', *Past and Present*, 196, 3–36.

Collins, B. 2018. 'Pittsburgh synagogue shooting suspect threatened Jewish groups', NBC News, 27 October.

Colombo, E. 2021. 'Human rights-inspired governmentality', *Critical Sociology*, 47(4–5), 571–81.

Comaroff, J. and J. Comaroff. 2013. 'Writing theory from the south: The global world from an African perspective', *World Financial Review*, 13 November.

Connolly, G. 2020. 'Enemies of the state', *Independent*, 25 August.

Cooper, L. 2021. 'Authoritarian protectionism in central, eastern and south-eastern Europe', *LSE IDEAS*, June.

Cooper, R. 2002. 'Why we still need empires', *Observer*, 7 April.

Cornelius, W. 2001. 'Death at the border', *Population and Development Review*, 27(4), 661–85.

Coronese, M. et al. 2019. 'Evidence for sharp increase in the economic damages of extreme natural disasters', *PNAS*, 116(43), 21450–5.

Corson, W. 1968. *The Betrayal*. W. W. Norton and Co.

Coscarelli, J. 2017. 'Kellyanne Conway admits "Bowling Green Massacre" error', *New York Times*, 3 February.

Costello, A. 2020a. 'A public inquiry into the UK's coronavirus response would find a litany of failures', *Guardian*, 1 April.

— 2020b. 'Despite what Matt Hancock says, the government's policy is still herd immunity', *Guardian*, 3 April.

— 2021. '"Living with the virus" makes no sense', *Guardian*, 7 July.

Cramer, C. 2006. *Civil War Is Not a Stupid Thing*. Hurst & Co.

Cunningham, D. and A. Warwick. 2013. 'Unnoticed apocalypse', *City*, 17(4), 433–48.

Cutler, P. 1989. 'The development of the 1983–5 famine in Northern Ethiopia', PhD, London University.

Cuttitta, P. 2017. 'Repoliticization through search and rescue?' *Geopolitics*, 23(3), 623–60.

Daily Mail. 2015. 'Inside "Sangatte 2"', 25 March.
Dalglish, S. 2020. 'COVID-19 gives the lie to global health expertise', *The Lancet*, 395, 1189.
Danner, M. 2016. 'The magic of Donald Trump', *New York Review of Books*, 26 May.
Davidson, N. and R. Saull. 2017. 'Neoliberalism and the far-right', *Critical Sociology*, 43(4–5), 707–24.
Davies, C. 2016. 'The conspiracy theorists who have taken over Poland', *Guardian*, 16 February.
Davies, T., A. Isakjee and S. Dhesi. 2017. 'Violent inaction', *Antipode*, 49(5), 1263–84.
De Leon, J. 2015. *The Land of Open Graves*. University of California Press.
de Waal, A. 1997. *Famine Crimes*. James Currey.
— 2000. 'Democratic political process and the fight against Famine', IDS Working Paper, Sussex University.
— 2007. 'Sudan: The turbulent state', in de Waal (ed.) *War in Darfur – and the Search for Peace*, Justice Africa/Global Equity Initiative, 1–38.
— 2015. *The Real Politics of the Horn of Africa*, Polity.
Denman, D. 2020. 'The logistics of police power', *Society and Space*, 38(6), 1138–56.
Défenseur des Droits. 2015. 'Exiles and fundamental rights the situation in the territory of Calais', October.
Dershowitz, A. 2003. *Why Terrorism Works*. Yale University Press.
Dodd, V. and J. Grierson. 2020. 'Terrorism police list Extinction Rebellion as extremist ideology', *Guardian*, 10 January.
Dodge, T. and B. Wasser. 2014. 'The crisis of the Iraqi state', *Adelphi Series*, 54(447–8), 13–38.
Doward, J. 2020. 'Far right hijack coronavirus crisis to push agenda and boost support', *Guardian*, 25 April.
Duffield, M. 1994a. 'Complex emergencies and the crisis of developmentalism', *IDS Bulletin*, 25(4), 1–14.
— 1994b. 'The political economy of internal war', in J. Macrae and A. Zwi (eds), *War and Hunger*. Zed Books/Save the Children.
— 2001. *Global Governance and the New Wars*. Zed Books.
— 2007. *Development, Security and Unending War.* Polity.
— 2019. *Post-Humanitarianism*. Polity.
Ebner, J. 2017. 'Austria's full-face veil ban is a kneejerk reaction to the rise of the far right', *Guardian*, 1 February.
Elias, N. 2000. *The Civilizing Process*. Oxford: Blackwell (first published 1939).
Evans-Pritchard, E. 2002. *Witchcraft, Oracles and Magic Among the Azande*. Oxford University Press (first published in 1937).
Facebook. 2020. 'Anti-lockdown protesters harass Covid-19 nurses at Arizona protests', 21 April. https://www.facebook.com/NowThisPolitics/videos/anti-lockdown-protesters-harass-covid-19-nurses-at-arizona-protests/516037812407183/
Factbase. 2016. 'Speech: Donald Trump in Henderson, NV – 5 October 2016.'
Fanon, F. 2008. *Black Skin, White Masks*. Pluto (first published 1952).
Fasenfest, D. 2019. 'A neoliberal response to an urban crisis', *Critical Sociology*, 45(1), 33–47.
Favila, M. 2001. '"Mortal thoughts" and magical thinking in "Macbeth"', *Modern Philology*, 99(1), 1–25.
Ferguson, N. 2020, Twitter, 22 March.

Ferguson, N. et al., 2020. 'Report 9: Impact of non-pharmaceutical interventions (NPIs) to reduce COVID-19 mortality and healthcare demand', Imperial College Covid-19 Response Team, 16 March.

FirstPost. 2022. 'Why farmers' protests that kicked off in The Netherlands are spreading across Europe' (FirstPost Explainers), 18 July.

Fletcher, R. 2012. 'Capitalizing on chaos', *ephemera*, 12(1–2), 97–112.

Foa, R. et al. 2022. 'The great reset', University of Cambridge, January.

Foglesong, D. 2020. 'With fear and favor', *The Nation*, 17 July.

Ford, R. and M. Goodwin. 2014. *Revolt on the Right*. Routledge.

Forsberg, T. and C. Pursiainen. 2017. 'The psychological dimension of Russian foreign policy', *Global Society*, 31(2), 220–44.

Foucault, M. 1977. *Discipline and Punish*. Penguin (first published 1975).

— 1980. *Power/Knowledge*, Harvester Press (1972–7).

Fournier, R. 2001. 'Bush heads for Asian summit, says world behind U.S.', *Tulsa World*, 18 October.

Fox, F. 2021. 'Britain's Covid experts are under attack, but they are just doing their jobs', *Guardian*, 8 August.

Frank, T. 2004. *What's the Matter with Kansas?*, Secker and Warburg.

— 2012. *Pity the Billionaire*. Harvill Secker.

— 2016. *Listen, Liberal.* Scribe.

Fraser, N. 2017a. 'The end of progressive neoliberalism', *Dissent Online*, 2 January.

— 2017b. 'Against progressive neoliberalism, a new progressive populism', *Dissent Online*, 28 January.

Freedland, J. 2019. 'This political crisis now goes far beyond Brexit – our very democracy is at stake', *Guardian*, 13 September.

— 2020a. 'Trump's narcissism has taken a new twist', *Guardian*, 27 March.

— 2020b. 'Under cover of coronavirus, the world's bad guys are wreaking havoc', *Guardian*, 15 May.

— 2021. 'Don't call it sleaze, call it corruption', *Guardian*, 16 December.

Freud, S. 1960. *Totem and Taboo*. Routledge & Kegan Paul (first published 1950).

— 1997. *The Interpretation of Dreams*. Wordsworth Editions.

Frum, D. 2020. 'This is Trump's fault', *The Atlantic*, April 7.

Garamvolgyi, F. and J. Borger. 2022. 'Trump shares CPAC Hungary platform with notorious racist and antisemite', *Guardian*, 21 May.

Gawthorpe, A. 2022. 'Conservatives want to make the US more like Hungary', *Guardian*, 20 May.

Gerges, F. 2005. *The Far Enemy*, Cambridge University Press.

Gerwarth, R. and S. Malinowski. 2009. 'Hannah Arendt's ghosts', *Central European History*, 42(2), 279–300.

Gessen, M. 2017. 'Russia: The conspiracy trap', *New York Review of Books*, 6 March.

Gilens, M. and B. Page. 2014. 'Testing theories of American politics', *Perspectives on Politics*, 12(3), 564–81.

Girard, R. 1977. *Violence and the Sacred*, Johns Hopkins University Press.

Giroux, H. 2006. 'Katrina and the politics of disposability', 14 September.

Giustozzi, A. 2004. 'Respectable warlords?' Working Paper 33, Crisis States Programme, LSE.

Global Terrorism Index. 2015. 'Measuring and understanding the impact of terrorism', Institute for Economics and Peace.

— 2016. 'Measuring and understanding the impact of terrorism', Institute for Economics and Peace.

Goepner, E. 2016. 'Learning from today's wars', *Parameters* 46(1), 107–20.

Gonzales, R. 2018. 'Trump says he'll send as many as 15,000 troops to southern border', NPR, 31 October.

Gordon, S. 2020. 'Regulating humanitarian governance: Humanitarianism and the "risk society"', *Politics and Governance*, 8(4), 306–18.

Gotham, K. 2012. 'Disaster, Inc.: Privatization and post-Katrina rebuilding in New Orleans', *Perspectives on Politics*, 10(3), 633–46.

— 2013. 'Dilemmas of disaster zones', *City and Community*, 12(4), 291–308.

Gotham, K. and M. Greenberg. 2008. 'From 9/11 to 8/29: Post-disaster recovery and rebuilding in New York and New Orleans', *Social Forces*, 87(2), 1039–62.

Graham, S. 2013. 'Foucault's boomerang', *OpenDemocracy*, 14 February.

Grandin, Greg. 2019. *The End of the Myth*. Metropolitan Books/Henry Holt and Company.

Grierson, J. and R. Scott, 2020. 'Extinction Rebellion listed as "key threat" by counter-terror police', *Guardian*, 19 January.

Guardian. 2020. '"A beehive of terrorists": Donald Trump threatens to deploy national guard in Portland', 31 July.

Guardian News. 2018. 'Laughter as Trump lauds politician's body slam of Guardian journalist', 19 October.

Guardian staff and agencies, 2021. 'FBI failed to fully investigate Kavanaugh allegations, say Democrats', 22 July.

Guardian/Associated Press. 2018. 'Barack Obama takes aim at Donald Trump for "making stuff up"', 27 October.

Gutiérrez, P. et al., 2021. 'How fires have spread to previously untouched parts of the world', *Guardian*, 19 February.

Hacker, J. and P. Pierson. 2010. *Winner-Take-All Politics*. Simon & Schuster (ProQuest Ebook Central).

Hagan, M. 2018. 'Disassembling the camp', MSc, University of Amsterdam.

— 2019. 'Inhabiting a hostile environment', *Society and Space*, 38(3).

Hanage, W. 2020. 'I'm an epidemiologist. When I heard about Britain's "herd immunity" coronavirus plan, I thought it was satire', *Guardian*, 15 March.

Hancock, S. 2021. '"Who do we not save?"', *Independent*, 26 May.

Harrell-Bond, B. 1986. *Imposing Aid*. Oxford University Press.

Harris, J. 2022. 'The Tories' bellicose posturing on Ukraine is dangerous – and unfair to us', *Guardian*, 20 March.

Harrington, M. 2022. 'Why we need the apocalypse', *Unherd*, 21 July.

Harvard Law Review. 2015. 'Policing and profit', 128(1706), 1723–46.

Harvey, Daina 2016. 'The discourse of the ecological precariat making sense of social disruption in the lower ninth ward in the long-term aftermath of Hurricane Katrina', *Sociological Forum*, 31(S1), 862–84.

Harvey, David. 2004. 'The "new" imperialism: Accumulation by dispossession', *Socialist Register*, 40, 63–87.

— 2020. 'The authoritarian turn', in J. Camp and C. Caruso (eds), *The Anti-Capitalist Chronicles*. Pluto Press.

Haslett, A. 2016. 'Donald Trump, shamer in chief', *The Nation*, 24 October.

Hattenstone, S. 2020. 'The Tories' call to "protect the NHS" is a disgraceful hypocrisy', *Guardian*, 4 April.
Haug, S. 2021. 'A Thirdspace approach to the "Global South"', *Third World Quarterly*, 42(9), 2018–38.
Hellewell, J. et al., 2020. 'Feasibility of controlling COVID-19 outbreaks by isolation of cases and contacts', *The Lancet*, 28 February.
Helm, T. 2021. 'Brexit one year on', *Guardian*, 25 December.
Henley, J. and S. Jones. 2020. 'Do not let this fire burn', *Guardian*, 13 March.
Herbert, B. 2004. 'Shirking America's problems', *International Herald Tribune*, 3 August.
Hurst, Greg. (2020) 'Coronavirus: Care homes become the hidden front line in Britain's fight against Covid-19', *The Times*, 13 April.
HIAS. 2018. 'HIAS rescues people whose lives are in danger for being who they are', 27 October, Silver Spring, MD.
Hickel, J. 2015. *Democracy as Death*. University of California Press.
Hinton, A. 1998. 'A head for an eye', *American Ethnologist*, 25(3), 352–77.
Hitler, A. 1939. *Reichstag speech, January 30*. The International School for Holocaust Studies.
Hochschild, Adam. 2022. 'Who's to blame?' *New York Review*, 12 May.
Hochschild, Arlie Russell. 2016. *Strangers in Their Own Land*. The New Press.
Hofstadter, R. 2008. *The Paranoid Style in American Politics and Other Essays*. Vintage (essays from 1965).
Honig, B. 2014. 'Three models of emergency politics', *boundary 2*, 41(2), 45–70.
Horowitz, A. 2014. 'Hurricane Betsy and the politics of disaster in New Orleans's Lower Ninth Ward, 1965–1967', *Journal of Southern History*, 80(4), 893–934.
Horton, R. 2020a. 'Offline: COVID-19 – a reckoning', *The Lancet*, 395, 21 March, 935.
— 2020b. 'Offline: COVID-19 – bewilderment and candour', *The Lancet*, 395, 11 April, 1178.
House of Commons Library (UK). 2020. 'Research briefing: The prorogation dispute of 2019', 24 September.
House of Commons Science and Technology Committee (UK). 2021. 'The UK response to Covid-19: Use of scientific advice', 8 January.
Hoyos, H. 2012. 'Aftershock: Naomi Klein and the Southern Cone', *Third Text*, 26(2), 217–28.
HRW (Human Rights Watch). 2017. 'Like living in hell', July.
Hunter, D. et al. 2022. 'Reforming the public health system in England', *The Lancet*, 7, 797–800.
ICG. 2007. 'Sri Lanka: Sinhala nationalism and the elusive southern consensus', 7 November.
Ignatieff, M. 2004a. *The Lesser Evil*. Edinburgh University Press.
— 2004b. 'Could we lose the war on terror? Lesser evils', *New York Times Magazine*, 2 May.
Intercepted, 2019. 'The day after Mueller', 27 March.
IOM (International Organization for Migration). 2019. 'Mediterranean migrant arrivals reach 12,174 in 2019; deaths reach 356', 4 May.
Isaac, J. 2019. 'Beyond Trump?' *Philosophy and Social Criticism*, 45(9–10), 1157–69.
Islam, F. 2020. Video clip of Halpern, https://twitter.com/faisalislam/status/1238097745971421184 (March 2020).

ITV News. 2020. 'Coronavirus: Cheltenham festival and Liverpool Champions League game "likely increased suffering and death"' (itv.com), 26 May.

Jackson, D. 2016. 'Donald Trump accepts GOP nomination, says "I alone can fix" system', *USA Today*, 21 July.

Jaspers, S. M. 2018. *Food Aid in Sudan*, Zed.

Jaspars, S. M. and Buchanan-Smith. 2018. 'Darfuri migration from Sudan to Europe', Overseas Development Institute. August.

Jessop, B. 2014. 'Repoliticising depoliticisation', *Policy and Politics*, 42(2), 207–23.

Johns Hopkins Bloomberg School of Public Health/Nuclear Threat Initiative. 2021. Global Health Security Index, December.

Johnson, J. and A. Barnes. 2015. 'Financial nationalism and its international enablers', *Review of International Political Economy*, 22, 3, 535–69.

Johnston, J. 2020. 'Matt Hancock insists "herd immunity" not part of government's plan for tackling coronavirus', *PoliticsHome*, 15 March.

Jones, L. 2015. 'Jungle Diary, Calais', blog, 16 November.

Jones, O. 2012. *Chavs: The Demonization of the Working Class*. Verso (first published 2011).

— 2020. 'The prurient headlines about Neil Ferguson are a huge distraction', *Guardian*, 6 May.

Jones, R. 2016. 'How "values voters" became "nostalgia voters"', *The Atlantic*, 23 February.

Jukes, P. 2020. The coronavirus crisis: Herd immunity infected UK policy, but who was patient zero for this toxic transatlantic idea?' *Byline Times*, 3 April.

Kaldor, M. 1998. *New and Old Wars*, Polity.

Africa Watch. 1991. *Evil Days*.

Kallis, Aristotle. 2013. 'Far-right "contagion" or a failing "mainstream"?' *Democracy and Security*, 9(3), 221–46.

Kalyvas, S. 2004. 'The paradox of terrorism in civil war', *Journal of Ethics* 8(1), 97–138.

Keegan, C. 2021. 'Black workers matter', *Urban Geography*, 42(3), 340–59.

Keen, D. 2003. 'Demobilising Guatemala', Crisis States Research Centre LSE.

— 1991. 'A disaster for whom?' *Disasters*, 15(2).

— 1994. *The Benefits of Famine*. Princeton University Press.

— 2005. *Conflict and Collusion in Sierra Leone*. James Currey.

— 2006. *Endless War?* Pluto.

— 2008. *Complex Emergencies*. Polity.

— 2012. *Useful Enemies*. Yale University Press.

— 2013. 'When "do no harm" hurts', *New York Times*, 6 November.

— 2014. '"The camp" and "the lesser evil"', *Conflict, Security and Development*, 14(1), 1–31.

— 2017, *Syria: Playing into Their Hands*, Saferworld.

— 2021. 'The functions and legitimization of suffering in Calais, France', *International Migration*, 59(3), 9–28.

— (forthcoming) *The Politics of Shame*. Princeton University Press.

Keen, D. and R. Andersson. 2018. 'Double games', *Political Geography*, 67, 100–10.

Keen, D. and L. Attree. 2015. 'Dilemmas of counter-terrorism, stabilisation and statebuilding', Saferworld.

Keller, E. and N. Kelly. 2015a. 'Financial deregulation, and the new gilded age', *Political Research Quarterly*, 68(3), 428–42.

— 2015b. 'How republicans and democrats enhanced inequality by undermining financial regulation', LSE, blog, 8 July.

Kellner, D. 2007. 'The Katrina Hurricane spectacle and crisis of the Bush presidency', *Cultural Studies – Critical Methodologies*, 7(2), 222–34.

Khan, M. et al. 2021. 'Trump and Muslims', SAGE Open, 1–16, January–March.

Khomami, N. 2016. '*Daily Mail* publishes correction to story about "migrants from Europe"', *Guardian*, 17 June.

Kim, T. 2020. 'Why is South Korea beating coronavirus?' *Guardian*, 11 April.

Kirkpatrick, L. 2016. 'The new urban fiscal crisis', *Politics and Society*, 44(1), 45–80.

Klein, N. 2007. *The Shock Doctrine*, Allen Lane.

— 2015. *This Changes Everything*. Penguin.

— 2017. *No Is Not Enough*. Penguin.

— 2018. 'There's nothing natural about Puerto Rico's disaster', *The Intercept*, 21 September.

— 2020. 'How big tech plans to profit from the pandemic', *Guardian*, 13 May.

Kornai, J. 2015. 'Hungary's u-turn', *Journal of Democracy*, 26(3), 35–48.

Krastev, I. 2016. 'The unravelling of the post-1989 order', *Journal of Democracy*, 27(4), 5–15.

Krause, W. et al. 2022. 'Copying the far right doesn't help mainstream parties', *Guardian*, 13 April.

Kristof, N. and S. Thompson. 2020. 'Trump wants to "reopen America"', *New York Times*, 25 March.

Kumar, D. 2020. 'Terrorcraft', *Race and Class*, 62(2), 34–60.

Kundnani, A. 2014. *The Muslims are Coming*. Verso.

Kuttner, R. 2022. 'Free markets, besieged citizens', *New York Review of Books*, 21 July.

Kuzmarov, J. 2008. 'From counter-insurgency to narco-insurgency', *Journal of Policy History*, 20(3), 344–78.

Larking, E. 2012. 'Human rights, the right to have rights, and life beyond the pale of the law', *Australian Journal of Human Rights*, 18(1), 57–88.

Laughland, O. 2018. 'Trump suggests he will end birthright citizenship with executive order', *Guardian*, 30 October.

Lawrence, F. et al. 2020. 'How a decade of privatisation and cuts exposed England to coronavirus', *Guardian*, 31 May.

Lazar, M. 2020. 'Politics of the "South"', *Discourse and Society*, 31(1), 5–18.

League of Nations, 1933. Convention of 28 October, relating to the International Status of Refugees, Treaty Series, CLIX, 3663.

Lerer, L. and N. Corasaniti. 2020. 'Four years later, Trump still portrays America as under siege', *New York Times*, 28 August.

Lerner, M. and C. Simmons. 1966. 'Observer's reaction to the "innocent victim"', *Journal of Personality and Social Psychology*, 4(2), 203–10.

Levine, S. 2021. 'Republicans are shamelessly working to subvert democracy', *Guardian*, 19 December.

Levitsky, S. and D. Ziblatt. 2019. *How Democracies Die*. Penguin.

Lewis, M. 2018. *The Fifth Risk*, Penguin/Random House.

Lincicome, S. 2021. 'Manufactured crisis', CATO Institute, 27 January.

Lind, D. 2018. 'The conspiracy theory that led to the Pittsburgh synagogue shooting, explained', *Vox*, 29 October.

Liu, A. 2020. 'Blaming China for coronavirus isn't just dangerous. It misses the point', *Guardian*, 10 April.

Loewenstein, A. 2017. *Disaster Capitalism*. Verso.

Luce, E. 2020. 'Premature US reopening plays Russian roulette with its workers', *Financial Times*, 6 May.

Lukyanov, F. 2020. 'Trump may be leaving, but Russia sanctions will stay', Carnegie Moscow Center, 20 November.

McCoy, D. 2020a. 'Faith in coronavirus modelling is no substitute for sound political judgment', *Guardian*, 10 April.

— 2020b. 'Coronavirus has exposed the dangerous failings of NHS marketisation', *Guardian*, 5 May.

McGreal, C. 2020. 'Federal agents show stronger force at Portland protests despite order to withdraw', *Guardian*, 30 July.

McKie, R. 2022. 'Britain got it wrong on Covid', *Guardian*, 2 January.

McQuarrie, M. 2017. 'The revolt of the Rust Belt', *The British Journal of Sociology*, 68(S1), S120–S152.

Macwilliams, M. 2016. 'Donald Trump is attracting authoritarian primary voters, and it may help him to gain the nomination', blogs.lse.ac.uk, 17 January.

Mahase, E. 2020. 'Covid-19: UK death toll overtakes Italy's to become worst in Europe', *BMJ*, 369, 6 May.

Malik, K. 2021. 'If you thought the right to protest was inalienable, then think again', *Guardian*, 14 March.

Mamdani, M. 2001. *When Victims Become Killers*. Princeton University Press.

Manjoo, F. 2008. *True Enough*. John Wiley and Sons.

Markus, S. 2017. 'Oligarchs and corruption in Putin's Russia', *Georgetown Journal of International Affairs*, 18(2), 26–32.

Marriage, Z. 2006. *Not Breaking the Rules. Not Playing the Game*. Hurst & Co.

Marten, K. 2020. 'NATO enlargement', *International Politics*, 57(3), 401–26.

Masco, J. 2017. 'The crisis in crisis', *Current Anthropology*, 58(15), S65–S76.

Maxeiner, J. 2020. 'America's Covid-19 preexisting vulnerability', *Theory and Practice of Legislation*, 8(1–2), 213–35.

Mayer, J. 2020. 'How Mitch McConnell became Trump's enabler-in-chief', *New Yorker*, 12 April.

Mbembé, J.-A. 2003. 'Necropolitics', *Public Culture*, 15(1), 11–40.

Mencken, H. L. 2009. *In Defense of Women*, Cosimo Classics (first published 1981).

Menkhaus, K. 2012. 'No access: Critical bottlenecks in the 2011 Somali famine', *Global Food Security*, 1, 29–35.

Mennell, S. 1990. 'Decivilising processes', *International Sociology*, 5(2), 205–23.

Menon, R. and J. Kucik. 2020. 'We're not all in it together', *Boston Review*, 18 May.

Michaels, W. 2008. 'Against diversity', *New Left Review*, 52, 33–6.

Miller-Idriss, C. 2021. 'From 9/11 to 1/6', *Foreign Affairs*, September/October.

Mishra, P. 2017. *Age of Anger*. Allen Lane.

Mkandawire, T. 2001. 'Thinking about developmental states in Africa. *Cambridge Journal of Economics*, 25, 289–314.

— 2010. 'Aid, accountability, and democracy in Africa', *Social Research*, 77(4), 1149–82.

Mohdin, A. 2020. 'People were abandoned', *Guardian*, 27 June.

Mollat, M. 1986. *The Poor in the Middle Ages*. Yale University Press (first published 1978).
Monbiot, G. 2020. 'When secret coronavirus contracts are awarded without competition, it's deadly serious', *Guardian*, 15 July.
Morris, S. 2020. 'Cheltenham cited Boris Johnson's rugby outing as a reason for festival go-ahead', *Guardian*, 8 April.
Mouffe, C. 2005. *On the Political*. Routledge.
Muana, P. 1997. 'The Kamajoi Militia', *Africa Development*, 22(3–4), 77–100.
Mueller, B. 2020a. 'Doctors say UK is ill prepared for Coronavirus', *New York Times*, 5 March.
— 2020b. 'As Europe shuts down Britain takes a different, and contentious, approach', *New York Times*, 13 March.
Müller, J.-W. 2016. *What Is Populism?* Penguin.
Nelson, L. 2017. 'Conway: Judge Trump by what's in his heart, not what comes out of his mouth', *Politico*, 9 January.
Netflix. 1977. *Hitler – A Career*.
— 2017. *White Right: Meeting the Enemy*.
Newsnight/BBC. 2020. 'Coronavirus: Can herd immunity protect the population?', 13 March.
Newton, J. and D. Boyle. 2016 'Illegal immigrants aiming to cross the Channel say Brexit will make it EASIER to sneak into Britain because France will no longer try to stop them', *Daily Mail*, 24 June.
Ni, V. 2022. 'Nancy Pelosi's visit to Taiwan risks upsetting Beijing to no advantage', *Guardian*, 2 August.
Norberg, J. 2008. 'The Klein Doctrine', CATO Institute, 14 May.
NPR. 2018. 'Is Trump the toughest ever on Russia?', 20 July.
O'Loughlin, B. and M. Gillespie. 2012. 'Dissenting citizenship?', *Parliamentary Affairs*, 65, 115–37.
O'Toole, F. 2018. *Heroic Failure*. Head of Zeus.
— 2020a. 'Coronavirus has exposed the myth of British exceptionalism', *Guardian*, 11 April.
— 2020b. 'Trump has unfinished business', *Irish Times*, 26 December.
Ogden, T. 2010. 'On three forms of thinking', *Psychoanalytic Quarterly*, 79(2), 317–47.
Osnos, E. 2018. 'Only the best people', *New Yorker*, 21 May.
Oxford Dictionary of English. 2010. Oxford University Press.
Packer, G. 2020. 'We are living in a failed state', *The Atlantic*, June.
Pallister-Wilkins, P. 2020. 'Hotspots and the geographies of humanitarianism', *Society and Space*, 38(6), 991–1008.
Parker, G. et al. 2020. 'UK's chief scientific adviser defends "herd immunity" strategy for coronavirus', *Financial Times*, 13 March.
Parten, B. 2021. 'The paranoid style', *Los Angeles Review of Books*, 13 July.
Pegg, D. et al. 2020. 'Revealed: The secret report that gave ministers warning of care home coronavirus crisis', *Guardian*, 7 May.
Perle, R. 2003. *The Spectator*, 22 March.
Petley, J. 2009. 'Whose rights? Whose responsibilities?' *Soundings*, 43, 77–88.
Piketty, T. 2014. *Capital in the Twenty-First Century*. Harvard University Press.
Pilkington, E. 2022. 'What is "great replacement" theory and how did its racist lies spread in the US?' *Guardian*, 17 May.

Ponder, C. and M. Omstedt. 2022. 'The violence of municipal debt', *Geoforum*, 132, 271–80.

Press Association. 2020. 'Chaos and panic', *Guardian*, 28 March.

Putzel, J. 2020. 'The "populist" right challenge to neoliberalism', *Development and Change*, 51(2), 418–41.

Rangasami, A. 1985. 'Failure of exchange entitlements' theory of famine: A response', *Economic and Political Weekly*, 12 and 19 October, 1747–51, 1797–1800.

Rangel, J. et al. 2020. 'COVID-19 policy measures', *Journal of Evaluation in Clinical Practice*, 26, 1078–80.

Ray, R. 2017. 'A case of internal colonialism?' *British Journal of Sociology*, 68(1), 129–33.

Rector, J. 2017. 'Accumulating risk: Environmental justice and the history of capitalism in Detroit, 1880–2015', PhD, Wayne State University.

Refugee Rights Data Project. 2016. 'The long wait.'

Reich, R. 2016. 'Want to reverse sky-high inequality?' *Guardian*, 27 January.

Rigi, J. 2012. 'The corrupt state of exception', *Social Analysis*, 56(3), 69–88.

Roberts, J. 2020. '*Telegraph* journalist says coronavirus "cull" of elderly could benefit economy', *Metro*, 11 March.

Robinson, A. et al. 2021. 'This is your disease', LSE, June.

Rubin, O. 2009. 'The merits of democracy in famine prevention – fact or fallacy?' *European Journal of Development Research*, 21(5), 699–717.

Ryan, F. 2021. 'During Covid, to be "vulnerable" is to be told your life doesn't matter', *Guardian*, 24 June.

Sabbagh, D. 2022. 'Western war aims are growing', *Guardian*, 27 April.

Saddique, H. 2021. 'New bill quietly gives powers to remove British citizenship without notice', *Guardian*, 17 November.

Saez, E. and G. Zucman. 2016. 'Wealth inequality in the United States since 1913', *Quarterly Journal of Economics*, 131(2), 519–78.

SAGE secretariat. 2020. 'Current understanding of COVID-19 compared with NSRA Pandemic influenza planning assumptions', 26 February.

Said, E. 1991. *Orientalism*. Penguin.

— 2003. 'A window on the world', *Guardian*, 2 August.

Sakwa, R. 2021. *Deception*. Lexington.

Sample, I. 2020a. 'Immunity to Covid-19 could be lost in months, UK study suggests', *Guardian*, 12 July.

— 2020b. 'Secrecy has harmed UK government's response to Covid-19 crisis, says top scientist', *Guardian*, 2 August.

Sandri, E. 2018 'Volunteer humanitarianism', *Journal of Ethnic and Migration Studies*, 44(1), 65–80.

Savage, C. 2021, 'Incitement to riot?' *New York Times*, 10 January.

— 2022. 'Was the Jan. 6 attack on the Capitol an act of "terrorism"?' *New York Times*, 7 January.

Schaffer, B. 1984. 'Towards responsibility', in E. Clay and B. Schaffer (eds), *Room for Manoeuvre*. Heinemann Educational Books.

Scherer, M. 2017. 'Read President Trump's interview with TIME on truth and falsehoods', *Time*, 23 March.

Schmitt, C. 2005. *Political Theology*. University of Chicago Press (first published 1922).

Schreiber, M. 2022. 'Vastly unequal US has world's highest Covid death toll – it's no coincidence', *Guardian*, 6 February.

Sen, A. 1984. *Poverty and Famines.* Oxford University Press (first published 1981).

Sen, A. and J. Drèze. 1989. *Hunger and Public Action*. Oxford University Press.

Serwer, A. 2018. 'Trump's caravan hysteria led to this', *The Atlantic*, 28 October.

— 2020. 'The coronavirus was an emergency until Trump found out who was dying', *The Atlantic*, 8 May.

Shaxson, N. 2018. *The Finance Curse: How Global Finance is Making us all Poorer*. Vintage.

Shipman, T. and C. Wheeler. 2020. 'Ten days that shook Britain – and changed the nation for ever', *Sunday Times*, 22 March.

Shorrock, T. 2020. 'How South Korea triumphed, and the US floundered, over the pandemic', *The Nation*, 20 March.

Siddiqui, S. 2019. 'What the Mueller report tells us about Trump, Russia and obstruction', *Guardian*, 18 April.

Sinclair, I. and R. Read. 2020. 'A national scandal', *Byline*, 20 April.

Singh, G. 2020. 'We are being treated as cannon-fodder', openDemocracy, 19 March.

SIPRI (Stockholm International Peace Research Institute). 2022. 'Trends in World Military Expenditure, 2021', April.

Smith, A. 2019. 'Trump says congresswomen of color should "go back" and fix the places they "originally came from"', NBC News. 14 July.

Smith, D. 2017. 'Trump paints himself as the real victim of Charlottesville in angry speech', *Guardian*, 23 August.

— 2018. 'Why is that racist?' *Guardian*, 27 October.

— 2020. 'Trump appears to stoke protests against stay-at-home orders', *Guardian*, 17 April.

Smith, D. and D. Agren. 2018. 'Trump accused of stoking immigration fears by sending 5,200 troops to border', *Guardian*, 29 October.

Smith, H. 2003. 'Blix: I was smeared by the Pentagon', *Guardian*, 11 June.

Smith, M. 2005. 'Blair planned Iraq war from start', *Sunday Times*, 1 May.

Snyder, T. 2021. 'The American abyss', *New York Times*, 9 January.

Sommer, W. et al. 2018. 'Trump's own team knows his caravan claims are bullshit', *Daily Beast*, 24 October.

Sommerlad, J. 2022. 'Freedom convoy', *Independent*, 17 February.

Spencer, J. 2008. 'A nationalism without politics?' *Third World Quarterly*, 29(3), 611–29.

SPI-M-O. 2020a. Consensus view on public gatherings, 11 February, 1.

— 2020b. Consensus statement on 2019 novel coronavirus (Covid-19), 17 February.

— 2020c. Consensus statement on 2019 novel coronavirus (COVID-19), 2 March.

Spielthenner, G. 2010. 'Lesser evil reasoning and its pitfalls', *Argumentation*, 24, 139–52.

Stanley, J. 2018. *How Fascism Works*. Random House.

Stephan, M. and E. Chenoweth. 2008. 'Why civil resistance works', *International Security*, 33(1), 7–44.

Stein, H. 2009. 'Death imagery and the experience of organizational downsizing or, *is your name on Schindler's list?*' in B. Sievers, B. (ed.) *Psychoanalytic Studies of Organizations*. Karnac Press, 123–51.

Stern, S. 2022. 'Dire straits', *New York Review of Books*, 23 June.

Stevenson, J. 2019. 'Right-wing extremism and the terrorist threat', *Survival*, 61(1), 233–44.

Stewart, H. and M. Busby. 2020. 'Coronavirus: Science chief defends UK plan from criticism', *Guardian*, 13 March.

Stoakes, E. 2017. '"Humanitarian catastrophe" unfolding as Myanmar takes over aid efforts in Rakhine state', *Guardian*, 15 September.

Stockman, Farah. 2021. *American Made*. Random House.

Stockton, N. 1998. 'In defence of humanitarianism', *Disasters*, 22(4), 352–60.

Stubbs, P. and N. Lendvai-Bainton. 2019. 'Authoritarian neoliberalism, radical conservatism and social policy within the European Union', *Development and Change*, 540–60.

Suskind, R. 2004a. *The Price of Loyalty*. Free Press and Simon & Schuster.

— 2004b. 'Without a doubt', *New York Times*, 17 October.

Swinford, S. 2021. 'Boris Johnson "said he would let Covid rip" in lockdown row', *Times*, 27 April.

Sylves, R. 2006. 'President Bush and Hurricane Katrina: A presidential leadership study', *Annals of the American Academy of Political and Social Science*, 604, 26–56.

Tapper, J. 2020. 'Recruit volunteer army to trace coronavirus contacts now, urge top scientists', *Guardian*, 4 April.

Tapsfield, J. 2020. 'So who IS to blame for testing fiasco?' *MailOnline*, 2 April.

Taylor, A. 2015. 'Italy ran an operation that saved thousands of migrants from drowning in the Mediterranean. Why did it stop?' *Washington Post*, 20 April.

Taylor, M. 2021. 'Environment protest being criminalized around world, say experts', *Guardian*, 19 April.

Telegraph reporters. 2020. 'When will coronavirus peak in the UK? How to prepare and what to expect', *telegraph.com*, 16 March.

Telegraph, foreign staff. 2020. 'Trump threatens to pull US out of WHO, branding it "a puppet of China"', 19 May.

The White House. 2001. 'President George W. Bush: Address to a joint session of congress and the American people', 20 September.

— 2022. 'Remarks by President Biden on protecting the right to vote', 11 January.

Thomas, K. and B. Warner. 2019. 'Weaponizing vulnerability to climate change', *Global Environmental Change*, 57, 1–11.

Tierney, K. 2015. 'Resilience and the neoliberal project', *American Behavioral Scientist*, 59(10), 1327–42.

Tilly, C. 1985. 'War making and state making as organized crime', in P. Evans et al. (ed.) *Bringing the State Back In*. Cambridge University Press.

Todorova, M. 2009. *Imagining the Balkans*. Oxford University Press.

Topping, A. 2017. 'Sweden, who would believe this?' *Guardian*, 19 February.

— 2020. 'UK minister admits less than 10% of contact tracers recruited', *Guardian*, 17 May.

Townsend, M. 2017. 'Trafficking laws "target refugee aid workers in EU"', *Observer*, 11 November.

Truss, Liz. 2022. Foreign Secretary's Mansion House speech, 27 April.

Tsygankov, A. 2018. 'The sources of Russia's fear of NATO', *Communist and Post-Communist Studies*, 51, 101–11.

Udall, T. and J. McGovern, 2020. 'Trump and Barr used a loophole to deploy the National Guard to US cities', *NBC News*, 7 August.

United Nations, 2020. *COVID-19 and Human Rights*, April.

UN Panel of Experts, 2011. 'Report of the Secretary-General's panel of experts on accountability in Sri Lanka', 31 March.

Van Dorn, A. et al. 2020. 'COVID-19 exacerbating inequalities in the US', *The Lancet*, 395, 19 April, 1243–4.

Varoufakis, Y. 2021. 'Greece's deadly wildfires were sparked by 30 years of political failure', *Guardian*, 29 August.

Vazquez, M. and D. Judd. 2020. 'Trump predicts "most corrupt election" in US history while making false claim about mail-in voting', CNN, 24 June.

Venugopal, R. 2009. 'The making of Sri Lanka's post-conflict economic package and the failure of the 2001–2004 Peace Process', CRISE Working Paper 64, Oxford University.

— 2018. *Nationalism, Development and Ethnic Conflict in Sri Lanka*. Cambridge University Press.

Verhoeven, H. 2011. 'Climate change, conflict and development in Sudan', *Development and Change*, 42(3), 679–707.

Vogel, K. and K. Kelly. 2021. 'G.O.P. Donors Back Manchin and Sinema as they reshape Biden's agenda', *New York Times*, 21 November.

Volokh, E. 2017. 'Trump incorrectly says "the murder rate in our country is the highest it's been in 47 years"', *Washington Post*, 8 February.

Wade, R. 2009 'Robert Wade on the global financial crisis', interviewed by Alex Izurieta, *Development and Change*, 40(6), 1153–90.

Walker, A. 2020, 'Coronavirus: UK economy could be among worst hit of leading nations, says OECD', *BBC News* (bbc.co.uk).

Walker, P. 2020. 'No 10 denies claim Dominic Cummings argued to "let old people die"', *Guardian*, 22 March.

Ward, B. 2020. 'It's not just Neil Ferguson – scientists are being attacked for telling the truth', *Guardian*, 6 May.

Waterson, J. 2020. 'Broadband engineers threatened due to 5G coronavirus conspiracies', *Guardian*, 3 April.

Watts, J. 2021. 'Climate scientists shocked by scale of floods in Germany', *Guardian*, 16 July.

Wehner, P. 'The Trump presidency is over', *The Atlantic*, 13 March 2020.

Weigel, D. 2020. 'The Trailer: The resistance to stay-at-home orders rises from the right', *Washington Post*, 16 April.

Weiss, F. 2012. *The Cage*, The Bodley Head.

Weissman, F. (ed.). 2004. *In the Shadow of 'Just Wars'*. Hurst & Co.

— 2011. 'Sri Lanka: Amid all-out war', in C. Magone et al. (eds), *Humanitarian Negotiations Revealed*. Hurst & Co.

Werleman, C. 2020. 'The coronavirus crisis: Enter the far right', *Byline Times*, 20 March.

Wertheim, S. 2020. 'How Trump brought home the endless war', *New Yorker*, 1 October.

White House task force briefing. 2020. 19 April.

White, J. 2015a. 'Emergency Europe', *Political Studies*, 63, 300–18.

— 2015b. 'Authority after emergency rule', *Modern Law Review*, 78(4), 585–610.

— 2019. 'Proroguing parliament is bigger than Brexit', *Guardian*, 3 February.
Wilde-Anderson, M. 2016. 'Democratic dissolution', *Fordham Urban Law Journal*, 39.
Wise, A. 2020. 'Trump admits playing down coronavirus's severity, according to new Woodward book', NPR, 9 September.
Wisner, B. 2001. 'Risk and the neoliberal state: Why post-Mitch lessons didn't reduce El Salvador's earthquake losses', *Disasters*, 25(3), 251–68.
Wodak, Sebastian. 2019. 'Entering the "post-shame era"', *Global Discourse*, 9(1), 195–213.
Woodward, B. 2002. *Bush at War*, Simon & Schuster.
Woodward, S. 1995. *Balkan Tragedy*, Brookings Institution.
Worldometers, 2020. Coronavirus update (Live), 27 May.
Wyman, D. 1984. *The Abandonment of the Jews*. Pantheon.
Yong, E. 2020a. 'How the pandemic will end', *The Atlantic*, 25 March.
— 2020b. 'How the pandemic defeated America', *The Atlantic*, September.
Zuboff, S. 2019. *The Age of Surveillance Capitalism*. Profile Books.

Index